Mario and Franco
and the Trattoria Revolution

Alasdair Scott Sutherland

foreword by Len Deighton

First published in 2009. Updated and reprinted in 2013
PRIMAVERA BOOKS LIMITED



British Library Cataloguing-in-Publication Data.
A CIP record for this title is available from the British Library.

ISBN 978-0-9557892-0-5

Designed by Willie Landels.
Typesetting and artwork by RMA Design.
Production by B&G Porteous.
Printed and bound in Great Britain by Halstan Print Group.
Papers used by Primavera Books are naturally recyclable.
products made from wood grown in sustainable forests.
The manufacturing processes conform
to the environmental regulations of the country of origin.

Primavera Books Ltd, London
www.primaverabooks.co.uk

To Felicity

**felí city** noun 1 being happy; intense happiness;
thing causing happiness

*Oxford English Dictionary*

and in memory of
Mario Cassandro 1920 – 2011
and
Mara Berni 1932 – 2012

**CONTENTS**

# FOREWORD

John Barker knew everyone and everything about everyone but you would never have guessed it from his appearance. John was lost somewhere in my vast, unquantified category of "older than me" but looking back I'm sure he was a young, energetic man. He wore carefully cut pin stripe suits, starched white shirts and dull-patterned ties. His hair was dark, cut short and brushed tight. He spoke quietly and was polite and self-effacing even when explaining to me that the client wanted changes to an illustration that we both knew could only make my drawing worse.

I had spent six years studying, had graduated from the Royal College of Art as an illustrator and been in New York selling my drawing to such desirable clients as *Esquire* magazine, *Good Housekeeping* and Arrow Shirts. I had even managed to steal a job from Andy Warhol when a magazine art director wanted a drawing of a crippled boy in a wheelchair that wouldn't frighten his female readers. Somehow I made him happy. Making clients happy was a vital part of being a successful illustrator and it was the reason I was represented by John Barker of Artist Partners, the most successful artists agents in London, in fact in Europe.

I knew Soho. I studied for three years at St Martin's School of Art. I had lived in one cramped room in Moor Street. I worked there as a waiter and so knew what the streets were like at two o'clock in the morning when law-abiding people were abed. I knew the all-night motorised coffee and sandwich van likely to have an available burglar (always delicately referred to as "builders") when I locked myself out. I had followed restaurateurs as they rummaged through the garbage of rival restaurants to discover who their suppliers were. I watched traffic wardens being paid off and hungry policemen fed. I knew something of Soho.

John selected the newly opened Trattoria Terrazza for lunch. Like all his fellow directors at Artist Partners, the gastronomic facilities of central London were not something he was likely to get even slightly wrong. At the end of a delicious lunch, John signed the bill. I had seen rich, busy businessmen sign their restaurant bills before, but that didn't make it less impressive. "Would you like an account here?" he asked casually.

That's how it all began. When John took one of his artists to La Terrazza and suggested to Mario and Franco that he should open an account for them, they knew that John was with someone who was unlikely to default on a month's spaghetti lunches and dinners. It did happen, of course, but many years later Mario told me that the artists and designers of that period were the most reliable clients he had ever had.

In 1960 Allen Lane brought the dynamic if not to say explosive personality of Germano Facetti to London, to totally revise the covers and overall appearance of Penguin Books. One of the artists and designers that Facetti contacted remembers: "After a drink we strolled for lunch to Trattoria Terrazza, a recently opened Italian restaurant which was just around the corner [from the York Minster pub] in Romilly Street. The food was very good and so was the wine. Franco joined us at the table for coffee and brandy."

I don't have to draw a diagram, do I? Germano did not like his office; he liked to work in places where life went on around him. It was an Italian point of view and Germano proved how well it worked. Others followed his working style. I wrote chunks of my books sitting in La Terrazza comforted with fresh pasta, grappa and powerful espresso. While Germano was changing the face of Penguin Books, the Italian artist, cartoonist and interior designer Enzo Apicella started to change the face of restaurants.

The Trattoria Terrazza was the place to find him. Usually, despite Mario's constant objections, Enzo was drawing on the tablecloth. His ideas, about table positions and sizes, about noise levels and creating easily changed spot lighting for each table, brought fundamental change that other restaurateurs would ignore at their peril. Enzo never took the tablecloths away with him and I sometimes wondered if he did it just to annoy Mario.

The Trattoria Terrazza was founded upon a clientele of artists and designers brought in by agents and art editors. Agents also brought commercial photographers. They brought pretty models and after them came advertising men armed with seemingly unlimited expense accounts.

Well-designed magazines were created: *Town*, *Queen*, *The Sunday Times Colour Supplement* and then *The Observer Magazine*. Colour printing was essential and artists and designers brought glamour and excitement. Advertisements brought money.

In the sixties Hollywood came to London. Show-biz corres-pondents, notably Peter Evans, brought top American film stars to La Terrazza. With the instinct that made them a world-wide success, Mario and Franco didn't put their stars on display but tucked them away in the inaccessible Positano Room. It was a canny move. Even when the Positano Room held only wannabees like me, the buzz said that Frank and Liz were downstairs and Cecil Beaton had been stopped at the door for carrying a concealed camera.

In London during the sixties there were half a dozen great restaurants where the spirit of Escoffier ruled. French cooking may or may not be the greatest cuisine in the world but it remains the only one which is so ordered, scientific and systematic that it demonstrates the logic of cooking. At that time cooking was still a profession to which serious students devoted their whole lives. To become a Maître Chef des Cuisines meant spending some years studying at an established hotel school and more years as a dogsbody in the kitchen of a three-star chef in France. As the English language became more important in the hotel business, a year or two in a fine London restaurant became desirable for young ambitious cooks from the Continent. The kitchens of the Savoy Hotel were, at that time, turning away fifty skilled applicants a week with even greater numbers of experienced waiters seeking a job in the Savoy dining rooms (where the fourteen-year-old Franco started work). As the success story of La Terrazza spread, Mario and Franco could choose from a constant supply of white- and black-coated men from the Savoy and other fine London restaurants such as the Mirabelle, from which they themselves had recently come. Without this pool of skilled professionals La Terrazza might have been very different.

The kitchen staff was highly skilled, but Mario and Franco did not want to offer the sort of food served at the Mirabelle. They had created a Neapolitan Trattoria and that implied localised Italian menus more simple than those of a ristorante. The resulting food was excellent and consistent: the gnocchi and the fresh egg pasta – for ravioli and fettucini – were made in La Terrazza kitchen and the osso buco was just like your old Italian mother made. There was no chasing of fashion, posturing personality chefs, "fusion food" or pretentious "signature dishes." And despite the famous faces to be seen there, La Terrazza maintained its position on the basis of modest prices, which enabled penniless painters and writers to eat there alongside the rich and famous.

The *Petto di Pollo Sorpresa* is the dish for which La Terrazza is best remembered. The customer was strongly advised to let the waiter stab into the chicken and brave the spurt of hot garlicky butter. The way that Mario and Franco encouraged the interaction of waiters and customers was an important part of the restaurant's success. "At La Terrazza I could talk to the customers," is a frequently heard fond memory. Amid a traditional menu, the pollo sorpresa was a rare instance of a Terrazza speciality. In the 1920s kotlety po-kievski, a Russian delicacy, had arrived in Paris along with displaced aristocracy. A stuffed, breaded and deep-fried chicken breast, it had become an international favourite by the time Franco adapted it by adding grated parmesan cheese and garlic to the butter filling and omitting the traditional finely chopped mushrooms.

I was having an early coffee with Mario in an otherwise empty restaurant on that morning when Mario went into the kitchen to be sure a newly engaged chef made the sorpresa in the way that Franco had prescribed. The chef not only declined to add cheese but chased Mario out, wielding a large knife. Mario emerged from the kitchen white faced. He sat down opposite me and gulped his espresso. "He wants to kill me," said Mario, but the enraged chef had already departed and Mario's narrow escape was forgotten as he energetically marshalled the resources of the kitchen to prepare for the lunchtime customers despite the absent purist. It was little wonder that La Terrazza kept to traditional Italian recipes.

The Italian revolution that Mario and Franco brought to London in the sixties is fondly revisited by Alasdair in this book. It is a tale of passion and possession, vendetta and repentance, a story of triumph, disaster and betrayal. It is an opera and one more like *Rigoletto* than *Die Fledermaus*. But I love them all: the incomparable Mario, Franco, Enzo, Pasquale, Alvaro, Germano and Mimmo. They became my life-long friends and skewed my dull, dyspeptic English view of the world to a vivid Italian panorama. They showed me how to live, love, argue and eat. What more is there?

Oh, yes, and in 1966 I first met my wife Ysabele in the Trattoria Terrazza.

**Len Deighton**
**Portugal**

# THE SPAGHETTI TREE

## THE MAIN CHARACTERS

| | |
|---|---|
| Antoniazzi,Osvaldo | La Terrazza chef |
| Apicella, Enzo | restaurant designer, creator of "Trattoria Style" |
| Benet, Fabio | waiter at La Terrazza, Alvaro, partner-manager of Barbarella |
| Berni, Mara & Lorenzo | proprietors of San Lorenzo |
| Betti, Dante | waiter at La Terrazza, manager of Aretusa, partner in Factotum, proprietor of Beccofino |
| Buonaguidi, Franco | partner in San Frediano group, proprietor of Vin Santo |
| Calzolari, Valerio | waiter at La Terrazza, manager of Mr Chow, partner in Scalini |
| Carluccio, Antonio | TV chef; proprietor of Neal Street Restaurant, founder of Carluccio's |
| Cassandro, Mario | founder partner in La Trattoria Terrazza |
| Contaldo, Gennaro | chef at Neal Street, partner in Passione, mentor to Jamie Oliver |
| Cornoli, Giulio | proprietor of Verbanella |
| Galassi, Sergio | chef-partner of San Frediano |
| Lagattolla, Franco | founder partner in La Trattoria Terrazza |
| Locatelli, Giorgio | chef-partner in Olivo, then Zafferano, proprietor of Locanda Locatelli |
| Lunghi, Pasquale | waiter at La Terrazza, manager of Trattoo, Meridiana, Pontenuovo, partner in Medusa |
| Maccioni, Alvaro | manager of La Terrazza, proprietor of Alvaro, Aretusa, La Famiglia |
| Mariti, Walter | proprietor of Pontevecchio, Meridiana, Factotum, Ponte Nuovo |
| Mattera, Mimmo | waiter at La Terrazza, manager of Aretusa, proprietor of Mimmo d'Ischia |
| Nobilio, Giulio | manager of Terrazza Manchester, proprietor of Giulio's Terrazza, manager of San Carlo |
| Orsi, Walter, | Savoy headwaiter, manager of Tiberio, partner in Medusa |
| Paglierani, Luigi | waiter at Mirabelle, proprietor of Don Luigi, partner of Mario and Franco |
| Paggetti, Mario | waiter at La Terrazza, manager of Mr Chow, proprietor of Signor Sassi, Scalini |
| Pardini, Franco | assistant-manager Trattoo, Terrazza Leeds, proprietor of Flying Pizza, partner in Brio |
| Parlanti, Mino | partner in Dolce Vita, Il Porcellino, San Frediano, Santa Croce |
| Pizzala, Antonio | waiter at Hatchett's, partner in Pizzala restaurant |
| Serpussi, Franco | waiter at La Terrazza, manager of Alvaro's, proprietor of Franco's |
| Taboro, Peppino | waiter at La Terrazza, manager of Mr Chow, Montpelier, Sambuca, La Finezza, partner in Trattoria Conti |
| Taruschio, Franco | chef-proprietor of The Walnut Tree |
| Tobi, Sandro | waiter at La Terrazza and Alvaro, manager of Mr Chow, proprietor of Sambuca, Sale e Pepe, Sandrini |
| Trapani, Antonio | waiter at San Lorenzo, proprietor of Montpeliano, Toto's |
| Vollono, Mario | headwaiter at Savoy and Tiberio, manager of La Terrazza |

## ROMILLY STREET, SOHO, 1964

"*Questo, Mario, è il mio fratello Alasdair.*" My elder brother Robin and I were at the door of La Trattoria Terrazza. He was attempting to show off his restaurant Italian, as I shook hands with the smiling man who greeted us.

Robin, seven years older than me and already working in London, was taking me, together with his half-Italian girlfriend Maggie, for my first visit to the most fashionable restaurant in London. It was 1964 and entering this glamorous place aged eighteen, having grown up in the country and accustomed to ordinary English food, was an extraordinary experience, both sensually and gastronomically.

The man at the door – who, it turned out, was also the owner, Mario Cassandro – told us our table wasn't ready and took us upstairs to wait in the bar. Seated on a black leather sofa, I drank my first Campari and surreptitiously pocketed a postcard which depicted the owners and the two dining rooms. On the back of the card, was printed "PS: We also hope to see you soon, Mario e Franco." (Forty years later, after my mother died, I found in her desk several of these cards on which I'd written messages like "Will be down at the usual time on Saturday," and on one of them, "I am sitting right next to Brigitte Bardot.")

After about ten minutes, as we were escorted downstairs to the Positano Room, then shown to our table, I tried to stay cool while I gazed around at the other customers. I recognised one or two familiar faces from newspapers and TV. Robin, who had lived in London for several years, pointed several out to me – the actor Laurence Harvey, The Duke of Bedford and his glamorous French wife, Nicole; the fashion designer Gina Fratini, the James Bond film producer, Cubby Broccoli, as well as photographers, artists – even a government minister, Ernest Marples.

Entering La Terrazza's atmosphere was like being handed a glass of champagne. Each table stood in a small sparkling pool of light, creating its own little world which guests could either simply, solely inhabit, or from which they could share the enchantment and excitement of the whole room. It would feel intimate and romantic, or you could transcend your space, look around and feel that you were taking part in a night at the theatre. While we feasted our eyes, unfamiliar aromas wafted from the kitchen, arousing our tastebuds in anticipation of the meal to come.

Having grown up in the years after the Second World War, it was hardly surprising that my palate went mad at La Terrazza. School food had consisted of porridge, pies and sausages, plus cod on Fridays, and at home it was much the same, though with more green vegetables. Here were delicious, exotic dishes, with ingredients, textures and flavours that I'd never experienced before.

The headwaiter, in his blue jacket and white polo-neck, came up to take our order.

"Robin, how are you?"

"*Ciao*, Pasquale, very well, thanks. And you?"

"*Molto bene, grazie*."

I was completely unused to this informality and when I confessed to Pasquale that it was my first visit, he laughed, telling me, "Then you must have the *Pollo Sorpresa*."

I remember that as a starter I ordered the *Fritto Misto Mare*, a pile of crisp, clean-tasting, mixed octopus, calamari, goujons and scampi, deep fried in the lightest of batter and lemon scented. I was completely reduced to silence by the sheer sensation of the complex flavours. Having cleaned my plate, what would become La Terrazza's best-known dish was placed before me.

When our waiter gently cut open the stuffed breast of chicken and the scent of garlic, herbs and parmesan spread upwards from the plate, it was gastronomic heaven. The chicken was accompanied by the most delicious potatoes – oven roast with rosemary – and spinach, briefly tossed in oil and garlic, a far cry from the watery stuff I knew.

I had never before tasted Italian wine. Robin ordered an Antinori and as we sipped the deep red Chianti, I gazed around me as customers left and new ones replaced them. I recognised the actor Terence Stamp, with his girlfriend the model Jean Shrimpton and another exotic couple. Despite my replete contentment, I couldn't resist staring. Later, after my first real espresso coffee, as we collected our coats at the door, Princess Margaret and her husband Lord Snowdon arrived and I watched Mario greet them like old friends. For a teenager, La Terrazza's customers were almost as fascinating as the food.

The "Trat" as I began to learn to call it, was so alluringly different from the dreary, over-decorated, boring restaurants that I'd been to with aunts and godmothers and after family weddings. I couldn't wait to go back as soon as I could afford to – or even before.

I still have the bill for the first time I ventured there without my brother's protection – with my girlfriend Pippa. We were both nineteen and the account came to two pounds and sixteen shillings (£2.60), not including service. I was working as a messenger boy in a West End public relations agency, was paid £12 a week and our dinner cost twenty percent of my week's wages. Long before the days of credit cards, I carefully wrote out a cheque, which was honoured by my bank manager, though he wrote me a not wholly discouraging letter to advise me that my overdraft "had gone far enough."

To have eaten at La Trattoria Terrazza, at the golden moment when a revolution was all just beginning, was, I realise, worth a million bank manager's letters. The memory of that experience was enough to make me want to return to it forty-five years later, to start to write this book.

## 2009: A LIFETIME OF SPAGHETTI

Since that first visit to La Terrazza in 1964, I have eaten in Italian restaurants, mainly in London, about three times a week. During that time, millions of English words have been written about Italian food, but the causes of its original popularity and growth in the United Kingdom have been forgotten. Today, when young British food writers reminisce about the overcooked spaghetti or tasteless veal that they remember when they first ate out, and they imagine, from their experiences, that authentic Italian food just didn't exist here before they discovered it at The River Café – I realise how few people are aware of how it all started.

It's easy to measure our ignorance of the subject, thanks to the BBC. In the 1950s, many Italian exports – their cars, scooters, espresso machines, design, furniture, even their film stars, like Sophia Loren and Marcello Mastroianni, had become popular and fashionable. But, on the food front, it was still a pretty safe bet that most Britons had never eaten spaghetti except from a tin, and that few knew where it came from. When BBC television's *Panorama* programme was broadcast on 1 April 1957 about an unusually heavy spaghetti harvest in southern Switzerland, most people didn't spot the hoax. As they watched a family of farmers picking pasta from trees, viewers heard the august voice of Richard Dimbleby, the man who had held the nation in reverence with his commentary for the televising of the Coronation of Queen Elizabeth II only four years earlier.

"Many of you, I'm sure," he intoned, "will have seen pictures of the vast spaghetti plantations in the Po valley." The film closed with shots of young Swiss tenderly picking strands of spaghetti, as we were told how each year's harvest ends with a traditional celebration dinner of spaghetti and tomato sauce.

Although it didn't take long for some viewers to realise that they'd been taken in by an elaborate and expensively staged April Fool's Day joke, for others, belief was suspended rather longer. Soon after the transmission ended, the BBC began to receive calls from baffled viewers who requested verification that spaghetti really did grow on trees, some even asking for a leaflet which would show them how they could start their own plantation. *Panorama's* producers replied that they should "place a sprig of spaghetti in a tin of tomato sauce and hope for the best," adding "Spaghetti is not a widely eaten food in the UK and is considered by many as an exotic delicacy."

Subsequently, cookery writers have done much to educate Britain on Italian food, through books, magazine articles and television series. But as their food gained in popularity here, and the number of visitors from Britain to Italy rose to between four and five million in 2008, I realised how few people are aware of how it all started.

Antonio Carluccio, whose TV series and books on Italian cookery have been accompanied by his chain of café-delicatessens across the country, gives most credit to Elizabeth David for the early acceptance of

*BBC television's Panorama broadcast, on 1 April 1957, had the nation fooled. Only a few years after the end of food rationing, and long before mass-market travel, most British viewers had never eaten anything foreign. And if you couldn't believe Richard Dimbleby, who could you? BBC Photo*

foreign cooking in post-war Britain. "Although England has wonderful food products and ingredients," he asserts, "they were swept under the carpet after the war and others became more fashionable. Because of Elizabeth David's books, the British started cooking French and Italian instead of English."

But was Mrs David's *Italian Food* the spark that ignited our love of Italian cooking? Not when it was first published in 1954. The hardback edition reached a certain middle-class reader, but many of the ingredients required for the recipes – peppers, ricotta, courgettes, fennel, aubergines, garlic, rosemary, basil – were almost impossible to find in England. We had a copy at home. But I'm pretty sure that my mother read it as fiction. As she and other readers stood in queues for the family's weekly rations, they could only fantasise about cooking such exotic recipes. The book's real impact happened ten years later, after a number of other factors had set the ball rolling. When the Penguin paperback edition came out in 1963, imported vegetables were already much more available and, once the raw materials existed, the book became much more useful. As our taste for Italian grew, it was reprinted twice more in the 1960s.

The River Café, on the Fulham-Hammersmith Thames waterfront, was another significant influence. But when I asked the chef-partners Rose Gray and Ruth Rogers for their views on the origins of the popularity of Italian food in Britain, Gray suggested that they had brought the first authentic Italian gastronomic experience to London.

"From the 1950s to the 1980s," Gray said emphatically, "there were no Italian restaurants in London which did anything more than straightforward food, not regional, not seasonal, no nod to what real Italian cooking is about and the food you ate was just spaghetti and veal Milanese, with breadcrumbs – those sort of dishes."

In the glow of their success, Ruth and Rose can be forgiven for overlooking the influence of the restaurant which, thirty years before their River Café opened, sparked Britain's love affair with Italian food. Much more perceptive was Fay Maschler, restaurant critic of the London *Evening Standard*, who noted in a 1975 column, that back in the sixties:

> **One Italian restaurant began to serve the sort of food which Italians remembered from home, instead of the mock-Italian which could be found in many of the pre-war Italian restaurants in London.**

The restaurant in question, was, of course, Mario and Franco's

La Trattoria Terrazza, in Romilly Street, in Soho.

The chef-restaurateur Alastair Little, often called the "Godfather of Modern British cooking," now the proprietor of Tavola delicatessen, in Westbourne Grove, also tasted his first authentic Italian food at La Terrazza. "The trattoria revolution," he told me, "was the biggest influence on British cuisine since Escoffier."

A little while ago, at a dinner party given by Willie Landels, we were discussing Italian food, restaurants old and new and the people who ran them. Willie, born in Venice, came to England in the 1950s and became an influential artist, designer, art editor of *Queen* magazine and later the editor of its successor, *Harpers & Queen*.

"In the fifties, when I was quite young," Willie remarked, "going to a restaurant was still a formal occasion. When I took my mother out to lunch, she always wore a hat."

As he spoke, Willie was stirring a risotto, which emitted the heady scent of porcini.

"But," he said, "the Terrazza put a stop to all that. Everything changed after the Terrazza."

I knew what he meant. Willie had been one of the first regulars, and many different worlds in early sixties London – artists, writers, actors, designers, journalists, politicians, film, advertising and business people – had all merged at La Terrazza's tables. As Mario and Franco's empire spread, many of the young waiters at La Terrazza left to open their own ventures, and are now the grey-haired proprietors of respected Italian restaurants throughout London, and as far from Soho as Leeds and Bristol. They have played an important role in the lives of many generations, because these trattorie were so much more than just somewhere to go for lunch or dinner – they transformed the UK restaurant landscape.

"Really, Alasdair," Willie went on, placing the steaming bowl of risotto on the table, "you were there, you knew all these people, you must write this story. Mario is in his eighties now, go immediately to see him. I'll give you his address."

So I wrote to Mario Cassandro, explaining the idea. Within a day or two, the telephone rang and Mario, his voice huskier now, but still with its distinctive warmth and rich accent, said, "Alasdair… I remember you. Come and see me tomorrow."

That was the spur that got me going on the story of the Trattoria Revolution.

## PICCADILLY, 1953

In the mirror of the staff locker room of Hatchett's restaurant in Dover Street, Franco Lagattolla carefully checked his appearance one last time.

Tall and thin, with straight dark hair brushed back from his high forehead, his black-framed glasses enhanced his angular face. In his tail suit, stiff-fronted dress shirt and black bow tie – a real one, he reminded himself, not the fake kind that upstart younger waiters wear – he was, he thought, correctly and perfectly dressed for his new position at this prestigious establishment.

Hatchett's, originally a coaching inn for travellers bound for the west of England, was well known during the Second World War as a basement restaurant which offered protection from the Blitz and traditional English food. It catered to well-heeled Mayfair residents and Secret Service employees from nearby Curzon Street.

At twenty-five, Franco had already amassed several years of professional experience. Well trained and completely bilingual, he had found it easy to make this latest step up the ladder towards his goal of becoming a restaurant manager in a top establishment. Now, as a station headwaiter, he would be in charge of a section of five tables, not yet the best in the room, but that would come later. Hatchett's was much more upmarket and exclusive than the Bagatelle in nearby Stratton Street, where he had previously been employed. Brushing away imaginary fluff from his impeccable lapels, he set out for his first day's work.

Upstairs in the dining room, Franco solemnly and studiously inspected the station of tables to which he had been assigned and with his two assistants checked that everything was ready for the luncheon service. The glasses gleamed, the cutlery shone and the elegant cream linen reflected a Mayfair establishment of quality. Around the room he could see other waiters going quietly about their preparations. At the door, the distinguished white-haired restaurant manager, Mr Claude, and the imposing headwaiter, supervised the scene as they awaited their first customers. Gazing at all this formality, Franco knew that he had arrived in a dignified and elegant restaurant, one which would help him achieve his goal of reaching the pinnacle of his profession.

Suddenly there was a commotion. Everyone turned to watch as a jovial character bounced through the staff entrance and waltzed across the room, nearly tripping over his long, black, wine-butler's apron. He gathered up the apron's hem and, with a wide smile, dropped Mr Claude a full curtsey. The whole staff grinned, as, with a glance and a nod to Franco, the new arrival slapped another colleague on the back, exchanged a few phrases with him in a rough accent (which Franco immediately recognised as Neapolitan), before skipping to his station at the other side of the room.

Franco was appalled. This little man, whoever he was, looked more like a comedian than a professional waiter. How had someone of this sort come to work at a top-class restaurant like Hatchett's? Franco's dream of a career in a truly British quality establishment seemed over before it had even started. Hatchett's, he realised, was after all, no different to any other upmarket London restaurant he'd worked in – staff all Italians and clowns at that. But, as he pondered this, his first customers began to arrive and he turned to his duties.

Not long after his induction, as Franco was walking slowly and pensively towards the Hyde Park bus stop in the afternoon sunshine, he felt someone touch his arm. It was the animated Neapolitan wine-butler, who introduced himself as Mario Cassandro and asked whether they could walk together. "Of course," Franco had replied, although he wasn't at all sure if he wanted this crass comic for a companion. But Mario turned out to be charming and entertaining. And as they strolled and talked, Franco soon felt at ease with him.

It quickly became clear that they both had ambitions to open their own businesses. Franco explained to Mario that he needed first to work his way up the ladder, so that when he finally did start his enterprise, he would have gained experience at the highest level.

"Why can't we begin now? This week or this month?" Mario asked impatiently. He wanted to open a coffee bar. (The first espresso machine had been invented in Italy just after the war and coffee bars were becoming popular in Britain.) That, he felt sure, was where a man could make a fortune, with hard work and some good luck. Franco disagreed. He wanted a proper restaurant, the kind of place where people would come first for the food, then return time and again for the atmosphere and value for money.

Their conversation became more and more heated and complex. Often, they stopped in the street, turned and shouted at each other, arguing loudly as passers-by stared and tiptoed around them.

By the time they had reached Knightsbridge they had become friends and had agreed on a compromise solution. When they had earned enough, when they had saved enough, when they had found the right place, when they were ready, they would combine their ideas – they would meld the cheerful informality of a coffee bar with an unpretentious restaurant serving real Italian food – something like a modest roadside eating house in southern Italy. They'd open a real trattoria in London.

At the bus stop, before setting off in different directions, they turned and shook hands. "Agreed, then?"

"*D'accordo*. Agreed."

"*Ciao*, Franco." "*Ciao*, Mario. See you this evening."

Sitting at the back of the bus on his way home to north London, Franco rotated the coins in his pocket and wondered if it would ever happen. How could he save enough money? It would surely cost at least a thousand pounds to get hold of a place. He was only making six pounds a week.

Franco Lagattolla was one hundred percent Italian, but had been born and raised in middle-class Highgate, north London, to which his parents had migrated from Minori on the Italian Riviera. He thus spoke Italian at home and English at school, with an excellent English accent. Although the Lagattolla family lived in Britain, Franco had been brought up in the Neapolitan style. His mother Lisetta made sure that he enjoyed the southern Italian food that she had grown up with and whenever they could afford it, the family took holidays back in Minori.

Franco's first job in catering was in his great-uncle Peppino Palumbo's café, beneath a railway arch in Camden. At fourteen, counselled by his family to start at the bottom of a high-class establishment, Franco applied to the head hall porter at the Savoy Hotel, for work as a page. But he was tall for his age and once it became clear that they had no pageboy uniforms that would fit him, he was instead sent to the restaurant headwaiter to see if he would take him on. He was told to come back with black shoes, a short café-jacket, black dinner trousers, a washable celluloid shirt-front and an apprentice's white bow tie. In 1942, having done as he was bid, he began to learn the Savoy way – the correct way – how to dress properly, how to address his superior colleagues, how to approach a table, how to clear a table, how to serve different dishes, how to speak to a customer...

Careful and thorough, Franco steadily gained in confidence as he acquired these disciplines. For him, they were necessary in order to become a master of his craft, so that he could eventually achieve his ambition to run a great restaurant. Franco, as a British boy, had been obliged to do National Service and was called up at eighteen, just at the end of the Second World War. After two years in the army he returned to his restaurant career and soon he began work at the Bagatelle, moving from there to Hatchett's.

Was he cut out to be his own boss? Franco wasn't sure he had the nerve. But he knew that this new job would give him yet more valuable experience. It was, he felt sure, just a matter of time.

Mario Cassandro had started at Hatchett's a few months before Franco. Well-built, with a pleasant countenance, he was of medium height with thick curly brown hair, clear blue eyes and an optimistic temperament. In his first thirty-two years he had already experienced more than most of us do in a lifetime. His family (his mother, like Franco's, was from Minori and his father from Brescia near Milan) existed on almost the bottom rung of the poverty ladder.

Born in Naples in 1920, Mario was the third of four children. "When I was a kid, we used to have to steal food, just to feed ourselves. We'd nip past the market stalls and pinch some fruit or a vegetable," he recalls. When he was nine, his father died, so he left school to help his mother support his siblings. His first job was to run through the streets of Naples, delivering olive oil from heavy cans carried on a yoke across his shoulders.

In 1938, at eighteen, he was called up into the Italian army and shipped to North Africa, where he took part in Mussolini's empire-building foray into Abyssinia and Libya. When the Duce, having seen Hitler's success in the Low Countries, rashly declared war on England and France on 10 June 1940, Mario's unit was stationed in Garianne, near Tripoli. That morning, he'd argued with his sergeant major and, as punishment, he was tied to a pole and left to stand in the sun until dusk. Half dozing, he suddenly realised that everyone was moving, boarding the unit's trucks.

"What's happening, where's everybody going?" he yelled. "The war has begun," someone shouted back. "We're at war with France." Someone else cut him loose and he jumped onto the tailgate of the last truck to leave.

Soon he was promoted to corporal. But six months later, his military career came to an abrupt halt. Still four months short of his twenty-first birthday, most of his regiment were taken prisoner at the Battle of Sidi-el-Barrani. As the Italian army crumbled at Tobruk, Mario, one of more than 150,000 Italian prisoners of war captured by the British, was shipped to Aden and then to a prison camp in Bangalore.

In 1943, the Italian government crumbled, the dictator, Mussolini, fell and Italy changed sides and joined the Allies. In his Indian prison camp, Mario had received a letter from his brother urging him to stay on and try and obtain a job with the British forces. This, his brother wrote, would be far better than coming home to war-torn Italy. In fact, Mario had no choice, since the beleaguered British had no resources to ship Italians home and, anyway, conflict still raged in the Apennines. So Mario took his first step towards success and enrolled in a Basic English course. Then, using his new linguistic skill, he found work as an army ambulance assistant, transporting casualties returned from the campaign in Burma.

Mario's second break was to meet a pretty, red-haired, Irish nurse, assistant matron at the hospital. The first time he tried to flirt with her, she called for help and had him removed. But Mario was kind, charming, funny and, above all, persistent. By the time he was allowed to return to Italy, he and Mary MacDonnell had become close.

There was not much opportunity for socialising in India, let alone mixing with high society. But if there was one, Mario was the sort of boy who would find it. While working at the hospital, he made friends with a local tailor and ordered himself a suit, so that, when off duty, he would not be recognised as a former POW. When, early in 1945, Lady Mountbatten made an inspection visit to the hospital as head of the St John Ambulance Brigade, Mario was ready. After her tour of the facility, Lady Mountbatten and her entourage attended a morale-raising event for hospital staff and the recuperating soldiers. After the official welcome, an aide shepherded them towards some staff members, believing them all to be young British lads. Camouflaged in his blue suit, the newly released Italian POW found himself making easy conversation with the wife of the Supreme Commander of the Allied Forces South East Asia.

After the fall of Japan, it still took a year to repatriate all the prisoners from India and it wasn't until June 1946 that Mario finally returned home. He was already twenty-six years old, but, in spite of his loss of freedom, the time in prison camp had not been wasted. He now had the determination to succeed and an ability to make the best of the cards he had been dealt. He had mixed with foreigners and people of all types, he had worked in a disciplined environment, his English was good and his experiences had given him a strong sense of his own ability to make a success of his life. The past years had not been wasted, but he knew it would be a struggle to find work at home.

## FROM NAPLES TO MAYFAIR

"*Biglietti, Biglietti.*" The conductor was working his way down the packed tram as it clattered through the shambolic streets of Naples. A year after the war had ended, the town was still in chaos, with little food in the shops, bomb craters and ruined buildings everywhere and no sign of the planned reconstruction which might have provided work. Mario was on his way to apply for a job, but he had no money for the tram fare.

"*Biglietti, Biglietti.*"

The conductor stopped in front of him.

"I have just returned home," Mario told him. "I have no money for a ticket. I was a prisoner of war."

"We are all prisoners here," replied the conductor quietly and passed on down the tram.

"*Biglietti, Biglietti...*"

Mario realised that he would have to find an occupation elsewhere. He had continued his courtship of his red-haired nurse and they had planned that she would join him in Italy. But now, because he could speak English and because post-war Britain seemed to offer better opportunities, he decided to go to London. Their engagement enabled him to obtain an entry permit.

Mary sent him four of the large white five-pound notes of those days. But when Mario went to the Naples *cambio* to change the notes into lire for the train fare to Britain, the money-changer agent vanished with his cash, so he had to borrow the fare again. He finally set out for London in 1947 with introductions to several Italian families who lived there.

Soho and Clerkenwell, with established Italian communities and their own businesses, were in those days the first destinations for all Italians arriving in London. The area north of Shaftesbury Avenue, around Wardour, Dean, Greek and Frith streets had enjoyed a bohemian reputation for more than a century. Soho was a district to which groups of immigrants had flocked in the seventeenth and eighteenth centuries and this gave its narrow streets and little mews, yards and alleyways an air of cosmopolitan diversity, which it had never lost. More recently, in the years leading up to the Second World War, several Italian, French and German restaurants and delicatessen shops had opened and the area became known for its "Continental" atmosphere, for raffish and slightly seedy pubs, drinking clubs and jazz cellars. In the late forties, there were occasional news stories about crooked police and the Maltese gangs who tangled over the ownership of strip clubs and prostitutes.

Within a week Mario found his first job, at Parmigiani Figlio, a provision store in Old Compton Street. He would be paid four pounds a week, a good sum in those days. He rented a room in the East End in Clapton and started devising the best ways of getting to work and home again at different times of the day.

With his charm and improving English, Mario was good with customers and his kindly boss soon suggested that he might make more money as a waiter. Mario knew someone who knew Mr. Giannini, the manager of The Ivy, the most celebrated of the theatre district restaurants and, at the late age of twenty-eight, Mario began his new career there.

With better wages, he and Mary could marry and they managed to

*Soho, spring 1959, at the corner of Old Compton and Frith streets. Almost everything is or looks Italian – fruit shop, coffee shop, valet service and one of many indifferent Italian restaurants. Photo: Popperfoto/Getty Images*

organise a wedding just a few days before his original six-month permit expired. In due course, he received a residency permit and their first son, Piero, was born in 1948. After three years at The Ivy and a brief spell working for a young Hungarian émigré, Egon Ronay, manager of the Society, in Jermyn Street (Egon Ronay had trained as a lawyer, come to London from Hungary in 1946 and in 1952 opened the Marquee in Kensington), Mario found himself at Hatchett's in 1952.

A year later, as he walked to the Hyde Park bus stop with his new colleague Franco Lagattolla, their destiny began to shape up.

Mario remained at Hatchett's for eight years, until his temper got him sacked. One of the restaurant's regulars, Lord Scott, was well known to the staff for his arrogance, bullying those who could not talk back. Nobody wanted to have to serve him and one day a wine-butler colleague of Mario's had had enough of the Milord. Stamping back to the waiters' station, puce in the face, he told the manager that if he had to speak to Scott again he would probably kill him. Kindly, but perhaps unwisely, the manager asked Mario if he would mind looking after the wine at Scott's table for the rest of the meal.

"May I pour you some wine, my Lord?" Mario asked Scott, picking up the decanter as the customer concentrated on his liver and bacon.

Sour-faced Scott replied, without raising his head, "Of course, you stupid little idiot."

Mario hesitated for a second, then, reddening, he stepped forward.

"What did you call me?"

Scott did then raise his head and, coldly, looking straight at Mario for the first time, said, "You're a stupid idiot, Now get on with it."

"What makes you think you can speak to me like that?" Mario shouted, pulling Scott out of his chair and attempting to strangle him. No one ever treated Mario like that and got away with it. Not even the King.

But there could be only one winner in that kind of argument and, within an hour, Mario, a husband and by now a father of two, was out on the street looking for another job.

"Some of those customers saw us as second rate, not even humans," he remembers fifty years later. "They treated us like dirt."

After five years in London, Mario had built up a good list of contacts, so his next job, at the Café de Paris, located in Coventry Street, came through another London Italian. The Café de Paris had suffered terribly during the Blitz when a bomb had cascaded down the main staircase to explode in the entrance, killing thirty-four people and injuring eighty-two more. It had re-opened in the late forties and survived mainly because of its position between Piccadilly Circus and Leicester Square. It was at first hand for the hundreds coming out of the nearby theatres. But the food, supposedly traditional French dishes, was fake. Pork was used instead of veal and margarine and ersatz cream made up for the lack of fresh ingredients. Also, by the end of the fifties, its traditional offering of dining, dancing and cabaret was no longer in fashion.

Again, Mario looked out for a new job and in 1956, when a vacancy for an experienced wine waiter came up at the Mirabelle, one of the most prestigious West End restaurants, paying a pound a week more than the Café de Paris, he took it like a shot.

*The Café Royal team in the annual Waiters' Race, Paddington Park, 1932. It was a hard life, as Italian waiters in London at the time were not employed, but paid their employer for the job and earned their income exclusively from tips. Photo: G Guarnieri*

## CURZON STREET, MAYFAIR, 1958

At the Mirabelle restaurant, the waiters' lunchtime shift normally finished a few minutes after 2.30 p.m., but if customers wanted to linger over the remains of their Château Cheval Blanc '37, the duty staff had to stay on. One early summer's day, there was just one party left on Mario's section and as he waited for them to leave, he gazed out of the window, beyond the heavy tapestries and silk curtains, to the Mirabelle's Spanish garden, with its fountain and rockery. It was early summer and no time to be stuck indoors in a uniform and bow tie. Finally, the last group was ready to leave.

"Thank you. Keep the change."

"Thank you very much, sir. Good afternoon."

Mario would be back on duty at six, but once his station was prepared for the evening, he could get away for a few hours of fresh air between the long shifts. He changed into his street clothes, slipped out of the staff entrance and turned left up Curzon Street, heading for the Serpentine. Having crossed Park Lane and entered Hyde Park, he turned right and, as he approached the lake, he could see that there were already several boats out on the water. Grey-uniformed nannies walked their charges and young couples drifted across the lawns. He found a spot in the sun beside the lake, lay on the bank, put his jacket down beside him, folded his hands behind his head, shut his eyes and started to think about his plans.

The Mirabelle was Mario's fourth restaurant job since his arrival in Britain and each had paid better than the last. At thirty-eight, Mario had by now worked there for more than two years and was one of four wine waiters, a respectable and senior position. He made good money; nine pounds a week plus tips. He had contacted his friend Franco when a vacancy for a headwaiter came up and now they were working together again. Off duty and on duty, they endlessly talked about the future.

Admittedly, Mario thought, the Mirabelle wasn't so bad, although a few customers were rude. He was always popular with his regulars and besides, when you worked with friends like Franco, good fun was often to be had. You could laugh together at the customers' fantastic behaviour and at the prices they paid – 25 shillings (£1.25) a head for lunch, or six pounds for a bottle of good French wine, more than he had earned in a month back at home in Naples.

He now had over a thousand pounds in his account at the Midland

Bank in Cambridge Circus and the kind manager would always say hello when he went to deposit part of his wages. For more than five years he had managed to save something every week. One of his regular Mirabelle customers, Percy Shaw – who had made a fortune inventing road safety cat's eyes – had suggested that Mario should buy Burmah Oil shares. He had invested two hundred pounds and the shares had risen substantially.

But how long should he go on saving and when should he make the break? Opening a restaurant would be a huge gamble. But he knew he had to take the risk. Should he try and do it on his own, or would Franco, determined to succeed but still timid about going solo, really be persuaded to join him? If not Franco, would one of his other good Italian friends from the Mirabelle come in? He had made many contacts, customers certainly liked him and some might well frequent a new place, but would that be enough? Did he have the temperament to cope with the pressure? His short fuse had caused him problems at Hatchett's, but now, more mature, he was pretty sure he could control it. He didn't bear grudges and, as Mary knew well, his outbursts always evaporated. They were forgotten as quickly as they had flared up.

Lying in the warm sun reminded him of the Mediterranean, of Naples and home. Thinking all these faraway thoughts made him drowsy and he fell fast asleep.

*"Si, è vero. Non c'è la cucina italiana a Londra. Ci sono tutti questi piatti francesi con nomi italiani."*

*"Certo, io sono qui da tre anni e la cucina napoletana mi manca molto!"*

The voices penetrated Mario's dream and he awoke. Not ten paces from him, two men were chatting in the familiar Neapolitan accent. One of them, who looked about thirty-five, had a dark moustache under a large, distinguished hooked nose and wore an expensive yellow jacket. He constantly gesticulated as he spoke. The other man, well dressed and darkly tanned, seemed to Mario to be the playboy type. Mario eavesdropped as they gossiped about Soho, about Greenwich Village in New York and about opening a night club or a discotheque. But over and over, they returned to the subject of food. Both, it seemed, were suffering from the lack of a decent Italian trattoria in London.

Mario sat up and ventured, "Excuse me… are you Neapolitan?" And of course they were and were delighted to meet a compatriot. So he moved over to join in their conversation. "I heard what you said," he told them, "and I agree… I am thinking of opening a real trattoria myself…"

The man with the moustache introduced himself as the cartoonist and designer, Enzo Apicella. He had, he said, been in London for a couple of years, doing some cartoons, a few advertisements and newspaper illustrations. His companion, Nino Falanga, a professional racing driver also from Naples, was his guest here in London for a few days. (Four years later Falanga would be driving near San Bernardino, California, when his car crashed and his passenger, the radiant young British film actress Belinda Lee, was killed.)

Mario shared the two Neapolitans' views on the poor quality of Italian food to be found in London. He said, though, that he was going to do something about it. He was still only a waiter at the Mirabelle. But he had saved some money and he planned to open his own restaurant.

Later, when it was time for Mario to return to work, the three men strolled over the grass, under the budding cherry and maple trees, towards Hyde Park Corner. As they parted at the park gate opposite St George's Hospital, Mario said that when he opened his own restaurant, he wanted a mural of the bay of Naples with grapes growing on a vine all over the wall. Then, as they shook hands, Apicella handed Mario his number.

"When you're ready," he said, "call me and I'll come and design it for you."

Mario would soon be ready. But could he count on his prospective partner?

That evening at the Mirabelle, Mario talked through his plan with Franco. Franco was still not certain he was ready to make the break. With his parents' comfortable family home in the background, he didn't entirely share Mario's hunger for success. He was a less enthusiastic entrepreneur than his friend, who had a great deal to gain and only his savings to lose. As Mario saw it, there was no shame in having a shot.

"If it all goes wrong," he said, "we can always go back to being waiters again."

"Are you sure we can do it?" Franco worried. "What if nobody comes? Who will we get as a chef? How will we trust him? Will the chef do what we tell him? What if we lose everything?"

Certainly, Franco's anxiety was well-founded. But Mario knew he was a worrier by nature and since he was impulsive, this aspect of Franco's character could only help them. In the Mirabelle's strait-laced environment, where Franco was at ease, Mario had learned to control his tendency towards informality. Franco was always correct, at home in a large establishment, seemingly not the entrepreneur type. But, Mario thought, he could fix that. He had the energy. He would have to be the one who pushed, who carried Franco along with his enthusiasm. He was convinced that they were about to make the right choice.

Franco, for his part, also knew his friend's strengths. He was always amazed at how Mario remembered so many names and faces and loved the social side of restaurant work – dealing with customers, getting to know them and their favourite dishes and drinks. He, himself, had become a highly knowledgeable restaurant professional. In addition to his skills at table service, he knew at this stage a great deal more than Mario about menu planning and the business side of the trade. Through dedication, diligent pursuit of his craft and careful observation not only of his own kitchen colleagues, but also of French Maître Chefs such as Raymond Oliver of Le Grand Véfour, who had guested several seasons at the Mirabelle, Franco had learnt a great deal about menus, food and presentation. His English accent impressed not only the Mirabelle's management and its customers, but also Mario, who was aware that his prospective partner was way ahead of him in matters of sophistication and presentation. Because of his Savoy training, Franco had a habit of standing at attention, feet together, leaning slightly forward, with his hands either round his order book or behind his back and peering solicitously at the customer with his eyebrows raised. This was also partially because his eyesight was not good and he often refused to wear his new glasses, but the impression he made was excellent.

When Mario took Franco home to east London for a rare Sunday lunch, his wife Mary, now working as a district nurse, very much encouraged her husband to persuade Franco to join him. Franco, she said, was the right partner – a little reserved, perhaps, but thoughtful and reflective whereas Mario wanted to rush ahead. Mary saw that their different but complementary personalities, combined with their strong respect for each other's talent and by now four years' experience of working together, would make an ideal combination.

At one stage there might have been three partners, as another Mirabelle headwaiter, their friend Luigi Paglierani, was also thinking of starting his own business. Tall, thin, balding and slightly stooped, Luigi had come to Britain in 1951 from Rome, then spent six years at the Savoy before moving on to Hatchett's, where they'd all met. Luigi was hardworking, honest to the point of naïveté and still somewhat shy; it was mostly thanks to his supportive English wife Patricia, that he had become more focused on success. Although it became clear that he was not yet ready to set out on his own, Mario and Franco would never lose touch with Luigi, nor with Antonio Pizzala, their other headwaiter friend. Both Luigi and Antonio reappear in this story.

Although, encouraged by Mary, Mario and Franco had finally agreed to go into business together, Franco still had no contribution to match Mario's savings. He fretted that they were starting out as unequal partners, but Mario told him not to worry. He was determined that whatever happened, they would share everything 50–50. So, in February 1959, they set out to look for a site for their new venture.

*"One day I will open my own place, with grapes growing on a vine up the wall." Waiters at the Mirabelle, 1958. Left to right Luigi Paglierani, Mario and Franco. They would never lose touch with Luigi and their other Mirabelle headwaiter friend, Antonio Pizzala. Photo: courtesy of Mario Cassandro*

## READY FOR A CHANGE

Initially, Mario and Franco had no way of knowing whether their dream of a real Italian trattoria, with food as authentically Italian as possible, would prove right for the moment. But the state of British restaurants and food was dire and London was certainly ready for something new.

By 1959, Italians had been working in English restaurants for at least a hundred years, but until Mario and Franco made Italian cooking fashionable, their countrymen had always been the ones in charge of the "salle" or dining room, while their French colleagues ran the kitchen. At the turn of the twentieth century, London was perhaps the greatest city in the world, capital of both the most powerful and earliest industrialised nation, which resulted in much new wealth and many new people able to afford new houses and the servants to staff them. But the majority of available British and Irish workmen were engaged in building the many new public and private buildings, in the West End, Belgravia, Kensington and Notting Hill and many of their wives and sisters were already in service. The solution to the shortage of labour lay in immigration.

For the first time, in the late nineteenth century, English restaurants emerged that might be recognisable today. Before 1890, no woman of position could be seen dining out in public, but when César Ritz, manager of the newly opened Savoy Hotel, began to offer dining rooms for private entertainment and hospitality, the practice very soon became fashionable. If such notables as Lady Randolph Churchill and Consuela Vanderbilt, Duchess of Marlborough, could be seen to arrive at the Savoy's private rooms to dine on Maître Chef Auguste Escoffier's concoctions, it would not be long before everyone else was ordering from the same menu, in public, downstairs. Dining out in company became not only acceptable, but respectable and, eventually, positively chic. This increased the demand for catering staff.

Very soon, Italian waiters were serving French food to English customers; the catering field, from the grandest hotels to humble corner cafés, became an open door for immigrant labour in Victorian Britain.

In 1861 there were a mere 4,500 Italians in Britain – mostly craftsmen and professionals – but the trickle of peasant emigrants who trudged across Europe to seek a new life turned into a flood after the unification of Italy, as in the space of next thirty years, the British Italian community doubled and, in the 1890s, demand for waiters led to a further increase to just over 20,000, four times more than in 1861. Ten years into the new century, there were several thousand Italian waiters, chefs, bakers and confectioners in London alone, while 500 Italians owned cafés and restaurants and at least another thousand were in domestic service. The Ritz Hotel opened in 1905 and, as in the other grand palaces, its restaurant served an Anglo-French menu, with French titles and French wines. Like the others, it was managed and mostly staffed in front of house by Italians and in the kitchens by Frenchmen. It was Sir George Smith, chairman of the Savoy Group of hotels in the 1930s, who first coined the phrase "*Dans la salle les Italiens, dans la cuisine les Français.*" For nearly seventy years, this was the system which worked so well in British restaurants, both grand and less so. It was not an easy life. Italian waiters in London were not really employees. On the contrary, they paid their employer for the privilege of having the job and their income came exclusively from tips. It would be a while before English middle-class diners regarded foreign staff as individuals and fellow human beings.

When Mario and Franco decided to start up on their own, the catering and restaurant business was still stuck in a pre-war time-warp, on the whole with very low standards. In hotels and restaurants, the Second World War had become the perfect excuse for a lack of everything, including courtesy and when Mario had arrived in London in 1947, bread, petrol, sugar, bacon, jam, oatmeal, semolina and macaroni were still all rationed. Restaurant meals were limited to three courses, which always included soup and cost a maximum of five shillings (25p). Short of food and luxuries during the war, the British had learned not to complain. If anyone did, the reply was always "Don't you know there's a war on?" Little remained of former grand restaurants beyond out-of-date ceremony. Only a few family-run hotels and restaurants, in which the food was prepared by a dedicated professional, maintained anything approaching 1930s standards.

In post-war Britain, convenience food was still unknown and everything had to be made at home. Nobody had yet shopped in a supermarket or bought a pre-packed portion of meat, a fish finger, a hamburger, or frozen peas; there was no instant coffee, or sliced bread and no breakfast cereals; the weekly meat ration, if taken as a chunk of fillet steak, would fit into a box of matches; satisfaction was a matter of quantity, rather than taste and actually to have obtained enough food to feed the family, let alone guests, was in itself a triumph. After a meal, the polite guest would say to his hostess that he "couldn't eat another thing."

The journalist Raymond Postgate had been so furious with the British people's disinterest in what they ate that in a 1949 magazine article, he proposed the creation of a society for the prevention of cruelty to food, pointing to an obvious tell-tale clue – every restaurant or café across the country provided bottled sauce on the table, assuming that people would want, or need, to disguise the taste, or absence of taste, in what they were about to order. Postgate's Good Food Club offered free membership to anyone who cared about what they ate. The only stipulation was that they should write to him with comments about restaurants which they had visited. The first edition of his *Good Food Guide* was published in 1951.

As a pub-going nation, Britain had never enjoyed a restaurant or café society culture. While eating in a restaurant was a luxury at the top end of the market, for most people a visit to a tea shop or a milk bar was the nearest they would come to a meal away from home. Most pubs did not, in those days, serve food and at the very cheapest level there were fish and chip shops, the early curry houses, Chinese takeaways, or working men's cafés serving egg, sausage and chips. The idea of a real restaurant offering interesting freshly cooked food, at everyday prices, was unheard of in most parts of the country.

In May 1950, hotels and restaurants were de-restricted from the five-shilling (25p) limit on the cost of a meal and the number of courses that could be served. But for all except a privileged few, a meal out was functional, not a pleasure and dining well was rare in London and a bleak prospect elsewhere. In London, the choice was either to dine at the Mirabelle, the Savoy, The Ivy or the Caprice, with its flocked wallpaper, gilded mirrors and claret-satin quilting, or at the other end of the scale, you could eat at a greasy spoon café. For families, there were very few restaurants outside larger towns and choice was, on the whole, still limited to hotel dining rooms, department store restaurants and the ubiquitous Lyons Corner Houses. Except for a few faux-French restaurants – where, besides the name on the door and the words on the menu, there was nothing very French – there was little in between. Natural, simple Mediterranean food had not arrived in London and French was the only respected cuisine.

In the 1955 edition of the *Good Food Guide*, the Three Horseshoes Hotel in Rugby offered an à la carte menu with a wide range of dishes, many with exotic names, but what is extraordinary to modern eyes is the amount of ingredients required to make what seem to us unnecessarily complicated dishes. For example, "Sole Walewska" at 7/6d (38p) would involve lobster tails, flour, butter, white wine, cognac, shallots, tomato puree and more. Today, that looks like a complete waste of a fresh sole, but the French influence was still all-pervasive and menus were a peculiar polyglot affair. The Three Horseshoes dinner menu at 9/6d (48p) offered a choice of "noodles Champenoise," grapefruit or soup, then "plaice Meunière," chicken casserole, braised ox-tongue in Madeira sauce, grilled lamb cutlets, scampi or grilled salmon, followed by various sweet dishes and cheeses. Down the road at the Warwick Arms, operating at an altogether simpler level, the chef made excellent Indian curry and some "noteworthy simple Italian dishes such as spaghetti and ravioli."

One newly arrived young Italian waiter, Sandro Tobi, simply gave up:

> The first time I came from Italy to London the food was terrible, awful. None of the food actually tasted of anything. At the Coq d'Or they fed us staff on chicken wings, every day of the week. One day I was walking along Piccadilly and I saw a sign saying Spaghetti, it was outside a Lyons Corner House. So I went in and the waitress came up and I ordered the spaghetti. It was tinned and it came served on toast. I said to myself, I have to leave this country, now! So I left the next day.

It was not until the mid-fifties that rationing ended. By this time, the British had suffered food deprivation for thirteen years, longer than any other Western European country. Although more exotic vegetables such as courgettes, red and green peppers, fennel and endives and fruit such as melons and figs were gradually becoming available at Covent Garden market, it would still be a long while before any appeared in homes or on menus beyond London. Not only restaurateurs, but also private cooks suffered from the lack of ingredients which were necessary to give authenticity to their recipes.

Although there was still nothing new to be found in the field of French or Italian cooking in Britain, several other foreign influences on Britain's tastes were beginning to emerge. That same 1955 *Good Food Guide* reviewed Chinese restaurants in Brighton, Liverpool and Manchester, an Indian in Manchester, a Greek in Nottingham and in the London section two Chinese, six Indian, one Burmese and four Greek or Turkish.

There was one group of enterprising Italians which introduced a new food concept to Britain, albeit not an Italian one. In the aftermath of meat rationing, steak became understandably popular. Frank and Aldo Berni, originally café owners, took over a Bristol pub and reopened it as the Berni

Inn with a menu costing less than eight shillings (40p). For this sum, their customers could enjoy a prawn cocktail, a half-pound steak with chips and peas and Black Forest Gateau or cheese. The brothers' chain of Berni Inns succeeded because a visit to one of them made a meal in a restaurant, still seen by the vast majority of Britons as a luxury, affordable.

Other than Soho Italian families, their own friends and a few Mirabelle regulars who might visit a new venture, Mario and Franco had very little idea of their potential clientele. Britain in the mid-fifties was still very much a polarised society. For most older middle-class Londoners, an "evening out" in 1958 would have meant men dressing up in black tie and dinner jackets and women in evening gowns. Perhaps they might meet first for cocktails at a smart hotel, then go on to the new Terence Rattigan or Hugh and Margaret Williams play – perhaps *Plaintiff in a Pretty Hat*. Then they would repair to a formal West End restaurant, maybe the Coq d'Or in Stratton Street and later perhaps to a cabaret nightclub to be entertained by Hungarian gypsy musicians or Cossack dancers. They would not have dreamt of dinner in Soho.

Social classes, whether stratified by position, by money, education or profession, still led entirely separate lives. A sportsman, a hairdresser, musician, or dancer would know exactly where he or she might expect to be at ease in a club, restaurant or café, surrounded by like-minded people. Doctors, lawyers, journalists, editors, gallery owners and high society all had their own favourite, exclusive establishments. The groups didn't mix.

Some small new restaurants did begin to offer good food in less grand surroundings. They catered for the large numbers of Londoners who now found themselves living in smaller houses than before, with fewer, if any, staff; people who didn't want to bother to dress up and go to the West End for dinner. The Ox on the Roof, opened at 353 King's Road in 1950 by Alfred, a Slav, and his London-born wife Ruby, was informal and cosy. The *Good Food Guide* noted its snails, grilled scampi and mixed grill. The psychotherapist, Dr Hilary James, opened Le Matelot restaurant in Elizabeth Street in 1952, with a mostly amateur staff ("with overtones of RADA" sneered the 1957 *Good Food Guide*) and was soon sufficiently busy to add a second, La Bicyclette (staffed by "flashing young men and dramatic young women," according to the *Guide*), next door.

Perhaps the earliest example of an Englishman copying the small bistros of the South of France was Bill Stoughton's La Popote, opened in Walton Street in 1955. At the end of the decade, Nick Clarke opened

Nick's Diner, in Ifield Road, Chelsea. Originally a workman's café, providing only breakfasts and lunches, Nick's Diner morphed into a proper restaurant at night, serving French bourgeois cooking mostly gleaned from Elizabeth David's recipes.

These were the first to break another long-standing convention – formality. In most hotel restaurants throughout in the country and in every "professional" restaurant in London, dining out was still an elaborate performance. The process known as "silver service" denoted a serious restaurant and every restaurateur thought they must offer it in order to prove that they were worth taking seriously. In what has been described as an "archaic and frustrating ritual," customers' plates were filled, in a slow step-by-step performance, by a procession of waiters and waitresses

*How it was – velvet, plush, and gilt at Le Caprice, 1950s. Note all the ladies in hats surrounding Trevor Howard, centre, and television star, Bernard Braden, centre left. Photo: Le Caprice archive*

delivering separate elements of the meal to the table.

Even if they were lucky enough to be taken out, many adolescents who, in the next decade, would become Mario and Franco's customers, must have spent family lunches and evenings bored stiff by formal restaurant meals. As children in Sussex, my brother and I would watch the silver service ritual during a family Sunday lunch treat at the Roebuck Hotel in Forest Row. When it came to the roast main course, the staff – senior waiters in traditional tails or dinner jackets and the younger waitresses and waiters in white shirts and black skirts or trousers – would first bring us hot plates, giving them one final polish as they slid them, always from the right, before each of us in turn. Then there was an embarrassing silence. We all stopped talking and watched the staff as they worked. With fork and spoon often wielded very inexpertly, slices of meat, together with a sprig of greenery, would be twitched off a precariously balanced silver salver and carefully tweezered onto each plate. It was then joined by portions of overcooked vegetables delivered in similar fashion. Then followed Yorkshire pudding, gravy, horseradish sauce, mustard, mint sauce or red currant jelly, laboriously spooned from silver salver, jug or jar, to complete the assembly.

Restaurateurs had adapted this method from a style common in country houses, known as Service à la Russe, which had been introduced to England in the 1870s, to replace Service à la Française, in which all the dishes appeared at once. Under à la Russe, country house staff proffered various dishes in turn and guests then helped themselves. But this sort of service was unworkable in restaurants, not least because portion control determined profitability.

Many excellent meals were served in "silver service" style. But by the time the food reached the customer's mouth it was usually cold. At banquets, a waiter might have to serve ten people per table with spoon and fork in one hand, keeping the serving dish balanced with the other. This took time to learn. "For anybody to serve and balance the great heavy dish at the same time was very difficult," said the Chef Anton Mosimann, remembering his early days at the Dorchester. "And with everything coming separately – mustard, mint sauce, jellies, it all took a great deal of time." Sometimes it took ten or more minutes to serve one table.

Mario and Franco had not for a moment considered this issue, or how they would handle it. By the mid-fifties, customers were ready for a change, but the restaurants were not yet there to satisfy them.

## THE COMPETITION: MOCK-ITALIAN OR HOLLYWOOD ROMAN

*"Italians, with the exception of Macaroni, have no specially characteristic article of food."*

MRS BEETON, *HOUSEHOLD MANAGEMENT*, 1861

In 1959, when Mario and Franco set out to open their own trattoria, there were two different kinds of Italian restaurant in London and, as their countryman Enzo Apicella had observed, most of them were inauthentic. There was the Mock-Italian and the rarer Hollywood-Roman type, based on films such as *The Robe* and *Ben Hur*.

The Mock-Italian offered a reproduction of an Italy which the *padrone* remembered from the home he'd left fifty years before. It idealised what a restaurant in Italy might once have been and to elderly customers it brought back memories of travel to a long-forgotten Italy which had existed before the Second World War. Most of these establishments were furnished with heavy curtains, thick carpets and dark wooden beams, straw-wrapped Chianti bottles and plastic vegetation hanging from the ceiling. Their proprietors had arrived in Britain in the early 1900s and had learned their trade in the great French restaurants of the Edwardian era. When they left to open their own restaurants, they had not enough confidence or pride in Italian cooking to offer only Italian food and, bowing to the perceived superiority of French cuisine, produced menus which combined pasta with French dishes.

Fanny and Johnnie Cradock's 1955 *Bon Viveur* guide listed six Italian restaurants in London, while the new edition of *The Good Food Guide* suggested seven. All were long-established, provided traditional dishes and formal service, very much in the pre-war mould. Leoni's Quo Vadis in Dean Street, founded in 1929, was the most celebrated and La Speranza in the Brompton Road was another. In St Martin's Lane, Brusa's was popular with hungry actors and actresses and the much smaller Continental Restaurant in the Earls Court Road was frequented by a regular clientele who had set nights every week for dining there. There were also Chez Ciccio, in a basement in Kensington Church Street, which clearly couldn't make up its mind whether it was French or Italian and Casa Prada, described in the *Guide* as "Milan crossed with High Holborn."

Valerio Calzolari describes his first London job at Leoni's Quo Vadis in Soho's Dean Street:

Coming from Bologna and only knowing about food from the village, for me to see this very, very old Italian restaurant with a mix of French and Italian dishes was very strange; I was very lost there. It was not Italian, it was not French. He used to take French dishes and put an Italian name, like Pollo alla Principessa instead of *Poulet à la Princesse*. That was not Italian food at all to me… but anyway I needed a job.

Guidebooks of the era provide many examples of "Mock-Italian" menus. One typical meal seems to have been enjoyed by a *Good Food Guide* inspector in 1955 at Romano Santi in Greek Street:

**Dinner, 6/9d (55p): consisted of spaghetti bolognese, sole meunière and peach melba, which was adjudged to be very satisfying. Veal escalope with mushrooms (4/6) and mixed grill (4/-) also praised. Carafe wines at 10/6d (red and white Bordeaux and red Chianti)… Little attempt at décor…**

In addition to the Italian pasta and a French recipe for sole, these menus also offered half-breed dishes, spelt in neither language, such as "Gnocchi Romaine," "Saltinbocco alla Zingara," and "Lasagne Imbottite with rocotta mazarella." An omelette was offered alongside "Artichokes in Hollandaise." One of Leoni's popular dishes was "Pollo alla Yolanda," a chicken breast, beaten flat, coated with egg, flour and parmesan, fried in oil and served with asparagus tips and butter on top, finished under the grill.

"Hollywood Roman"-style restaurants evolved from Tinseltown's idea of Italy and were to be avoided by all except wannabe emperors, handmaidens and centurions. The worst offenders were the Villa dei Cesari in Grosvenor Road, near the river Thames and The Roman Room at 171 Brompton Road. At these "restaurant experiences" your wine waiter wore sandals, a short white smock and a glued-on beard. The headwaiter wore a heavily braided velvet-rimmed Roman toga, while glamorous blonde waitresses wore one-shouldered white dresses. There were mosaic table tops, antiquey Roman statues and concrete archaeological relief fragments attached to the walls. Cooking was done on an open fire and the profusion of thick guttering candles would have done credit to a scene from *Gladiator* or *Spartacus*. There were wooden platters and silver goblets and the menus and wine lists were written in cod Latin. But the food – Scampus Tartarus or Taurus Stroganofum – was clearly frenchified.

Into this bogus, formal, over-stuffed and weary environment, Mario and Franco prepared to launch their new venture.

## SOHO, SPRING 1959

*"We can certainly do a lot better than this!"*

On his afternoons off, Mario started to search for premises and, when he could, Franco joined him and they tramped around, looking at the possibilities together. After a month, they had scoured all the obvious London zones – Hampstead, Highgate, Chelsea, Kensington, Notting Hill Gate, Pimlico and the City – but everything they saw and liked was either too small, too large, had too short a lease or too high a premium.

One midweek March day in 1959, they met in Soho for another afternoon of research. They began with a quick meal in a Frith Street Italian café-restaurant run by a Florentine whom Mario knew from when he'd worked nearby at Parmigiani Figlio. Mario ordered a simple pasta with tomato sauce, while Franco decided to try the house speciality, an escalope of veal with onions – "*alla Veneziana*" – and, as they waited, they caught up with each other's news. Piero's eleventh birthday had been a great success, Mario said. After a panic about changing his shift, he had, after all, been able to get home in time for the cake.

Then, their orders arrived and they started to eat. But after one mouthful they looked at each other and put down their forks. Two sets of eyebrows were raised.

"It's tasteless and thin. The pasta's pre-cooked and reheated," exclaimed Mario.

"Mine's awful," agreed Franco. "It's gristle, it's greasy and the onions are watery."

"We can certainly do a lot better than this," they said in unison.

They became convinced that they were on the right track. And the more they talked and the more they searched, the more they also became convinced that it had to be Soho. With its regular supply of Italian immigrants, its Italian butchers and provision stores, its constant stream of visitors, its access to the nearby theatre districts of Shaftesbury Avenue and Covent Garden and with no worthwhile competition, Soho would be the ideal location for their trattoria.

Another week of Mario's exploration narrowed their focus. One distinct possibility was the Two i's Coffee Bar in Old Compton Street, where Tommy Steele, Britain's first Rock 'n' Roll singer, had been discovered; but the lease premium was too expensive. The next day, anticipating another afternoon plodding the streets, their rendezvous was at the Palm Club, in Romilly Street near the corner of Dean Street. Franco had joined the club but had rarely visited it.

The Palm was the traditional meeting place for London's top chefs and a few headwaiters, all from the West End's best restaurants. They would convene there in their off-duty hours to play chess, dominoes and cards. Franco had been made a member by Antonio Pizzala, who had convinced the owner that though not a chef, Franco was a respected headwaiter.

The Palm Club contained five marble-topped tables, a zinc bar counter, an upright piano and a parrot. Its members, mostly Italians who worked at Claridges, the Savoy and other grand establishments in the West End, relaxed there between their shifts. Since most of them worked in French restaurants, the opportunity to enjoy home cooking was welcome and at the same time every afternoon, the member whose turn it was would retire to the back yard (which had been covered with a leaky corrugated iron roof) and, on a large stove, he'd carefully prepare a meal. The result, usually a pasta dish from his home region, would be brought to the downstairs club room and consumed, with much critical comment by his fellow members. It was impossible to find this sort of sustenance outside Italian homes; not surprisingly, it was reputed to be the best eating place in London.

Mario and Franco walked into the bar together, greeted friends and ordered coffees. The Palm was owned and strictly run by Signora Botti, an elderly woman who made sure that there was no nonsense and closed the door promptly at eight each evening. In spite of its culinary reputation, the club was not a successful commercial venture.

"Hello, Franco, how are you? It's been a while," Signora Botti greeted them.

"Fine, thank you, Signora. Yes, I'm working much further away, across town now. And how are you?"

"Tired," she sighed. "I'm tired and I'm going to retire. It's time to stop all this."

The partners turned to each other, blank faced, betraying nothing, even though Franco did raise an eyebrow.

The site at the corner of Dean Street, they both instantaneously realised, would be ideal. It was just a few paces from Shaftesbury Avenue, with easy access to buses and Leicester Square and Piccadilly Circus tube stations. To its north was Old Compton Street, with its Italian butchers, grocery and provision shops and wine merchants. In particular, as Mario remembered from his days working round the corner, three of the most frequented haunts of journalists, writers, artists and bohemian types were right next door – Gaston Berlemont's York Minster, always known as the French pub, the Coach and Horses on the corner of Greek Street and Romilly Street and the Colony Club, Muriel Belcher's louche, after-hours drinking den, next door to the French on Dean Street. (Drinking clubs in those days existed to get round the licensing hours, which were much stricter than now. Pubs closed in the afternoons and at 10.30 or 11 p.m. The Soho drinking clubs were often clandestine and fairly sleazy, but that was part of the fun.)

Signora Botti was, she reiterated, getting too old for all this. She seriously intended to put the lease up for sale. Franco glanced at Mario and received the glimmer of a nod in return. Together, they turned towards her.

"We might be interested, Signora," Franco said cautiously.

Two days later, the old lady had agreed to sell them the business for £500, including goodwill, fixtures and fittings. Out of Mario's £1,200 savings, the partners would also have to pay £500 to the landlord to take over the lease. This would leave only £250 to turn the Palm Club into a restaurant.

On Mario's 39th birthday, 14 April 1959, the duo was to meet at the landlord's solicitor's office in Soho Square. Franco had agreed to bring a solicitor to represent them, but he turned up late, on his own and looking wan. He drew Mario outside.

"I've changed my mind. I don't want to go on, I don't want to come into the business," he muttered.

"Whaaat? Franco, what you talking about?"

Mario grabbed him by the shoulders. "You get fifty per cent of everything. Don't worry about it. I don't mind you don't put anything in yet. You still have fifty per cent of our business. Please. Come on. Let's do it. We're nearly there." Mario urged. "If it doesn't work, so what? We can just go back and be waiters again."

Franco caved in, persuaded by Mario's certainty.

"OK," he said. "But I hope to God we know what we're doing."

They both crossed themselves. Mario took Franco's arm and they walked back inside and signed the lease.

Finally, they had their own place. Franco, having decided to make the plunge – then made it – was suddenly transformed and, as excited as boys with new toys, they danced out of the lawyer's office and into Soho Square.

The partners had often talked long into the night about how their restaurant should look. They knew what they didn't want – a dark, beamed room like Gennaro's or Leoni's Quo Vadis or those other old-fashioned places – but all they knew that they did want was a mural of the Bay of Naples, to remind them and their customers of their southern Italian origins. Mario, remembering his meeting with Enzo Apicella, found the designer's card and called him. But either Enzo had written the number down wrong or else it was out of date. So Mario rang a French architect-designer, who had recently redesigned the garden room at the Mirabelle and drawings and plans were quickly created.

Next stop was Mario's bank manager, Sidney Boswell, at the Midland Bank, in Cambridge Circus.

"Come and look. I have found a place, " Mario invited him.

Boswell knew how hard Mario had worked to save a relatively small sum. So naturally he had questions about the site and the partners' business plan. But Mario urged him to look at the Palm Club before allowing scepticism to take over.

"Please. Just come with me," he pleaded and Boswell, against all instinct, found himself, together with Mario and Franco, walking straight out of the bank, down Shaftesbury Avenue and into Dean Street. Having peered through the window, Boswell turned and said, "Alright, I will help you. Go and find out how much you'll need to turn it into what you want."

That night, Mario called his wife's cousin, a builder, and asked him to meet them on site the next day. But after viewing it and the plans, the builder was discouraging. If he were to follow their design (creating a restaurant on the ground floor, with kitchens at the back), it would cost at least seven thousand pounds, maybe seven and a half. Mario returned to his bank manager to tell him what they needed. A few days later, Boswell rang him and told him that yes, they would have their money. Mario was, naturally, amazed at the decision, but he wasn't about to question it. He now quit his job, in order to supervise the building work full time. Franco, anxious to make a financial contribution, left the Mirabelle, too, and took an evening job at Harry Meadows' Churchill Club, sharing his weekly pay packet with Mario. Luckily Mary, now a district nurse, was earning a good living, so the Cassandro family wouldn't starve.

Construction began. Everything had to be done on a shoestring. Out came marble-topped tables, zinc bar, upright piano and the old bentwood chairs. And, having cleared the ground floor, the long, thin room suddenly seemed much bigger. At the back, in the open courtyard, the corrugated iron roof was extended to enlarge the kitchen area. The old Palm Club stove was kept and another large second-hand one was added. For £25 they bought a huge commercial fridge which the Mirabelle was about to jettison. As the restaurant gradually took shape, they bought new chairs and in second-hand stores and bankrupt premises they found tables, which they varnished and covered with felt. Once the restaurant opened, they planned to have a membership club, the Gatto Nero (Black Cat), in the basement, to take advantage of the Palm Club's former club licence.

One morning, Franco arrived on site to find Mario beside himself with rage. Work had ceased. Patiently, Franco extracted from his partner the news that the sanitary inspector had insisted that they had installed the wrong kind of kitchen tiles. Like most building problems, this was eventually solved.

As completion drew nearer, Franco left the Churchill to work with Mario on site for the last few weeks. Without his wage, they were penniless. Until they could open, there was nothing coming in and they had to rely on the generosity of their neighbours and the builders. "We used to go over to old Eugenio at King Bomba," Franco recalled, "and he'd give us bread and salami and we'd go back and share it with the workmen, who'd go to the pub across the road and bring us each back a bottle of Guinness."

A few weeks before the opening, Franco's football pools syndicate won him £1,250. Through this windfall, Franco could finally contribute to the project financially; he immediately put £800 into the business. As soon as it was time for the visual touches which Mario longed for, the mural of the Bay of Naples was commissioned from Polish George, a local Soho character, an artist who'd fought with the British against Hitler and had decided not to return to Warsaw. George insisted on working throughout the night and in addition to his fee, demanded enough brandy to accompany him through the small hours. So in the early evening, George was locked in with paints, a bottle of brandy for inspiration and, since the mural was supposed to be in relief, a large bag of dental cement.

The next morning, Franco turned up early to find Polish George slumped on a table, his head in his arms, with the empty brandy bottle by his side. His finished mural ran the whole length of a wall. From a terrace in the foreground, it transported viewers across the whole bay, taking in the sea, city, pine woods, right up to the mountains and Vesuvius beyond. But the sea was pale green, the sky white and the mountains were capped with snow. George, it turned out, had never been to the Mediterranean. That evening Mario and Franco briefed him on the colours and glories of *La Bella Baia di Napoli*. They gave him a highly coloured postcard of the area to copy and a large quantity of blue paint. The next morning, George was peacefully asleep in his usual position. Now, though, the view was in line with their idealised memories.

The night before the scheduled opening was predictably chaotic. Mario and Franco spent most of it on their knees, scrubbing and wire brushing the new tiles which had been mistakenly painted over. Their staff was unpacking cutlery, opening crates of china, stacking provisions, finding a shelf for stationery. Deliveries were continuously arriving while workmen struggled to finish and pack up. Technicians switched off lights, gas, or water, at crucial moments as dishes were being tested and sauces being tasted.

The basement was now ready to become the Gatto Nero Club. The ground floor, with seating for thirty-five, was La Trattoria Terrazza. Finally, Mario and Franco's career as restaurateurs could begin and on 2 June 1959, as they prepared to open for business, Franco put a sign outside on the pavement.

Their protracted preparations had attracted attention from neighbours as well as from passers-by. Curious onlookers, office workers, tradesmen and several inquisitive acquaintances gathered outside the door as Mario and Franco swept the floor for the third time and finished laying, then checking, the tables.

For a restaurant which, within a few years, would change the way that Londoners ate out, La Terrazza looked pretty similar to other small Soho establishments. On either side of the door, there were old-fashioned carriage lamps; on the left, stairs led down to the basement drinking club, under the sign **Gatto Nero Club, Members only**. From the street, you could just see through the panes of the original bow-windows into the restaurant. The front door gave onto a tiny corridor leading into the main room, where, on the right, behind the row of square tables, was the view from the trompe l'oeil terrace across to the Bay of Naples, framed by a trellis of plastic grapes which trailed over the faux balcony. Opposite it, rectangular tables were arranged under a long mirror which reflected the mural and made the narrow room seem larger. The floor was tiled and straw-wrapped Chianti bottles hung from hooks on the walls. Table settings were plain with white tablecloths, stainless steel cutlery and salt and pepper shakers. On each table there was a small basket of grissini and a Campari-branded ashtray.

Franco was twice forced to change the opening time, but finally he flung the doors open at 8 p.m. They were able to seat 35 people at eight tables. There was no great rush that first evening. But they welcomed a steady trickle of friends and well-wishers as well as some chance passers-by who had no idea it was the opening day of La Trattoria Terrazza.

Much later, a rumour circulated among La Terrazza's regulars that not only had Giovanni, the original head chef, once been the personal cook of Hermann Göring, but that Carlo, his deputy, had worked as Mussolini's private chef in San Remo. Whatever their backgrounds, they were fellow Neapolitans, very experienced chefs and very expensive. Giovanni was paid the then substantial wage of twenty pounds a week, Carlo was paid fifteen and the team was completed by a less costly kitchen porter and two waiters – another Carlo and another Mario.

Although the original idea had been that the menu would focus only on the south, Mario and Franco soon realised that adaptations would have to be made. Italian dishes would be popular with the British, but many of the ingredients of authentic southern domestic cooking were hard to find.

Fish and seafood from the Mediterranean coast, buffalo mozzarella from Lazio, fruit and vegetables from Basilicata, and citrus fruits from further south would appear on La Terrazza menu as soon as they could be sourced. Even if it would not offer exclusively Neapolitan food, Naples' culinary influence would be uppermost. Early menus featured southern dishes such as spaghetti with clams, or with a rich tomato, garlic and oregano sauce, linguine with sweet basil and garlic, toasted mozzarella sandwiches *(mozzarella in carrozza)* and mixed fried seafood.

It turned out that La Terrazza was the first trattoria in London to feature authentic dishes from all over Italy. As regional ingredients became readily available, its influence grew and Mario and Franco's format was copied extensively. There was pasta and bean soup from Tuscany, a casoeula – pork and cabbage stew – from Milan, gnocchi and saltimbocca from Rome, chicken Valdostana from the valley of Aosta in the north; Roman fettucine in a cream sauce and nodino – veal chop – from Lombardy. Not long after lemons had ceased to be a rare sight in England,

*La Trattoria Terrazza, 2 June 1959. Mario and Franco in front of their new restaurant. The original window is still there today. Photo: Apicella*

La Terrazza offered the Tuscan speciality *Bistecca alla Fiorentina*, always with lemon juice squeezed over the meat. But while Italian customers might order a speciality from their own region, then argue animatedly as to whether the recipe was exactly as it is at home, Mario and Franco's British clients had no idea where the dishes they enjoyed originated.

Mario and Franco always maintained that theirs was the first restaurant in London to serve several specialities – the pasta and bean soup and the linguini with fresh clams (*vongole naturali*) were soon favourites. Eventually, Mario found a factory in Amalfi which produced fresh clams in cans, so he placed a regular order for fifty cases. Quite soon there was a commis in the kitchen whose full-time job was to clean them.

La Terrazza's *Fracosta alla Pizzaiola* was also the real thing. "This is first time it's been prepared properly in England," Franco told customers. While some chefs made the dish with onions or with anchovies, really it should be a simple entrecote steak cooked in fresh tomatoes, olive oil, garlic and, most importantly, with fresh oregano. Somehow, a supply of this herb was found; without it the *Fracosta* would have been unauthentic.

At the end of their first week, Mario and Franco paid the wages, covered cash expenses and there were fifteen shillings (75p) left over. This was the most beautiful money either of them had ever earned.

A few weeks after the opening, Enzo Apicella happened to be standing near the intersection of Dean and Old Compton streets, waiting for his brother outside the Gamba delicatessen. After stocking up on Gamba's home-made ravioli, they planned to find somewhere handy for lunch. Enzo, a year after he'd run into Mario at the Serpentine, had steady work as a set-designer in a television studio in Soho and had definitely decided to stay on in London. Since his arrival in England with just £200 in his pocket, he had led a freewheeling life. He had planned a sojourn of two weeks. "I spent all the money on a big party. I invited all the Italians in London and all the money went on food and wine. The party lasted for fifteen days," he said later.

Unlike his fellow Neapolitan Mario, Apicella was from a middle-class family. He was schooled at the Liceo di Napoli, then studied languages at the Istituto Orientale, then served in the Italian Air Force, allegedly choosing it because by that stage of the war, there was only one plane left. But he wrote articles for flying magazines and after 1945, briefly studied film. He moved to Rome, worked as a journalist and found time to paint murals. By 1949 he was in Milan, running the art department of *Epoca* magazine. In Venice, in 1953, he co-founded a magazine on opera; it was after this folded that aged thirty-five, he made his first visit to England. Once his money had run out, Enzo concocted some poster ideas, sent them to Schweppes and to his surprise the company bought all of them, which started him off in freelance design. With hindsight, his unconventional early life and education seem to have given him exactly the right training for everything that happened in London.

Just as Enzo's brother arrived at Gamba's door, fifty metres away, Mario was pushing open the front door of La Terrazza. He was on his way to fetch a bottle of wine for a customer. Immediately, he recognised the man he'd met by the Serpentine and knowing that London Italians could be extremely important customers, he proudly invited the brothers to grace his new trattoria. "I have opened my own place now," Mario said simply. "Come and have a look."

Apicella winced at Polish George's mural, but, once comfortably seated, the brothers realised that on the food front, Enzo's dream of finding a trattoria in London which cooked just like his mother was a reality. Enzo looked up from his *Fracosta alla Pizzaiola*. "This is delicious," he told Franco. "The real thing. Where does your chef come from?"

"He's from Naples. Same as me," replied Franco. "But the recipe is my mother's. You have to have only fresh oregano. I taught him how to do it properly. Myself. Last week."

## FRACOSTA ALLA PIZZAIOLA
### Sirloin steak with tomato and oregano

This is the genuine Neapolitan dish that caught Enzo Apicella's attention on his first meal at La Terrazza, and went on to be a great favourite in all Mario and Franco's restaurants. It remains one of the very best ways to enjoy a good sirloin steak. The recipe is adapted from Franco's book *The Recipes That Made a Million*.

For four people, put four thin (125g ) sirloin or rump steaks into a pan with 450g of freshly peeled, chopped and drained tomatoes, one teaspoonful of chopped fresh oregano, two large sliced cloves of garlic, salt and freshly ground black pepper. Douse liberally with olive oil. Cook briskly over a high flame. Stir often. When the oil and the tomatoes have combined and turned into a fragrant sauce, it is ready (about 15–20 minutes of reduction). Serve with plenty of fresh crusty bread.

And so Apicella began to lunch at La Trattoria Terrazza nearly every day. He brought other Italian expatriates, artists and television people, as well as contacts from other worlds, and soon Mario and Franco, seeing how beneficial his friends and influence might be, were letting him eat for free.

*By 1961, the reputation of La Trattoria Terrazza had spread to Italy. Rossano Brazzi, one of Italy's biggest stars of the Fifties, dines with his wife Lydia (left). The immaculately suited Mario poses with them.*

## THE WORD SPREADS

Once Mario and Franco had become used to being their own bosses, they added some showbusiness to the equation. Mario, ever the showman, developed routines which enthralled new clients.

> We had the vine of fake grapes growing on the front on the wall of the restaurant and we had fresh grapes delivered every day. I used to take a piece of string and we put the fresh ones on the trellis with the others.

Once a young American woman couldn't decide what to order for pudding, so Mario said, "Would you like some fresh grapes?"

She was astonished. "What d'you mean? – I thought they were fake."

"Look in the corner there," Mario replied. "That's the vine growing up the wall."

"I don't believe it," she shot back.

> So I got a bowl with water and ice, I got a pair of scissors, I got on a chair and I cut the grapes one by one. People looking couldn't believe it. This woman said, "oh gee, oh my, I thought they were plastic." This became so popular, I had to do it all the time.

Customers left La Terrazza feeling that they'd had a great time and this was reflected in their tips. In the Italian restaurant community, it was soon no secret that waiters made more money at La Terrazza than at any other restaurant in London. Mario and Franco took orders and waited on tables themselves, but didn't take a share of the tips, so the first two waiters who joined them (Mario and Carlo), were effectively pocketing tips for four. "In those early days," recalls Mario, "we were guaranteeing our waiters £22 a week. Franco and I were taking home thirty shillings (£1.50) a week for ourselves."

Many early regulars customers have their own versions of how La Terrazza became so well known and these have become part of the Mario and Franco myth, difficult to separate fact from dinner-party fiction. Clearly, many of the first clients were London-based Italians, who appreciated Mario and Franco's authentic Italian menu – no more faux-French dishes. Enzo Plazzotta and A. Lubrani, the immaculately suited directors of Cosmopolitan Artists, an agency which represented Italian artists, designers and cartoonists, would bring Brian Duffy, their young studio assistant, to eat at La Terrazza. When Enzo Apicella first arrived in the UK, he was represented by Cosmopolitan and Plazzotta and Lubrani ate with him around town. At the end of each week Brian Duffy would go to collect his wages from an accountant's office in Villiers Street and (as soon as he could afford to) he'd head off into Soho for a meal at La Terrazza.

Duffy and Len Deighton had studied together at St Martin's School of Art and when Deighton started work as an art director at an advertising agency in Albemarle Street, and Duffy started to win photographic assignments for his clients, they began to meet for lunch at La Terrazza. As Len Deighton says in his foreword, he believes it was John Barker of Artist Partners, the agent for many of the best young freelance illustrators and designers, whose influence gave La Terrazza the push it needed. "The Trat owed its fame and fortune to John Barker," Deighton insists:

> He would take his commercial artists, like me and his photographers, and at the end of the meal say, "Would you like to open an account here?" which for most of us was like saying would you like to go for tea at Buckingham Palace?

Before credit cards existed, Mario and Franco had established the usual system of setting up monthly accounts for their regulars.

"Once you became known, you could open an account, sign the bill and then write them a cheque every month," Deighton remembers:

> Mario and Franco knew that anyone Barker okayed must be earning enough via the agent to settle restaurant accounts. It was good for all concerned. Models came with the photographers and so did wannabe models. Painters and intellectuals came with the commercial artists and soon it was the arty and chic place to be.

Deighton often dropped in to La Terrazza for a mid-morning espresso and chat with Mario before the beginning of the lunch service, and he worked on several of his early novels there. When *The Ipcress File* was published in 1962, it contained several references to the hero visiting La Terrazza and described Mario's treatment of his favourite clients. Deighton's hero takes his girlfriend Jean to dinner:

> **In London with a beautiful hungry girl, one must show her to Mario at La Terrazza. We sat in the ground-floor front under the plastic grapes and Mario brought us Campari-sodas and told Jean how much he hated me. To do this he had to practically gnaw her ear off. Jean liked it.**

As John Barker had brought in Deighton, so Duffy brought in his friend and fellow photographer, David Bailey. Bailey and Duffy were the instigators of a new kind of fashion photography and were making waves in the fashion world. From writers, artists and photographers, the word spread to Fleet Street and journalists, editors and newspaper art directors – always the first to identify a new trend – turned up at La Terrazza.

Hazel Evans, then writing for the *Daily Express*, remembers that:

> Because we were all working as fashion journalists we were always looking for something new and I heard there was this place called the Trattoria Terrazza, in Soho, an area we always thought of as rather downmarket. I was a bit thrown because it didn't have the grand cutlery, everything was very simple, very elegant and there was a completely new form of dress. There would be amused glances if you wore a hat and men didn't wear ties but they had designer jackets and shirts. We all went roaring down there, we were the pilot fish, the journalists and then we started seeing a smattering of film stars.

Another early word-spreading regular was Germano Facetti, the graphic designer from Milan. Just as Deighton was inventing a new genre of spy novel, so Facetti modernised the design of Penguin's book covers, enabling the publisher to morph into the sixties and remain the most recognisable imprint in the British publishing field. Authors, artists and designers from Bloomsbury were his frequent guests.

Mario and Franco did advertise La Terrazza in *What's On*, the contemporary listings magazine, but for the most part, word spread by mouth. Except for guidebooks, *What's On* and airline magazines, there were hardly any influential food and restaurant reviews. But with many journalists becoming regular diners, the daily newspaper gossip and showbusiness columnists started to mention parties which had just taken place at La Terrazza, so enticing curious readers to ring and book a table to see what the fuss was about.

Once La Terrazza was firmly established and had a track record of stability and good management, Mario and Franco could apply for a drinks licence. Without one, customers were obliged to pay for wine as they ordered it, then a waiter would run across the road to The Vintage House wine merchants in Old Compton Street, or if they wanted something stronger, to the French pub around the corner. According to the time of year, red wine would be cold, or the white too warm, and whenever it rained, the drinks were diluted well beyond the legal measure.

The solicitor who Mario and Franco first approached refused to make what he called an "unsupportable" application on their behalf, saying that the "demand was still insufficient," and that there was "no obvious hardship" if the restaurant had no licence. They then consulted the solicitor David Napley, who had been recommended by Franco's friend and former boss, Harry Meadows. Napley brought his family to dinner and satisfied himself that the new restaurant was being properly run and deserved the licence. When the application hearing came up, he dealt with the obstacles which, in those days, were placed in the way of new applicants – objections from rival licensees, restaurateurs, publicans, breweries and the ubiquitous representative of the Temperance Society – and La Terrazza's licence was granted.

So Mario focused on assembling a wine list. "Nobody featured Italian wine in those days," he later explained:

> At the Mirabelle or every other restaurant I was working in and even the so-called Italian places we visited, there was a huge wine list – with champagne – all French – white wine – all French – red wine, burgundy and claret – all French. At the very back of the list there was sometimes a small selection of Italian wines. Franco and I cut out all that. We made just a one-page list and whatever wines we had, we put the Italian first. It had never been done before. We had the best Italian wine and to begin with we never offered any French wine at all. Later, we put on a couple of French wines when we started becoming a little more adventurous.

*"Signora bella, would you like some fresh grapes?"*
*Apicella and the regulars were soon fed up with this charade. Photo: Apicella*

Having worked at the Savoy and the Mirabelle, where businessmen wore suits and ties and lunching ladies wore hats, the partners, accustomed to a decorous atmosphere, were initially worried by the appearance of their tie-less artistic customers and had admonished Enzo for introducing such apparent disreputables to their respectable establishment. But, as Enzo observed, artists – like himself – were not inclined to formality.

In 1961 *Queen* magazine engaged Quentin Crewe as its restaurant critic. He was hugely influential with readers and many of them were reliable customers of restaurants unable to depend on local or business clients. Crewe was the first journalist to review restaurants on the basis of whether he thought his friends would like them. He was concerned with the food and décor, but also with the identities of the other customers and how they and the staff behaved. Crewe wrote that he decided

> to get away from the use of the old fashioned words like morsel, tasty, portion and condiment and instead to write about the decoration, the owners, the waitresses and waiters and the other customers as if the whole event were a bit of theatre.

*Queen* established a new format for its restaurant advice, and this worked well for both newly opened and well-established concerns. In every issue there was a one-page review of two or three new restaurants, followed by a briefing section – *Queen's Counsel* – which provided a roundup of places previously reviewed, including reminders of their atmospheres, menus and prices. Throughout the sixties, Crewe encouraged restaurants, as, increasingly, did other restaurant columnists who had begun to appear in national and local newspapers, as well as in weekly guides such as *Time Out* (which had superseded *What's On*).

In 1960, Tony Armstrong-Jones married Princess Margaret, and when Jocelyn Stevens, the owner of *Queen*, where Armstrong-Jones's photography had first attracted attention, brought him to La Terrazza, Tony arrived tieless, in his trademark roll-neck shirt. Mario refused to let him in, but Franco, more up-to-date about London society, explained his significance, and all went well. For some time afterwards, Mario would hardly let in anyone wearing a tie. La Terrazza's customers seemed to welcome the new informality.

Apicella was still a constant regular and in addition to being a friend, he had become an adviser and confidant. With his ABC television office round the corner, he had lunch and dinner at La Terrazza most days. But every time he faced Polish George's mural, he became, he says, depressed.

Even if he sat with his back to it, the mirror on the other side of the room reflected it, as well as the trellis of plastic grapes which extended across the restaurant over the diners' heads. He spent hours telling Mario and Franco that they should change the décor and bring it more up to date.

"The food," Enzo said, "is so much better than the décor. This 'bunch-of-plastic-grapes-candle-in-Chianti-bottle-picture-of-Vesuvius-in-eruption' you have now. It is rubbish." Mario was clearly hurt. But Enzo persisted. "What is more," he said, "this show you do. This 'Bella Signorina, would you like some grapes' – every time any new client comes in. I am – we all are – embarrassed by this show."

Apicella argued that the excellence of La Terrazza's food contrasted so massively with its artificial environment, the improbable Vesuvius and the fake grapes, that clients might think the food, too, was fake. "Within this circus atmosphere, La Terrazza cannot be a serious restaurant," he warned.

For Mario and Franco, though, simply to have a full restaurant was the fulfilment of their dream. They weren't yet ready to make changes.

*Germano Facetti, the designer who led Penguin Books' 1960s resurgence, was an influential Terrazza regular. Photo: Lagattolla family*

*Mario and Franco and their chef in the Terrazza kitchens.*
*Photo: John Hodder, Sunday Times*

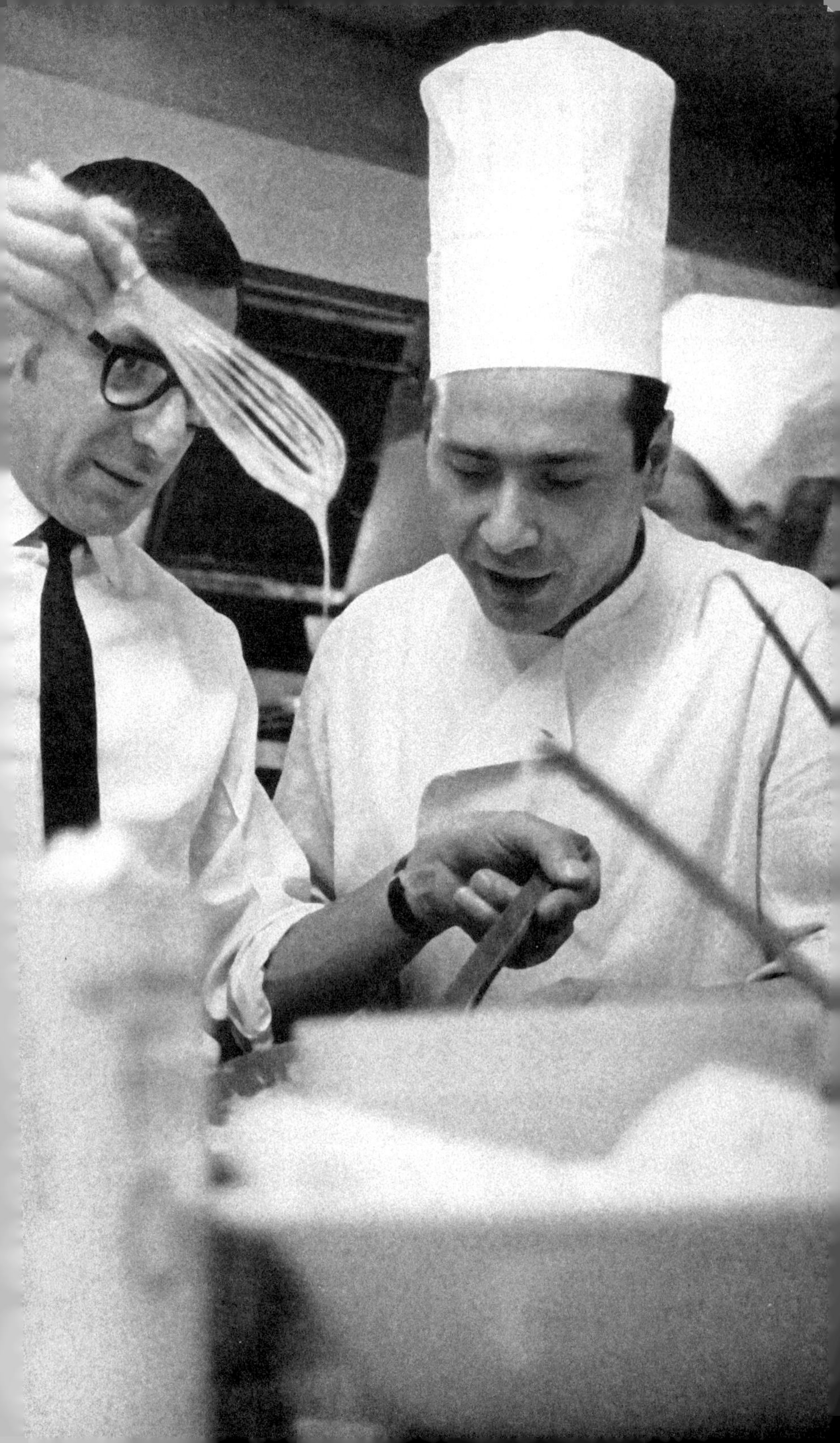

## 1960. CONVENTIONS BLOWN AWAY

"We can't always rely on the same regulars," Franco said one night, as they cashed up. "We've got to expand the business beyond the Soho crowd." The Gatto Nero Club had opened a few weeks after the restaurant itself and, within months, it prospered, supporting La Terrazza with its excellent cash flow. Many members of the Gatto Nero habitually ate upstairs. Almost every evening, there would be a spontaneous music session below in the club. Being, as he put it, the more experienced drinker of the partnership, Franco took responsibility for the Gatto Nero and would commute all evening between floors.

By now, Mario and Franco had an extensive list of account holders to whom they sent monthly bills and several of these customers were also members of the Gatto Nero. Many were already well known in their fields, people who appeared in the press and were doing much to change sixties Britain. This crowd was fundamental to La Terrazza's early success, but, clearly, it wasn't a good idea to remain reliant on a single small coterie.

"Let's have a look at the list," said Mario. "Perhaps if we give a discount to the regulars who bring in new customers it will help to spread the word?"

In addition to Len Deighton, Germano Facetti and Apicella, regulars included Adrian Bailey the illustrator and cookery writer; the fashion designer Gina Fratini; photographers Bailey, Duffy, John Deakin, Ted Ward Hart and Adrian Flowers; Malcolm Arnold, the composer; John Kasmin, the gallery owner; artists Pietro Annigoni, Francis Bacon, Barry Driscoll, Gianetto Coppola and Antonio Scorda; the actors John Slater and Terence Stamp; art directors Mark Boxer, Angela Landels, Tom Wolsey and Ray Hawkey; Sean Kenny, the stage designer; journalists Robert Pitman, Alan Hall, Quentin Crewe and William Davis; the socialite and jazz pianist Robin Douglas-Home; film-makers George Minter and Robert Brownjohn; fashion illustrator May Routh and art editor and artist Willie Landels.

"Those artist customers were really a club," remembered Mario, forty years later. "They all knew each other and were so influential for us. But, if we'd just had that one circle, we wouldn't have been able to develop the restaurant nearly so well."

The restaurant's client list soon began to include businessmen, lawyers and other professionals and, once political journalists and editors started to bring their contacts for lunch, Members of Parliament arrived too.

The ground-floor main entrance and the little internal corridor became increasingly crowded as people decided they had more chance of getting a table if they waited there than in the Gatto Nero downstairs. In order to manage the situation, Mario and Franco decided to stop taking reservations and instead, to seat on a first-come, first-served basis. The resulting queue became a familiar Soho sight and passers-by would stop to talk to their friends. Only the actress Elizabeth Taylor was allowed to jump the queue, so as to spare her the attentions of fans and autograph hunters.

With hindsight, it is clear that La Terrazza's mixed customer base was an early consequence of the breakdown of class barriers and the emergence of meritocracy in Britain. Business leaders, politicians and high society began to mix with photographers, artists, actors, pop singers, writers, designers, musicians, dancers and hairdressers. And, of course, with restaurateurs. As the American journalist John Crosby put it in the *Daily Telegraph*:

> **The working-class young were busting out of the lower depths and invading fields where they can make more money and the upper-class is breaking down walls to get into the lower depths where they can have more fun.**

Mario and Franco knew all their clientele, many of whom knew each other; the Italians were forging a reputation for fun, fashion and theatre. Soho, however, was still Soho and, on occasion, the partners would be reminded of the activities of its other residents. One evening Tony Mella, the Maltese gangster who operated a speakeasy round the corner from La Terrazza, was attacked and shot in the street outside the restaurant. Mario and Franco heard the gunfire and rushed to the door. As they watched, the good-looking and media-aware Mella, lying in the street in a pool of blood, managed to extract a comb out of his pocket, then straighten his hair for what could be his final photo opportunity.

Now that the business had begun to succeed, Franco's personal life took a new turn. He had often noticed a particularly beautiful girl in the Gatto Nero with a group of friends. One evening when he saw her there alone, wearing a green coat and little feathered hat, he decided to speak to her. Her name was Sara. She was also an English-born Italian and Franco was immediately entranced. That evening, uncharacteristically without hesitation, he decided to marry her and told her of his resolution.

Somehow, everything came to fruition and in 1960 Mario organised a guard of honour of Terrazza waiters and chefs brandishing long spoons and saucepans outside St Anne's Church, Soho, where Franco and Sara had just exchanged vows. Their first boy, Nicholas, was born in September 1961, and to celebrate, Franco decorated the front of the restaurant with the traditional Italian blue satin ribbons, handing out cigars to all the customers. The process was repeated a year later, when Nicholas was followed by Fabio.

The guidebooks were beginning to take notice of Mario and Franco's little restaurant:

SOHO AND WEST END 387

**(61) TRATTORIA TERRAZZA** 19 Romilly Street, W.1
*GERrard* 8991 *and* 3334

This trattoria is neo-Neapolitan, complete with vivid pictures of The Bay, a mock grapevine loaded with real grapes, *tarantelle* on the gramophone, opera-humming waiters, cramped tables, and pulsing, off-hand camaraderie. Not, obviously, for the sensitive and not, perhaps, for those who know Italy really well—but the food is pretty close to the real thing. Antipasti, 4/6 to 6/6; soups, 2/6 to 3/-; pasta, 3/- to 4/6; fish, 7/6 to 9/6 (try the squid—calamari alla Luciana, 7/6); meat dishes, 7/6 to 9/6. 'Robust' describes a cuisine which uses plenty of garlic and perhaps too much tomato. Specially approved: rolled and stuffed chicken breast (9/6); escalope di pollo Vesuvia (9/6); and the special pancake terrazzino—made to a secret formula which, however, at least one member claims to have penetrated. Licensed for beer and wine. Carafes from 11/6. Open 12–3, 6–12 all week. (*App. M. F. Perkins; Margit Owen; Maurice Elvey; Dudley Collard; Margaret Costa; T. L. Craven; Dr. D. Thorburn-Burns.*) **Map 13**

The first *Good Food Guide* review of La Terrazza, 1961–62 edition

Egon Ronay, too, was complimentary. His 1961 *Guide* entry read:

153 Map A

**La Terrazza**
*19 Romilly Street, W1. GERrard 8991 and 3334*
NOON-3 PM. 6 PM.-MIDNIGHT

My return visits to this tiny restaurant have convinced me that I was justified in praising it in the first place. It is an example of Soho's Phoenix-like spirit. At one time it seemed that this ancient eating district was yielding to garish slot machine joints, but enterprising young Italians keep bringing it up to date. Sport shirts take the place of stain-covered tails, silk lampshades give way to indirect lighting and space is perhaps a little less comfortable, only the wall paintings - here embellished with reliefs - are still inevitable. The Bay of Naples is of course the chosen theme of Neapolitan Mario and Franco, with cleverly disguised vine leaves and grapes hanging down from the ceiling. I have tried several dishes from the imaginatively compiled menu, one of them an Italianised and slightly garlicky version of chicken Kiev and other a stuffed pancake ("with a - sorry, secret - filling" says the menu). They were all very tasty. Add to this the whirlwind service, smiling reception and the fact that it is difficult to spend more than £1 per person without wine and you have a find.

*The new Mr and Mrs Franco Lagattolla,*
*St. Anne's, Soho, 1960,*
*with Mario (second on the left) and the waiters' guard of honour.*

Mario and Franco's success with La Terrazza was the beginning of a major change in the contact between restaurant customers, staff and kitchen. Across town at Hatchett's, the Mirabelle, the Savoy and the Café Royal, where tail-clad waiters continued to serve French food to formally dressed diners, clients might be familiar with the restaurant manager and with their own section headwaiter, but they never saw the kitchen staff. The kitchen brigade were hidden in a world of ovens and gas burners and they and front of house staff seldom met. "I was never ever allowed anywhere near the kitchens at the Savoy," said one former station headwaiter at the Grill Room, who went on to join La Terrazza.

In all the restaurants where Mario and Franco had previously worked, there had been receptionists, cloakroom staff, commis waiters, station waiters, chefs de rang, headwaiters, wine waiters and managers, who all had distinct roles and weren't allowed to touch another's responsibilities. Only the Maître d' could go into the kitchen, almost no one was allowed to speak to the chef and the headwaiter only became involved when there was trouble or if a customer was particularly special.

"If there was a problem in that type of place," the Terrazza waiter

Pasquale Lunghi remembered from his days at the Mayfair Hotel:

> the chef was never available, but the sous-chef would come and you'd explain the problem and he would try and sort it out. But in an Italian kitchen, if anything is not the way you want, you go and you have a row with the chef. And then the chef starts throwing pans and spatulas at you; this happens all the time.

At La Terrazza, the restaurant staff consisted of just Mario and Franco, two waiters and a wine waiter, with an extra waiter for days off. Mario explained:

> When we started, we cut away all these layers, it gave us much more direct contact with customers and because we didn't have separate jobs to begin with, we could manage everything ourselves. We did everything, take the orders, help serve customers, answer the phone, bring the food.

Mario and Franco's freshly prepared dishes, served on the plate, brought a new style to the restaurant business. They and their staff brought plates directly to the customers, then extras were served or placed on a dish on the table for the customers to help themselves. If the ingredients were fresh, quickly cooked and attractively arranged by the kitchen, then the old slow performance of silver service was obsolete.

One reason that everything tasted so fresh and unusual was because La Terrazza's kitchen was one of the very first to drop the English practice of cooking with lard. Only olive oil, or olive oil mixed with sunflower oil for frying, was used. Mario is sure their introduction of new tastes was another major reason for their early success. But La Terrazza also had a widening reputation for offering more than just good Italian food and wine. Franco's careful supervision of the kitchen, his insistence on buying only the best raw ingredients, combined with Mario's engaging personality and astonishing memory for names and faces, made an evening at the trattoria an experience. On one occasion, the food writer Adrian Bailey took a Canadian friend there and briefly introduced him to Mario. Two years later on the Canadian's next visit to England, they went again and Mario instantly greeted him by name.

The restaurant's thirty-five covers were now being turned over at least oncc at lunchtime and always twice a night. Serving more than a hundred customers a day meant that even with its low prices, the business loan could be repaid. Having made a loss of £350 in the first twelve months, Mario and Franco paid Midland Bank £7,500 at the end of 1960.

Part of Mario and Francos reputation in the trade was that they expected members of their staff to work for long hours, but they ensured that they'd always be properly fed and looked after. The partners wanted them to be informal, friendly with the customers, but always within reason and never to the detriment of standards of service.

"Listen to me," Mario said to a waiter who was about to join them:

> When I first started as a waiter we were always hungry. When I was working for other people, there was always food left over from the day before and every day they would always be throwing away food that was perfectly good. We would always try and take something to eat in the lavatory, because that's the only place nobody could see us. But here at La Terrazza,

he continued, looking the new man straight in the eyes, grabbing his wrist as he spoke:

> here, we don't do this. There is no need for you to steal. You can always have a meal and a drink before the first customers arrive. A glass of wine or a glass of water, ask for whatever you want. But don't pinch anything. If you pinch anything you are out in five seconds.

The partners, too, worked extraordinarily hard. They both did anything and everything in order to make the business go. In the restaurant, in the kitchen and in the club downstairs, they laboured from early morning to early morning – buying in the market, sweeping and cleaning, racking wine deliveries; washing up and laying tables, counting the laundry, serving in the club in the afternoons, before going back upstairs at six to prepare antipasti and salads; serving at tables for dinner, talking to the customers, making coffee, checking bills. Then it was downstairs again to the club until around 4 a.m.; having typed up the menu for the next day, they could snatch a few hours' sleep.

Eventually, they agreed that they had to add new personnel, perhaps even a manager, so they could take an occasional half day off. The first appointee was, later, to compete with them for the title of the most famous restaurateur in London.

## 1960. ENTER ALVARO AND ENZO'S FELT-TIP PEN

*In my youth there had been four things that we never talked about – food, sex, decor and money. Now, nobody talked of anything else.*

QUENTIN CREWE, "*WELL, I FORGET THE REST*"

One Sunday evening in May 1960, a smiling young Florentine waiter arrived at La Terrazza. He was not there to work, but out with his wife for their customary weekly dinner on his day off. The reputation of La Terrazza had spread among the London Italian community and, as a Tuscan and a former colleague of Mario and Franco, Alvaro Maccioni knew good food and where to find it.

Alvaro's friends and colleagues had realised several things about him since his arrival on the scene three years before. He was quick to learn, utterly charming, hard on himself and on his staff, ambitious and excellent with figures. He also possessed an entertaining ability to tell colourful stories about his life, although it had been sufficiently extraordinary not to require embellishment.

Born in 1937, Alvaro spent his childhood in the chaos of wartime Florence where his father was a wholesale food dealer, buying from farmers and selling to shops and restaurants. Although there was money for their own food, there was little left over and even though Alvaro won a scholarship at the age of eleven, his mother's poor health meant that, after only five years of schooling, he had to work. He found a job in a bar serving coffee, and in the autumn he would earn extra money in the grape harvest. Until he was fourteen, he gave his wages to his father, hiding his tips in a secret cubby-hole under the stairs.

Eventually, he says, he'd saved enough to send himself to hotel school for eight months. He then worked in big hotels around Italy, starting out as a lift boy, still sending his wages home, keeping tips, in order to finance a bookkeeping course. But, like all prospective hotel or restaurant managers, he needed to perfect his English.

Still only twenty, he applied to the Savoy, the Dorchester and the Mirabelle and was accepted, he claimed, by all three. He took the Mirabelle job, thus obtaining a UK entry permit, said *arrivederci* to his girlfriend Letizia, and, in October 1957 arrived with just ten shillings (50p) in his pocket and started as a commis waiter.

"When I first arrived in London, I didn't know anyone," Alvaro recalled, "and the first people I found who spoke Italian were at my new job – my immediate boss Franco Lagattolla and his colleague Mario Cassandro, the wine waiter. That first night I also met an Italian in the kitchens, with whom I'd worked before and he let me stay on the floor in his bedsit in Victoria until I found a place."

This commis (trainee or assistant) position was the first of several where Alvaro worked well below his capabilities and experience, but which would serve him well as a platform for the next phase of his career. At the Mirabelle, he soon developed respect for his two close contacts, Mario and Franco. However, they were to about to leave to open La Terrazza and, after progressing from commis to Chef de Rang, Alvaro accepted a headwaiter post at the Café Royal. "I was the youngest ever headwaiter at the Café Royal," he would tell people. But it was the Café Royal in Wimbledon, rather than Regent Street.

Letizia arrived in London in 1959; they married, and babies were soon on the way. They often came to Soho for a good meal and to catch up with his former colleagues.

That evening at La Terrazza, as they finished their dinner, Franco joined his former commis and offered the couple a grappa with their coffee. "How's it going in Wimbledon?" he asked Alvaro.

"It's OK. It's busy. But not like here. The food is French. Not really my thing. But the money's not bad. And you two? Where's Mario?"

"He's having a night off."

"How come he gets a night off?

"It's his first for two months. I'm supposed to be taking Wednesday off but I've just accepted two more bookings for tables of eight. We'll be full all night, so I've cancelled."

"You really are doing well," said Alvaro.

"Yes, we're OK, it's going OK. We need some extra staff though. We need another really good waiter. Can you think of anyone?"

"I'll think about it. Yes. Maybe. There's someone I know who might be interested."

"What about you?" Franco half joked.

Alvaro smiled his toothy grin, seemingly not even bothering to consider the offer. "I'm a headwaiter now, not a waiter anymore," he laughed.

"You'd make about thirty a week with us."

"What? As a waiter? Thirty?" Alvaro was astonished.

"Thirty. That's an average week. Sometimes more."

Alvaro, as ever the excellent mathematician, made a rapid calculation and an even faster decision. He smiled reassuringly at Letizia, stood up, shed his jacket and began to clear the table. "When do I start?"

And so it was that Alvaro joined La Terrazza, back in a jersey again as a simple waiter. His training had paid off. He was thoroughly professional, very good at his job and much liked by customers.

Early on, he spotted that Celestino, one of his new colleagues, was less than honest. He had seen him at one of the oldest restaurant scams. At some point in the evening, Celestino would take a bottle of whisky and put it in the bar dustbin. Then, when it was time to close, he'd put the dustbin out. Once the restaurant was shut and the owners had left, he'd return to pick up the bottle. According to the unwritten rules of the business, Alvaro said nothing to his bosses. Three months later, he was working hard, putting in all the hours and had become popular with customers. He had shown Mario and Franco that they could give him more responsibility.

Mario wanted immediately to promote him to manager, but Franco was cautious. "Let's give him another month. Then we'll see how it goes."

They agreed to wait. But a month later, at the end of a busy evening, as they were finishing up, Alvaro cleared his throat. Could he possibly have three weeks off in the following month, to return to Italy for his sister's wedding? Slightly surprised that he would be away for so long, they consented. He had only been with them for less than six months, so was owed only one week's wages, so he'd have to take the other two unpaid.

Wedding and celebrations in Florence over, Alvaro returned to London. As soon as he walked into La Terrazza, one of the waiters told him, "Mario Cassandro wants to see you upstairs." Alvaro was worried that he was about to be sacked for having been away for so long. Instead, Mario and Franco sat him down and, smiling at him, asked if he'd like to become their restaurant manager. "Of course. Thank you so much. Yes, I will do this very well. You will be proud of me."

He was on his way. He knew he was ready and that he deserved the promotion. He was becoming one of the family. The three of them shook hands and the partners kissed Alvaro on both cheeks.

The first thing Alvaro did was sack the whisky thief.

Now that it was possible to take a little time off, Mario and Mary went to see Mario's family in Naples. One evening, he was called to the telephone. In those days you had to book an international call well in advance and Franco had been trying to reach him for three days. "*Pronto?*" In the midst of his family, Mario felt a million miles from London life.

"Some Maltese have been in," Franco shouted down the line. The hairs on the back of Mario's neck prickled. Suddenly he was back in Soho. The Maltese gangs were the nearest thing that Soho had to a Mafia, but so far they had left La Terrazza well alone. "It's the basement. They've made us an offer to put in some slot machines and a pinball in the Gatto Nero. What do you think we should say? It could make us a lot of extra money."

Mario took less than five seconds to decide. "Tell them to fuck off," he shouted back. "We're doing well. We can close the club and expand the restaurant downstairs."

"I hoped you'd say that," came Franco's loud yell.

So, in late 1960, the Gatto Nero Club closed and La Terrazza expanded into the space downstairs. The second room would help Mario and Franco to reduce their queuing customers' waiting time.

Enzo Apicella, by now a regular customer and good friend, liked Mario and Franco's style and he loved their food. But he had different, firm ideas about the restaurant's appearance. Enzo had regularly suggested improvements to the décor, until, finally giving in to his constant pressure, they asked him to redesign the downstairs room.

Enzo had never received formal interior design training and it was his habit to use whatever materials came to hand, to illustrate ideas as soon as they came into his head. "Do you have a pen?" he'd say. Then, when a pen arrived, he would begin to draw on the tablecloth. Usually this meant that whenever he'd finished a meal the tablecloth was covered in drawings and sketches of whatever he'd been discussing over lunch. Now, the three of them sat down together, and he started to doodle, swiftly sketching his version of the downstairs room. His philosophy was indeed unorthodox, and very different from their expectations. But Mario and Franco absorbed his drawings, looked at each other and then at Enzo, then nodded simultaneously. As their partnership grew, Franco and Mario could instinctively agree whether or not something – an idea, a new dish, an employee – was right for them. In this instance, a mere glance passed between them, an eyebrow was raised, but no discussion was necessary.

From the beginning of his involvement, Enzo insisted to Mario and Franco that their customers must be the real decoration of the room. "You, the restaurateurs, are the ones who select them and arrange them, one by one," he told them.

He insisted they should have good lighting, clean lines, nice chairs and an environment which "projects an image of the kind of cuisine people are going to taste." Out went the Club's old furniture, carpets were thrown away, the zinc bar and tables were junked. In came the first example of what would become known as the Apicella style of modern restaurant design. There were green glazed ceramic floor tiles from Naples, rough brick and plaster walls painted white, with sculptured holes, arched ceilings, a giant lobster pot hanging in a corner and, instead of the usual light fittings on the walls, circular tube downlights which were positioned over the centre of each table. In spring, 1962, the Gatto Nero became La Terrazza's Positano Room.

Perhaps because of his limited design training, Apicella saw himself as a friendly customer-to-be, who would provide informed advice to a potential restaurant-owning client, rather than an interior decorator imposing a personal style. But as Adrian Bailey's photograph of Apicella in the new basement room reveals, even his first assignment manifests extreme simplicity and clean lines, essential features of an environment which will be filled by more than fifty people.

Enzo wanted to charge the partners a design fee of £300 for his transformation, which caused slight friction. The fee might have been reasonable, but since he had never paid for umpteen meals, Mario wasn't having it. "If you want to be paid for your work," he told Apicella, "from now on you start paying when you eat here."

Franco was worried. "Maybe we'll lose him both as a customer and as a friend."

"Nonsense," said Mario. "He knows he owes us much more than we owe him."

In fact, Apicella remained a friend and a customer and they let him sign bills up to the amount of his fee.

The original ground-floor restaurant was re-christened the Vesuvio Room and, with two dining rooms, Mario and Franco could go back to the more customer-friendly telephone-booking system instead of first-come, first-served. But on the Positano Room's first evening, the upstairs queue formed early and the Vesuvio ground-floor room had quickly filled up.

Having paid so much for the conversion, Mario and Franco were disappointed that the first people they showed into the Positano Room were neither particularly pleased nor impressed. They said that they missed the colour and warmth of upstairs and went back up to re-join the queue. This looked like a problem and immediate nerves didn't help.

"Do you want to be up in our old room?" Mario would ask their regulars. "Or in the new one downstairs?"

"How come you made us spend all this money and nobody wants to sit down there?" Mario and Franco complained to Apicella.

After about a month, the partners still found that few regulars wanted to eat downstairs and they worried about their investment. But Alvaro had worked at a place in Florence, where the owners had faced just such a problem.

"Can I use the same system we had there?" he asked Mario.

His boss shrugged. "We'll try anything."

"I will only do this if you promise not to interfere."

Mario smiled. "Why do you say that? I promise."

"From now on, when we pick up the phone and when people ask for a table for four, we say, 'Yes, certainly. But I can give you only a table upstairs, downstairs is already full.' "

"What do you mean?" Mario said. "Why not?"

"I'm sorry," insisted Alvaro. "We must say downstairs is fully booked."

That evening, the reception telephone rang and rang as usual. "Do you have a table for four tonight, about 8.30?"

"I am sorry, downstairs is fully booked," answered Alvaro, "but I can give you a table upstairs."

As he spoke, Mario jumped up and down beside him – literally hopping mad. "Madonna Mia, what do you mean, full? It's empty. You can't do that!"

Although Mario and Franco grew daily more nervous, Alvaro held to his resolve. He persisted for about a week and whenever anyone they knew well rang to book, Alvaro said, "I can't do downstairs. It's fully booked. Only upstairs." When off-the-street customers walked in, or there were new bookings from strangers, they were shown to the new room downstairs. Very soon, the regulars asked, "Please can I book a table for downstairs?" "I'm not sure," Alvaro hesitated. "Yes, perhaps. Yes, I can squeeze you in. I may be able to do it."

From then on, the Positano Room, where Alvaro was now in charge, was the hot spot. Non-regulars had to put up with a table on the ground floor.

Close to Wardour Street, La Terrazza had from its inception attracted film and television executives and the film industry was to have a major effect on its success and that of other new Italian restaurants. The producers Harry Saltzman and Cubby Broccoli had been in London since the 1950s. Their American studio, United Artists (UA), responsible for the James Bond films, opened a London office in 1961, to take advantage of cheaper British production costs. UA also produced other influential films: *Tom Jones* in 1963 and the Beatles' *A Hard Day's Night* in 1964. These and others introduced the frenzied, gaudy sixties style – a massive change from the gritty realism of British 1950s films.

As so many British-made films were successful, American studios and producers sensed that London was where they needed to be, so many of them opened subsidiary offices in London. Executives quickly caught on to where leaders like Saltzman and Broccoli lunched and dined and followed suit. An extension of Mario and Franco's and by now also Alvaro's job was to ensure that UA, Paramount and Colombia executives were seated sufficiently far from each other so they couldn't hear each other's conversations – though they had to be sufficiently close to note that their competitors were eating in the same room.

With two packed rooms, Mario now employed six waiters, all soon well known to the customers. Often these young Italians had arrived in England with only one or two words of English and started on the lowest rung of the ladder.

Peppino Taboro, who was to become one of Mario and Franco's most popular waiters, had started in England at the Bell Inn in Melton Mowbray. On his first week, he was alone in the restaurant at breakfast time. He spoke no English so he was unable to write down the orders and worse still

> the breakfast chef was Scottish, very hard to understand. So I listened very carefully to the customers' orders and I repeated the sounds to myself as I walked back to give the order to the kitchen. When a customer said to me, "Two fried egg, bacon, tomato, sausage," I walked back to the kitchen repeating again and again to myself, "two fried egg, bacon, tomato, sausage… two fried egg, bacon, tomato, sausage," and I said this to the chef, "two fried egg, bacon, tomato, sausage." The chef said to me, "No fockin' sausages." I didn't understand this, but I remembered what he said and I went back and I said to the customer, "no fockin' sausages."

Only a few years later, installed at La Terrazza, Peppino was, he subsequently told me, "making more money than the prime minister."

## JONI, GREGORY, PERRY AND JERRY, BURT, ELIZABETH, SAMMY AND FRANK

Romilly Street, a few paces from the Wardour Street film world, is only a little further away from Denmark Street, which, in the sixties, was still the centre of the music business. Musicians, many of whom knew each other well, began to frequent La Terrazza and it was through them that Mario and Franco's reputation became international. In particular, four American stars put the restaurant on the transatlantic map.

An early customer who spread the word was the Italian-American singer Joni James, who, in 1960, came to London to record an album at Abbey Road. Joni, who naturally liked Italian food, was brought to La Terrazza by her record producer and immediately became a regular. She invited many colleagues to eat with her and would always loudly inform her guests that Mario and Franco really did serve authentic southern Italian food. On the night before she returned to the USA, she appeared for a final dinner and presented the partners with a copy of her latest album. "I promise to make sure Frank hears about you before his next visit to London," she vowed.

The first Rolls Royce to park outside 19 Romilly Street disgorged Mr and Mrs Gregory Peck, in London for *The Guns of Navarone*. It was their first evening out in town and a small crowd was soon rubbernecking on the corner. Within minutes the word had spread and Franco saw a whole bunch of rival restaurateurs strolling, apparently indifferently, past La Terrazza's window. The Pecks returned at least two or three times a week.

A few well-chosen words from Joni James in the ears of the Los Angeles songwriters, Sammy Kahn and Jimmy Van Heusen, resulted in their visit and, for a while, they virtually took over the Positano Room, inviting their London friends from the worlds of film and theatre, musicals and television. When they left for California, they too promised they'd "make sure Frank gets to know about this great little place."

"I was first taken to the Trat by Riccardo Aragno, who was the London correspondent for the Italian newspaper *La Stampa*," remembers Lady Carolyn Townshend, who, in 1959, had just begun a career in television. "He told me that La Terrazza had the most authentic Italian food in London." Mario and Franco and the staff were a wonderful asset for Carolyn when, in her role as press agent, she found herself charged with taking care of American stars appearing in London. Many other restaurateurs would telephone the press as soon as a celebrity walked through the door, but she knew that Mario and Franco would put on a good show without compromising their visitors' privacy. She brought visitors like Perry Como and Jerry Lewis, who both loved the atmosphere and the Italian food, and liked to be recognised, but not mobbed. When Sammy Davis Jr arrived for a season at the London Palladium, Carolyn brought him to La Terrazza, which he found much to his taste. For the whole run of his show, he would come for an early dinner, requesting strange combinations of dishes – such as scampi with a side order of spaghetti alle vongole. On Sunday nights he would give a huge dinner and, before departing, he threw a farewell bash, promising, as he left, that he would definitely mention Mario and Franco to Frank.

All these recommendations finally achieved the result that Mario and Franco had dreamt of. During a trip to record his *In London* album in 1962, Frank Sinatra reserved a table for a party of fifteen.

It was Franco's evening off. But as soon as the reservation was made, Mario called him back to help supervise the menu and, as Franco remembered it, they prepared a long buffet table of southern antipasto specialities – garlic and chilli-spiked octopus salad, shrimp and scallop vinaigrette, fresh anchovies, black olives with garlic and fennel seeds, peperonata, cacio-cavallo cheese, coarse-cut salamis, aubergines al funghetto and bottles of his favourite Caruso Bianco and Rosato di Ravello wines.

Several days later, the same group booked the entire Positano Room and, as they left, Sinatra's generosity was to cause a stir in the offices of the Inland Revenue which waiters all over Britain have come to regret. After shaking hands with every member of staff who had served him, Sinatra finally came to Mario, turned and said to one of his associates, "Make sure the boys are well looked after."

The aide took an envelope from his pocket, which he gave to Sinatra who handed it to Mario. Mario paused and looked at it. "Thank you very much, Mr Sinatra." He turned and handed the precious envelope on to Alvaro.

"Put this in the tronc for the staff."

One of the waiters on duty that night was Peppino Taboro. "The tip in that envelope was a hundred pounds, in the days when a bill for thirty people would have been quite a bit less than that," he remembers.

The tronc is a box for all the tips, to be divided later according to the jobs and seniority of staff members. Somehow, this incident was reported in the *Evening News* diary a few days later and Her Majesty's Inspector of

Taxes came down on La Terrazza's waiters' tronc of tips like a ton of bricks. From then on, new legislation was brought in to ensure that waiters' tips had to be taxed together with their main wages and the existence of the tronc itself had to be registered and be subject to tax inspections.

One of the waiters' more important tasks was to serve the most popular dish on the menu – the rolled and stuffed breast of chicken that Franco had adapted from Chicken Kiev and re-christened *Pollo Sorpresa*. It was filled with butter and garlic and the boys had to make a theatrical gesture of cutting it open, taking great care as, if it were badly handled, it could cause problems. Many customers who turned down the waiter's offer to cut it open for them, went home with well-buttered ties.

"One day," recalls waiter Mario Paggetti, "it all went wrong. The chicken was hot and full of gas and the liquid butter came out like a jet across a customer's beautiful jacket. Of course, just my luck. The customer was Bruce Forsyth, a well-known TV star. I was almost in tears. I tried to wipe his jacket down, thinking, I've only been here two weeks and I'll get the sack right away."

But Forsyth calmed him. "You silly man," he said. "Don't worry, I've

**PETTO DI POLLO SORPRESA**

The recipe for La Terrazza's most famous dish. The story of how Franco adapted it from Chicken Kiev is told in his recipe book, *The Recipes That Made a Million.*

First, have your butcher cut and skin four tender breasts of young chicken, leaving the wing-tip bone. Carefully, without breaking the flesh, flatten them with a flat-sided mallet-cleaver, very, very thinly.

Place a 50g conical-shaped piece of well-chilled butter, which has been mixed with finely chopped garlic and parsley, a teaspoonful of grated parmesan cheese, salt and milled black pepper, in the centre of each piece of chicken.

Roll them up tightly leaving the bone exposed rather like a handle. Seal in the butter by pressing the edges very firmly. Roll the chicken breasts in flour, dip into seasoned beaten egg and then carefully cover with bread crumbs.

Deep fry the chicken breasts in hot oil until they are cooked and golden outside with the now melted savoury butter bursting to be released.

got two more at home like this." Soon Paggetti began to enjoy his new life.

Soon the appearance of stars at La Terrazza was unexceptional. A few nights after Sinatra had booked the Positano Room for his party of thirty, Elizabeth Taylor and friends arrived again for dinner. The table wasn't ready and since there was not yet a bar, they perched in the upstairs corridor while they waited to be seated. On another evening, Burt Lancaster ordered a large after-dinner Italian liqueur. "I don't think Lancaster had ever tasted Sambuca," recalls Peppino Taboro, who brought him the drink,

> but the man with him, an English, I think it was his agent, made him try it. Anyway I put in the coffee beans and lit the drink with a match, you know, to burn the coffee taste into the Sambuca and Lancaster just picked it up and drank it while it was burning. There were flames coming out of his mouth.

In 1962 the London *Daily Sketch* ran a "Who dines where?" feature, which noted that among the guests at La Terrazza, between 6.30 and midnight one evening, were Ingrid Bergman, Leslie Caron, Danny Kaye, David Niven, Gregory Peck, Laurence Harvey, Sammy Davis Jr, Michael Caine, Julie Christie, Terence Stamp, Carl Foreman, Pietro Annigoni and David Bailey accompanied by Jean Shrimpton.

"But," said Franco afterwards, "they missed Ari Onassis, who was quietly sitting in an alcove, enjoying a spiedino of lamb with a beautiful woman and a flask of Chianti."

As the restaurant business entered the jet age, many of Mario and Franco's regular customers came from thousands of miles away. From the early group of mainly London-based writers, media people, photographers, models and artists, the restaurant's customer list had extended to such internationally known names as Katharine Hepburn, the Maharajah of Cooch Behar, Sean Connery, Catherine Deneuve, Franco Zeffirelli, Charlie and Sidney Chaplin, Alex Korda, Jean-Paul Belmondo, Dirk Bogarde, Alan Ladd, Monica Vitti, Jack Palance, Sophia Loren, Marcello Mastroianni and Omar Sharif.

The presence of so many international stars among regular diners meant that the locals had to adjust to the fact that they were likely to see people at the next table who were very familiar from the big screen. To think that Franco or Mario knew us, as well as Onassis, Richard Burton or Gregory Peck, made the young, highly impressionable regulars (myself one of them) feel that to be at La Terrazza was to be at the centre of the

*In 1963, Ford advertised their new Ford Consul Capri with a series of ads, which featured a James Bond-style hero with the cool new car. As in Len Deighton's Ipcress File, the hero would take his girl to La Trattoria Terrazza, the coolest eating-place in town. This poster is from the episode 'A Bullet Travels Fast – And So Does a Capri.' Photos: John Chillingworth, from the collection of Ian Ingham, courtesy Stephen Wickham, Capri Classic Owners' Club.*

*The original Mario and Franco Terrazza postcard.*
*Contrast the clean lines of the new Positano Room, bottom right,*
*with the photograph of Le Caprice on page 33*

*Enzo Apicella in La Terrazza's new Positano Room,*
*the first example of his cool, modern restaurant design style.*
*Photo Adrian Bailey*

LA TERRAZZA 19 ROMILLY STREET LONDON W.1. TEL. GERRARD 8991-3334

# CARTA DEL GIORNO

COVER CHARGE 2-6 MINIMUM CHARGE 17-6

**Hors d'Oeuvres**

Lasagne al forno 8/6
BAKED LAYERED PASTA, STUFFED WITH MEAT BALLS CHEESE, EGG, TOMATO, CREAM SAUCE...

| | |
|---|---|
| PEPERONATA AL TONNO<br>ratatouille with tunny fish | 8-6 |
| UOVA AL TEGAME "TERRAZZA"<br>baked eggs with oregano and bel paese | 6-6 |
| MELONE DI STAGIONE<br>fresh melon in season | 7-6 |
| PERA AVOCADO AL GAMBERETTO<br>avocado pear with shrimps in cocktail sauce | 8-6 |
| INSALATA ALLA NIZZARDA<br>riviera style mixed salad | 9-6 |
| TERRINE DELLO CHEF<br>the chef's chicken liver paté | 6-6 |
| COCKTAIL POSITANO<br>sea-food cocktail | 7-6 |

SMOKED STURGEON 13/6

Lumache alla Borgogna 9/6
BUTTER STUFFED SNAILS

**Soups**

Pasta e fagioli 6/6
THICK PASTA & BEAN SOUP

| | |
|---|---|
| MINESTRONE ALLA MILANESE | 5-6 |
| PASTINA IN BRODO | 4-6 |
| ZUPPA TERRAZZA | 5-6 |
| STRACCIATELLA ALLA ROMANA | 4-6 |

Soffietti alla serpentaria 13/6
PIKE QUENNELLES WITH LOBSTER SAUCE

**Farinaceous**

Zuppa di lenticchie 5/6
THICK LENTIL SOUP

| | |
|---|---|
| SPAGHETTI AL RAGU' NAPOLETANO | 7-6 |
| SPAGHETTI ALLE VONGOLE | 7-6 |
| PENNE ALLA MATRICIANA | 7-6 |
| FETTUCCINE ALLA PANNA | 7-6 |
| SPAGHETTI ALLA CARBONARA | 7-6 |
| CARROZZELLA ALLA ROMANA | 7-6 |
| FUSILLI ALLA TERRAZZA | 7-6 |
| RIGATONI ALLE COZZE | 8-6 |

Zuppa di cozze 13/6
FRESH MUSSELS IN THEIR SHELL THE NAPOLI WAY

**Fish**

Calamari alla luciana 13/6
SAUTE OF BABY OCTOPUS, NAPOLI STYLE, WITH CROUTONS

| | |
|---|---|
| FRITTO MISTO MARE<br>scampi, baby octopus, goujons deep fried | 15-6 |
| SOGLIOLA GRATINATA<br>Baked Dover sole breadcrumbs parsley/garlic | 16-6 |
| SCAMPI ALLA CERTOSINA<br>scampi in rich creamy sauce and risotto | 17-6 |
| SCAMPI ALLA PROVINCIALE<br>scampi tomato/garlic/herb/parsley sauce | 16-6 |
| SPIEDINO DI SCAMPI "PESCATORA"<br>grilled skewered fresh scampis with mint | 16-6 |
| SOGLIOLA "TERRAZZA"<br>Dover sole in vermouth/cream sauce. | 17-6 |
| CASSEULA "FRUTTI DI MARE"<br>sea-food filled pastry, wine sauce, gratinee | 16-6 |

Rombo alla Palazzo 16/6
TURBOT WITH WHITE WINE SAUCE, TOMATO AND MUSHROOMS

**LE NOSTRE SPECIALITA'**

Trota in carrozza 15/6
FILLET TROUT WRAPPED IN PAN CAKE WITH AUBERGINES AND CHEESE SAUCE

| | |
|---|---|
| PETTO DI POLLO "SORPRESA"<br>rolled and stuffed chicken breast. | 16-6 |
| SCALOPPA DI VITELLO FARCITA<br>ham/mushroom filled escalope/cream sauce | 16-6 |
| STEAK ALLA TARTARA<br>raw spicely prepared, served with chipped potatoes | 19-6 |
| COTOLETTA DI POLLO ALLA VESUVIO<br>chicken escalope/aubergines/tomato/cheese | 16-6 |
| UCCELLETTI SCAPPATI "LOMBARDA"<br>rolled sauté beef olives with risotto | 16-6 |

Vitello tonnato 16/6
COLD SLICED VEAL WITH TUNNY FISH MAYONNAISE AND POTATO SALAD

**Entrees**

Carré d'agnello alla Sardadese 18/6
RACK OF LAMB, PARSLEY, GARLIC, BREADED PLAIN ROASTED, WITH SLICED BRAISED POTATO FLAN

| | |
|---|---|
| CERVELLA DI VITELLO ALLA MONTEVERDE<br>calves brains sautéed in special batter. | 13-6 |
| FEGATINI DI POLLO ALLA SIRACUSA<br>skewered chicken livers with special risotto | 13-6 |
| VALDOSTANA DI POLLO<br>chicken covered ham/tomato/melted cheese | 14-6 |
| ROGNONCINI CON FUNGHI AL BAROLO<br>sautéed calves kidneys/mushrooms/red wine sauce | 14-6 |
| ANIMELLE ALLA REALE<br>sweetbreads/mushrooms/cream sauce and asparagus tips | 14-6 |
| COTOLETTA DI VITELLO ALLA MILANESE<br>breaded veal escalope | 16-6 |
| FRACOSTA DI MANZO ALLA PIZZAIUOLA<br>sirloin steak tomato/garlic/oregano sauce | 16-6 |
| PICCATINE DI VITELLO ALLA MINORESE<br>veal scaloppines/oregano/tomato/garlic/green pepper sauce | 16-6 |
| CRESPOLINE DI POLLO "MARIA PIA"<br>stuffed chicken pancakes, cream sauce "au gratin" | 14-6 |
| FEGATO DI VITELLO ALLA VENEZIANA<br>calves liver with onion and white wine sauce | 14-6 |
| BISTECCA ALLA FIORENTINA<br>rib of beef cooked over charcoal, for one | 19-6 |
| SALSICCIE FRESCHE CON SPINACI<br>Italian sausages on spinach tossed in olive oil and garlic | 13-6 |

Escalope di vitello "Favorita" 17/6
VEAL ESCALOPE SAUTE: WITH HAM, TOMATO, ANCHOVIES, PARSLEY, GARLIC PIQUANTE SAUCE

**Vegetables**

PATATE E LEGUMI DEL GIORNO 3-6
ZUCCHINE FRITTI 3-0 PEPERONATA 3-6
FUNGHI AL SALTO 3-6 MELENEZANE/PARMIGIANA 5-6
CARCIOFINI DORATI 3-0 INSALATA MISTA 4-0

**Sweets**

COPPA CLO CLO 5-6 CASSATA SICILIANA 5-6
ZABAGLIONE 6-6 CREMA CARAMELLA 4-6
PESCA "MELBA" 5-6 ARANCIA "POSITANO" 5-6
ZUPPA INGLESE 5-6 GELATI 3-0 SAVARIN AL RHUM 6-6

Terrazzino 4/6

Hot rolled pancake - sorry - secret recipe!

FORMAGGIO 3-6 FRUTTA s.q. CAFFE 2-0

THE GATTO-CAT, CAPRI AND AMALFI ROOMS ARE AVAILABLE FOR YOUR PRIVATE LUNCHES, DINNERS AND MEETINGS

*The Terrazza menu in 1967.*
*By now Mario and Franco offered dishes from every region of Italy.*

universe. For waiters and staff as well, it was unreal. If you were sitting anywhere near the doors to the kitchen, it was easy to sense if there was someone famous in the room. There would be a gaggle of faces pressed to the little oval window of the kitchen door, trying to take a peek at the star.

Mario was still as impressed as a schoolboy when really big stars first booked a table at the Terrazza and he knew the other staff shared his excitement. "I was working upstairs one lunchtime when the internal phone buzzed," remembers the partners' secretary Pat Copeland, "and it was Mario, saying 'Get down here at once, bring me some papers to sign or look at. Anything. Just get down here as fast as you can!' When I arrived in the Positano Room, there was Mario talking to Rock Hudson and, of course, he introduced me to Mr Hudson and everyone in his party. I've never forgotten that moment."

Pat Copeland had arrived to work in Mario and Franco's upstairs office at the age of seventeen (and was still working for the Cassandro family forty-five years later). At first, she was in charge of the customers' monthly accounts and until credit cards started to become more common, would prepare and send out more than 750 monthly bills. "Up in the office it was often a madhouse," she remembered. "But we often had a celebration glass of Asti Spumanti and we were given salary increases every few months." For her birthday, Mario and Franco once gave Pat two tickets to see Andy Williams at the Albert Hall and dinner afterwards at the restaurant. When she got there, "I couldn't believe it, there was Andy Williams sitting at the next table."

As one of their very few female employees, Pat helped out the staff in quite a few unorthodox situations:

> One of the chefs was a very sweet young man from Naples, Mimi, he was only about four foot ten and very round, but he had a girlfriend back in Naples and he went back there, married her and brought her to London. He knew I was a mother and they both came into the office one day and asked me very shyly about how to get hold of the new contraceptive pill, so I sent them off to our doctor. But a few months later, Mimi was back in the office, looking halfway between delighted and horrified. It appeared that in spite of the pill, his wife was pregnant. "I can't understand it," he said. "I've been taking it every day."

Most of the waiters worked split shifts, five or even six days a week, with a break between three and six. This was one of the reasons why the Bar Italia, the Frith Street café, did so well in the afternoons. It was there that waiters would tell each other stories about the customers and their bosses, Mr Franco and Mr Mario. Quite a few of their stories about life at La Terrazza may well be true...

Marcello normally worked the lunchtime shift in the upstairs room. On his birthday, after the busy lunch service, he changed out of his striped uniform jersey and headed off into Soho with two of the other waiters. Like every Italian in that corner of London, they knew where to get an out-of-hours drink.

All afternoon, they celebrated, talking of football, of their girlfriends and their mothers and life in the sunshine back at home. By the time they came back on duty, Marcello was, alcoholically speaking, well past his best. That night, he was on the front station in the downstairs room. Here, in the best section of the most fashionable restaurant in London, only regulars could be sure of getting a table. Marcello's first party was composed of four familiar customers, who had booked a table before an evening at the Queen's Theatre round the corner. The two couples had met on the doorstep and were chatting non-stop as Franco ushered them downstairs to the table.

Marcello managed to hand round the menus and open a bottle of wine without spilling it. Franco, who had noticed nothing wrong, came to take their order. He put it through to the kitchen, then returned upstairs.

The group were still talking animatedly, oblivious to the first course as it appeared. The commis waiter brought the tray of dishes from the kitchen and Marcello, hazily, correctly placed three plates of cold antipasti. Then, with a pair of large wooden spoons, he served steaming *Linguine alle Vongole*, direct from the pan. Stepping back, he checked to make sure that everything was in place. There was, though, something wrong. It took him a while to focus, but suddenly he realised what it was. He had forgotten to put a plate beneath the linguine. The beautifully arranged portion was sitting on the tablecloth, its plate still on the tray.

Marcello's head abruptly cleared. He thought like lighting, then leant down and unobtrusively removed the antipasti dishes. While the four continued to gossip, he said, "Per favore, *signori*, *signore*, please lift your glasses to the health on my birthday."

"Oh wonderful, Marcello," replied the party's host, still unaware of the plate-less linguine in front of him. "Happy Birthday, Marcello and many happy returns. *Salute*!" All four raised their glasses to drink a toast to the beaming waiter.

Quickly and deftly, while their glasses were still aloft, Marcello tugged up all four corners of the tablecloth and whipped everything away. Cloth and its contents – water glasses, ashtray, side plates, cutlery, flowers, salt and pepper, grissini sticks, plus the linguine, were thrown in a bundle over his shoulder. With aplomb, he walked steadily towards, then through, the service door and disappeared from sight.

## THE TRANSFORMATION OF BRITAIN'S RESTAURANTS

| BEFORE MARIO AND FRANCO | AFTER MARIO AND FRANCO |
|---|---|
| Formal dress code | No dress code |
| Women lunched out in hats and gloves | Other women laughed at women who still lunched out in hats and gloves |
| Waiters in black tie and tails | Waiters in hooped Neapolitan jerseys |
| Silver service, food cold by the time it's all been served | Plated service, piping hot from the kitchen |
| Only headwaiter can speak to the chef | Everyone screams at the chef |
| Ersatz French food | Real Italian food |
| Wine lists offered French wines only, maybe one or two Italian | List offered Italian wines, maybe one or two French |
| Lard used for cooking | Olive oil used for cooking |
| Carpet on the floor | Tiles on the floor |
| Red plush velvet & flocked wallpaper | Rough plaster walls |
| Little red and gold chairs | Chunky rustic chairs with rush seats |
| Curtains | Wooden Venetian blinds |
| Chandeliers and silk-shaded wall lights | Spotlights |
| Indirect lighting | Downlights over each table |
| Atmosphere of muted seriousness | Atmosphere of exuberant enjoyment |
| Staff not allowed to look customers in the eye | Staff and customers become friends |
| Demarcation between jobs | Everyone does everything |
| The answer was "I will fetch your waiter" | The answer is always "Yes, immediately" |
| Customers rarely knew staff's names | Everyone knows everyone |
| Soho unfashionable, louche and seen as mainly for "slumming" | Romilly St/Dean St corner most fashionable address in London |
| Dining out was only for special occasions | Dining out is the new pastime |

## CHALLENGE TO THE MIRABELLE, 1962

*Before the sixties, London was an old man's town. Nightclubs were where you went if you wanted to hear people playing the violin.* PETER EVANS

Since La Terrazza, having been conceived as a simple trattoria, had grown to be the most fashionable and busy restaurant in London, Mario and Franco pondered what they should do next. Could Italy, with its simpler cuisine and penchant for informality, produce an authentic Italian restaurant which would compete with the luxury of the francophile Mirabelle? Could they take on Mario Gallati's Caprice and win? In 1962 they decided they would try and so began a massive gamble.

By the time the *Good Food Guide* and Egon Ronay's 1961 edition had appeared, the success of La Terrazza had inspired several new trattorie in Soho, Kensington and Chelsea. While some of them copied La Terrazza's menus and informal mode, many old-style Italian restaurants still existed. Out of 144 restaurants in his 1961 *Guide*, Egon Ronay listed twelve Italian establishments, but none beyond the boundaries of London. The top end of the restaurant market was as a whole dominated by French-restaurants-with-Italian-waiters. According to Ronay, the five best restaurants in London were Mario Gallati's Caprice and L'Écu de France, along with the Coq d'Or, Prunier and the Savoy Grill. Egon would probably have selected a very similar list had he published in 1951, 1941 or even 1931.

Mario and Franco knew that only in Mayfair would they be able to break into the highest level of the restaurant establishment.

Once they spread the word that they were looking for new premises, Harry Meadows, Franco's old employer and friend, owner of the Churchill Club in Bond Street, offered them a 21-year lease in a newly built office and apartment block in Queen Street, just round the corner from the Mirabelle. After a little hesitation, Mario and Franco decided to accept it and so began another make-or-break venture. After a series of tense meetings with bank managers, they embarked on their second major project, making what in those times was a colossal investment of more than £47,000 (equivalent today to about £1.8m) to create Tiberio, the best Italian restaurant outside Italy.

Called in by his friends for his first major restaurant commission, Enzo Apicella started sketching as usual on a series of tablecloths. He immediately discarded all the paraphernalia which was considered essential in those pre-sixties upmarket St James's and Mayfair restaurants – indirect lighting, candelabra, flocked wallpaper, deep pile carpets and heavy drape curtains. He insisted on his trademark tiled floors, white walls, downlights over tables and modern art on the walls. But he added extras that would signify an upgrade of the basic trattoria.

Although the restaurant would be in a basement, it was to have the grandest and most impressive modern entrance. Set into a panel on the external wall was a sensitively lit armoured Roman figure and just inside the glass doors on ground level, clients, as they walked downstairs, were to be soothed with the gentle sound of water running down one wall. The wall was to be covered in real lava from Mount Vesuvius. When Mario and Enzo flew to Naples to buy tiles and other materials, Mario hired a large truck and they drove up onto the mountain to collect lava. As they were loading the stone, an old woman stopped to watch them. Suddenly, there was an earth tremor. As it quietened, the old lady limped over to them, waving her stick. "It's a bad sign," she said, "you have disturbed the mountain."

At the foot of Tiberio's stairs a ticker-tape machine was installed so customers could check their stock prices – a direct crib from the Mirabelle – and, in the main room, Apicella set a new standard of glamour. The ceiling was composed of a series of rough plaster arches. Above each table the downlight consisted of a bulb inside a thin metal tube, producing Apicella's familiar circle of light. The kitchen would be divided from the dining room by a wall of thick red glass, which, for the first time in a London restaurant, allowed customers to watch the chefs and cooks in the kitchen, the fiery red glass making a ballet of even the most mundane kitchen activity. Elegant touches in the lavatories were panels of rosewood and Enzo's own graffiti – cartoons drawn directly on tiles, then glazed over.

The vaulted plaster ceilings would throw back the sound of the customers' voices, making them believe they were in noisy Italy. Apicella claimed this technique would solve the problem of people worrying that their conversations could be overheard. But when, a few months after opening, Quentin Crewe complained in a review that it was too noisy, Mario and Franco spent £1800 on making the ceilings noise absorbent.

Franco maintained that the best way to get mileage out of Enzo was to employ him just long enough to come up with ideas and then make sure he stayed well away. If not, he'd begin to fuss and change things around. But working with him was never boring. Once, badly delayed for a working lunch at La Terrazza with Tiberio's architect Geoffrey Crockett, whom he had met only once, Enzo arrived breathless. He rushed over to a man sitting alone at a corner table, mumbled his apologies and ordered himself a large drink and an even larger lunch. Their opening conversation followed the usual lines – weather, terrible traffic, that day's news – and Enzo finished the pasta course with his customary gusto. But halfway through the main course, he began to look around uneasily, mop his suddenly damp brow and loosened his top shirt button. Their conversation wasn't making too much sense and his companion gazed at him as though he was barking mad.

Enzo's worst fears were confirmed when the restaurant doors abruptly crashed open and the real Geoffrey Crockett puffed in, even later than Enzo, who straightened his tie, picked up his plate and glass and, muttering apologies, backed away from his unknown companion and joined Crockett at his table.

Mario and Franco decided that Tiberio would set a new high standard for Italian wine in the UK and again it was Mario's responsibility to concoct the list. He conducted animated and voluble negotiations, his Neapolitan shrewdness an antidote to any hint of English wine snobbery. Dealing with him was not exactly what the old-fashioned wine trade reps were used to. "You'll sell us *those* wines at *these* prices for three reasons," he would insist. "First, because you'll establish good business with us, second, because you're gonna be serving the best, most luxurious Italian restaurant this side of the Alps and third, because that's all you're gonna get!"

While Mario argued with wine suppliers, Franco focused on the food, determined that it, as well as the service, would be as good as, if not better than, at the Mirabelle and the Savoy. To take care of service, he hired Walter Orsi from the Savoy as Tiberio's manager. Orsi was a tall, distinguished-looking man who resembled a banker rather than a headwaiter; he had a large ego and a reputation for perfectionism. "Walter liked to be the god of the restaurant," says Mario Vollono, who joined Tiberio from the Savoy a year later. No fewer than five other senior Savoy headwaiters – Argenti, Lacchini, Balzaretti, Magnani and under-manager Dino Ribaudo – followed Orsi, turning in their black tail-coats for glamorous, Italian Riviera-style white linen jackets, to become Tiberio's core staff.

As building progressed, Mario and Franco's former Mirabelle colleagues began to take bets on how long it would be before the partners

*Tiberio's exterior was even more glamorous at night.*
*The specially commissioned ceramic statue was created by Lele Luzzati.*

came to a sticky end. However, when the glamorous flagship finally opened on 20 December 1962, it quickly became both a gastronomic and a fashionable success. Tiberio was full up on the first day and by the second it was completely booked for New Year's Eve. Within a few weeks, it was full every night and doing extremely well at lunchtime, due to the Mayfair business community.

With two businesses, both partners spent half their time at each restaurant. While Mario handled publicity and the front of house, Franco focused on working with the Tiberio chef to create a menu of the best Italian dishes, at their highest level of sophistication. The basic ingredients were the best obtainable. The menu was, as far as possible, composed of real Italian, rather than French, dishes. As Franco said,

> If you want Quiche Lorraine or roast pheasant, you go to the Coq d'Or. If you want fresh noodles with fresh truffles flown from Italy, quail stuffed with crayfish, zabaglione with fresh peach, you come to Tiberio.

The menu and its execution were quite simply spectacular and put paid to any residual ideas that Italian cooking could not compare to other major world cuisines. There were lobster cocktails in silver coupes, tissue-thin slices of sweet *Prosciutto di San Daniele* served with a glistening, brandied peach, baked Whitstable oysters, slices of pink Scotch smoked salmon accompanied by hot blinis, crisply gratinéed mussels, delicate pike in wine and tarragon sauce, home-made tagliolini with saffron-scented seafood, feather-light brioches with creamed lobster, glazed soufflé omelettes stuffed with chicken and crabmeat, dishes of crisply fried seafood, roasted honey-spiced duckling, braised chicken with truffle sauce, ribs of lamb served with Ligurian herbs, bowls of tiny wild strawberries served with fresh orange juice, fresh marinated raspberries with a sauce of port, curaçao and thick cream whipped to a deep magenta and silver Italian sweetmeat trays to accompany the espresso coffee.

Preparation, according to Italian custom, was not over-elaborate. Franco and his chefs set out to rely more on what the French call *déglaçage*, rather than thick sauces, actually one of the secrets of Italian cooking. This method is based on extremely light stocks or sometimes even plain water, to maintain the tastes of super-fresh and high-quality ingredients for the resulting sauce.

Tiberio immediately appealed not only to customers of the Mirabelle and to the richer section of La Terrazza's regulars, but also to customers of other nearby smart restaurants such as the Coq d'Or, Prunier and L'Écu de France. Certainly it gave the aristocracy and the British and Hollywood movie stars an opportunity to spend more money than in La Terrazza. Over the next year, Ronald Reagan, then governor of California, was brought by the American ambassador and, when other customers included Tony Curtis, Henry Fonda and David Niven, Mario and Franco and their staff tried hard not to let themselves be overawed by the world-famous faces.

"Mario," asked John Wayne, "could you have someone call the Connaught and send over my chess set?" The legendary actor was sitting after dinner with Edmund Purdom and his wife, the actress Linda Christian.

"Duke," admonished Mario. "It's ten past three."

That first New Year's Eve, the Tiberio brigade had just finished preparation for the evening. The whole room was full of flowers, balloons and Christmas crackers on the tables. Long before the first bookings arrived, a distinguished couple, the man in an outstandingly good suit with a beautiful woman in furs on his arm, walked down the stairs. Mario recognised Valerie Hobson from her films and John Profumo was, of course, defence minister. They had often graced La Terrazza, but were unaware of Tiberio. However, living nearby and having seen the new sign, they had come to ask for a table. Mario quickly walked over to greet them. "I'm afraid that because it's New Year's Eve everything is booked," he said, but since it was early and the place was still empty, he offered them a drink and they sat for half an hour or so and talked with Mario about his plans.

A few days later, the publicist Ronnie Maxwell arrived for the evening with two stunning girls, not perhaps as soignée or beautiful as Miss Hobson, but nevertheless conspicuous. When Mario went over to welcome his friend and find out what the well-known rascal was up to, Ronnie introduced him to Christine Keeler and Mandy Rice-Davies. These two "models" would be at the centre of the scandal which enveloped Harold Macmillan's government later that year and led to Profumo's resignation from the government after he lied to Parliament about his affair with Keeler.

Tiberio was undoubtedly glamorous, a complete break from most

*Tiberio's white-linen-coated headwaiters were all poached from the Savoy. Mario and Franco wanted to outdo the top French restaurants in every aspect of the business.*

usual convention, but in one way it catered to a taste which, though on its way out, was very traditional in Mayfair, namely: "Dinner and Dance." A pianist accompanied the main dinner service and a small band, Olaf Vas and his Orchestra, would start to play at about ten thirty through to closing at 3 a.m. On occasion there would be a cabaret show. The room fell silent when one evening an artist moved into the spotlight in the front centre of the bandstand and began his five-minute display of complex and rhythmic bongo drumming. Everyone craned forward as one elegant diner grabbed her partner and sallied onto the floor to perform a wild impromptu dance right in front of the musician, blocking him from view. Franco, watching from the back, instantly realised who was committing the faux-pas – HRH Princess Margaret and a member of her small party. Quickly he signalled to the band to end the solo so that she would not be embarrassed.

It was a taxi driver who brought home to Mario and Franco how celebrated Tiberio had become. Less than a year after its opening, they hailed a taxi in Shaftesbury Avenue one day and asked the cabbie to

"Take us to Tiberio restaurant in…"

"That'll be Tiberio in Queen Street, Mayfair", the driver interrupted. "You'll like it, everybody does. It's very good, Frank Sinatra goes there."

The Mirabelle staff members who'd bet against their survival had to

pay up. Nearly all Tiberio's customers were also fans of La Terrazza and, naturally, Mario and Franco's heads were slightly turned by the numerous aristocratic customers.

"There hasn't been a queen or a princess arriving from Europe who hasn't been to Tiberio," Franco said in 1965. "There are normally two or three dukes most evenings and always lords all over the place. We have the cream of society and we've done in three years what normally takes a restaurant at least forty."

The atmosphere, the food and the service were fantastic, but so was the bill. By then, the cost of a meal sitting next to exalted neighbours at Tiberio was circa eight pounds for two, about half my week's wages. I only went there twice, most memorably for dinner on my twenty-first birthday, when our party of eight was paid for by my incredibly generous elder brother. As soon as we arrived at the imposing entrance, we all knew the evening would be special and it turned out to be the best meal I had ever eaten and in the most memorably glamorous setting. Regrettably, I drank far too much and can't remember a thing about it.

The general opinion of the contemporary restaurant critics was that Tiberio was indeed as good as the Mirabelle or Caprice, perhaps better. In his column for *Queen* of 27 April 1966, a few months before my 21st birthday dinner, Quentin Crewe wrote, "People think I am obsessed with the place, but I must point out that I haven't mentioned it for a year. I can't think of a restaurant in London which gives one more strongly the sensation that they want you to enjoy yourself – they want you to like the food and want you to feel that dinner there is an occasion."

For more than a year, that same magazine ran the same short entry about Tiberio in its *Briefing* section which offered a monthly round-up of recommended places.

> **"Tiberio, 22 Queen Street, Mayfair. In the running for the best restaurant in London. £7 for two."**

Tiberio was the "most expensive and the most fashionable Italian restaurant in London" where Italian cooking became "closest to the subtleties of haute cuisine," opined the *Good Food Guide*. In its wisdom, the Guide described the décor as "Modern Capri style," and complained that while the bar was often crowded with the rich and famous, the tables were a little too close together. Dishes which had given greatest pleasure included lobster in piquant sauce, calamari, sweetbreads and veal. While

La Terrazza, having broken away from the old formality and made dining out fun, still offered simple Italian food, Tiberio with its *alta cucina* nudged Italian restaurants back onto the path of offering more classical cooking.

Mario and Franco's growing success and regular appearances in newspapers and magazines began to encourage more young Italians to think about opening their own establishments, relying on the same formula that had built Mario and Franco's reputation. More and more British diners were beginning to see that, in contrast to most of their culinary competitors, the Italians could not only promise a delicious meal, but would make sure that at the same time, you had a wonderful evening.

## EXPANSION IN ROMILLY STREET, 1964

After his early assignments for Mario and Franco at Tiberio and the Positano Room, Enzo's career as a designer began to flourish. His first new client came when Mario and Franco recommended him to their old friend and colleague Luigi Paglierani, who since he had left the Mirabelle had worked every winter in London and run his guesthouse near Rimini during the summer season. In 1963, he was ready to take the plunge and Apicella designed a cool, calm interior for a site on the newly fashionable King's Road, in Chelsea. Trattoria Don Luigi opened in 1963 and the normally staid and reserved Luigi Paglierani arrived at just the right time to find himself at the apex of sixties fashion. Egon Ronay's *Guide* noted the simple elegance of the design:

> **A modern Italian Trattoria with a warm atmosphere and a bare minimum of gimmicks. The modern paintings, crisp pink napery and background of green bottles give a pleasing freshness.**

Eighteen months after Tiberio had opened, Mario and Franco offered Enzo an even bigger opportunity.

At the corner of Romilly and Dean streets, next door to La Terrazza, was a well-known Chinese restaurant, the August Moon. Its owner, Mr Lee, had found larger premises in Queensway and was ready to discuss the sale of his freehold. Mario and Franco, dreaming of the possibilities of doubling the size of their trattoria, arranged a meeting with their neighbour.

Having exchanged pleasantries and compliments with Mr Lee, Mario asked what price he had in mind. As soon as he named it, one of Mario and Franco's silent board meetings ensued, during which they glanced at each other, raised and lowered their eyebrows, twitched, winked and eventually smiled. By now, as their staff had noted, they seemed to be able to read each other's minds and a decision was swiftly reached. With a new loan secured on the successful trading of La Terrazza and Tiberio, Mario and Franco once again turned to Apicella, who, as before, sat down with quantities of felt-tip pens and pink tablecloths to outline his ideas, not only for the proposed extension, but also for the redecoration and upgrading of the original Vesuvio room.

They had barely started work when a new occurrence caused them to change their plans completely. Neighbours on the other side of La Terrazza were also about to close their musical instrument store and wondered if Mario and Franco would like to be introduced to their landlord, a Mr Monnickendam, who was interested in selling the freehold. Their dream of doubling the size of La Terrazza was nothing compared to the possibilities offered by the prospect of uniting all three buildings, and a deal was quickly arrived at.

At last Enzo could start and, while he ordered more felt-tip pens, Mario and Franco considered the prospect. There would now be four separate dining rooms with a total seating capacity of 160, a far cry from the original thirty-five with which they'd begun in 1959. Upstairs on the first floor would be three private dining rooms and a bar, which they would christen the Gatto Nero Bar in honour of the original downstairs club. They would be able to extend both the kitchen and their offices above, where they would handle all the administration for both restaurants.

But first, they had to dispose of a piece of their heritage.

"Are you sure you want to do this? Quite sure?" Apicella queried, as he passed a huge hammer from hand to hand, gazing across the Bay of Naples at Mount Vesuvius and myriad buildings silhouetted against the blue evening sky.

Mario and Franco paced up and down behind him, anxiously chewing their fingernails. "Go ahead," Franco said finally. "We have waited long enough."

Enzo swung the sledgehammer and with six or seven rapid blows demolished Polish George's Vesuvius in a snowfall of plaster dust. The preposterous vine trellis with its fake fruit was much easier. It collapsed in seconds, the plastic grapes bouncing and scattering everywhere. After five minutes, Apicella, not normally given to violent exercise, or indeed to any exercise at all, was sweating and panting, his eyes stinging from the blizzard of plaster. He was, though, finally happy to have obliterated the hideous mural of his beloved home town.

The lead-up to the transformation of the Vesuvio Room had been anything but an overnight process. Enzo always had in his head a concept of how the restaurant should look, but he never managed to get it down on paper. As usual, his sketches were done on tablecloths and he was extremely reluctant – indeed not trained – to produce conventional drawings. But everything which had defined the room – floor, lighting, Chianti bottles, ashtrays – was to go; and once Apicella had finished his transformation, the new Vesuvio matched its sister the Positano Room downstairs.

The entire restaurant now incorporated the elements that have

*Mick Jagger – alone for the moment – at a table for two in the Positano Room, 1966. Photo: Mirror Pictures*

become Apicella's trademarks – glazed green ceramic floor tiles from Naples, plain white plastered wall-fittings, the spotlights – only rarely risked in restaurants before – to illuminate dark corners and highlight the abstract paintings which he chose for the white walls. Instead of the old wall-fittings, his trademark cylindrical downlights hung over the centre of each table, reflecting softly up from the pink tablecloths, onto the faces of diners; this enabled them to see what they were eating, but not the bags under each other's eyes. These simple downlights, here and at Tiberio, were a major change in restaurant design.

In addition to the décor, the metamorphosis gave Mario and Franco the opportunity to put more of Enzo's ideas to the test. The introduction of round tables in the Positano Room provided an illusion of much greater space than square or oblong tables, as well as making conversation easier and more intimate. The restaurateur's argument against round tables has always been that they cannot be pushed together or squashed up tight in a row; but the argument for them is that you can seat more people at each one and the restaurant does not end up looking like a railway carriage. They need to be exactly the right height. "It's the sort of thing customers don't notice unless you point it out to them. But they are certainly well aware if they are uncomfortable," Apicella noted. To give the lighting a focal point, he placed a tiny silver vase holding a single rose at the centre of each table. He designed a new menu, headed by the sunburst logo which was to become Mario and Franco's trademark; this was emblazoned on crockery, stationery and signage. He chose the art for the walls, in some instances doing quick drawings himself and, in addition to waiters' uniforms – traditional Neapolitan fishermen's jerseys, white with blue hoops, which he had suggested back in the early days – the four room managers were to wear white roll-necks and blue blazers. Like the décor, the waiters' striped jerseys became part of the restaurant's public identity, so much so that they were adopted or adapted over the next ten years by almost every new Italian restaurant in Britain.

One shadow which still hung over the business was that, while the new extensions were both freehold acquisitions, the original building was on a lease. While renovations was underway, Mario managed to do a deal with their landlord which enabled the expanding group to acquire the freehold of 19 Romilly Street; by the time the new premises were ready to open, all three buildings were owned by them.

For his contribution, Enzo was paid part in cash and part in free meals. He seemed to Mario and Franco to be uninterested in making money beyond satisfying his immediate needs. But as they observed from his constantly changing dinner companions, he was famously interested in and interesting to, women. As soon as he could afford it, every night of the week Enzo went dancing after dinner in the new fashionable clubs and discotheques, often accompanied by two girls "so they could take it in turns to rest."

"I did go out for dinner with him once," one date of Enzo's told me,

> and I do remember him as looking exactly like an Italian Renaissance painting. I don't remember any of the conversation. But as I thanked him and was about to leave, he seemed a little put out that I wasn't going to go to bed with him. "The only important thing is the fuck," he remarked.

Once, late for a train to Gatwick, he left his new Alfa Romeo Giulietta Sprint drophead outside the main entrance to Victoria station, even though a policeman had told him not to. ("Two minutes," he'd shouted as he belted towards the platform.) He'd spent two weeks in Italy before he remembered and called his friend, Adrian Bailey, who picked up a spare key, made his way to Victoria and found the Alfa still where it had been left.

Apicella's life seemed not to be touched by ordinary mortal cares and concerns, so that he would never send invoices, and when given a cheque, would forget to bank it. He would do a design, or have an idea for a restaurant and in exchange, eat for free; what could be simpler? The downside of this was that, generous on some occasions, he could be notoriously mean on others. Once, when a gallery organised an exhibition of his work, he was said to have demanded to be paid for drawing a poster to promote his own show.

With his design for Romilly Street finalised, the word "trattoria" in truth no longer applied to the business. Although Mario and Franco knew everyone would still call it "The Trat," the partners decided to shorten its name. On Apicella's advice, the whole exterior façade of the three buildings was painted white and his new logo, the cartoon sunflower, was mounted across the fascia, alongside the words "La Terrazza."

The extension opening was celebrated by Mario and Franco with a photo session. They stood in Dean Street traffic in smart new suits in front of their massive premises, looking like prosperous business executives, no longer the humble waiters of five years ago. In a concession to sixties vogue, Franco's hair now cascaded over his collar and was brushed forward; it was no longer combed back and brilliantined, 1950s style.

Money had worked its way into their private lives and, in 1961, they had both bought new Fiat 2100s. As well as all day in the office and all evening together, Mario and Franco now became neighbours. Franco and Sara moved out of their small house in Croftdown Road, Mario and Mary abandoned their council flat, and the two couples, each with two sons, moved into recently built Wates homes in a close in Sydenham Hill.

With four public dining rooms, bar and private rooms upstairs, plus extensions to the kitchen, Mario and Franco's Terrazza had become a substantial business, feeding more than 500 customers a day. From its inception, the partners had done everything themselves, including controlling the chef, and, as it grew, this system (or lack of a system), continued. In addition to Alvaro as manager, each room now had a headwaiter, but there was no job demarcation and, like Mario and Franco when they started out, Alvaro was involved in everything. There were barmen, receptionists and three or four waiters in each room, as well as a commis to fetch and carry; there were now eighteen members of the kitchen brigade. Being open seven days a week meant that with days off and holiday and relief cover, there were more than eighty people working at La Terrazza.

New young waiters found themselves in an environment where they had to work inordinately hard for long hours, keeping up Franco's high standards. But there was always a buzz, an atmosphere that made the experience more than bearable. "The service was very friendly," one of them told me later. "People were singing and it felt much more Italian than other places I had worked in."

The waiters' wages at La Terrazza may have been the best in London, but, as Pasquale Lunghi admits, the work was much harder than it had been in his previous job at the Mayfair Hotel.

> It was very tough, first of all because of the tiled floors. Up to then all the restaurants in London had carpets and going from walking on the carpets to then walking on the tiled floor made a lot of difference and gave you pain in your ankles. For the first couple of weeks I was literally in agony, I couldn't walk, it was terrible, but then you get used to it.

After a few months he became used to it and, consequently, was promoted to managing a room.

Another young Italian, who had earned £12 a week in a provincial English hotel, made £65 a week at La Terrazza. "In Bournemouth they told us about La Terrazza in London. They said the waiters make £80 or £90 a week," recalls Mario Paggetti, who went there in 1965. "I thought they must be joking. But my friend assured me, the work was hard but the money was good."

"You start at ten," he was told. "You finish at four. You start again at five thirty and you finish at one o'clock in the morning."

One day, he and a colleague caught a train to London and went straight to La Terrazza to ask for a job. His prospects were helped when he discovered that he came from the same part of Italy as Alvaro.

"Fine," Alvaro finally said. "You start tomorrow."

"Tomorrow? I've got to give a week's notice. I work in Bournemouth."

"You start tomorrow or you don't start at all," was the reply.

"*Madonna mia,*" Mario Paggetti muttered to himself. "What do we do?" Then he remembered that he had a friend who lived in Notting Hill, who might put him up. Paggetti contacted him, found accommodation and took the job.

For Dante Betti, originally from Bologna, the food capital of Italy, La Terrazza's cuisine was impressive.

> What most attracted the clientele was the simplicity of the food. It was genuine,

> presented well, reasonably priced. At the time the choice was only stiff French food or going to Lyons Corner House, so that Italian food, in between, was just what the people wanted. Compared with where I worked before, it had a very relaxed atmosphere and an informal friendliness; the staff could talk with the customers and that was the real success.

For many of the youths who arrived at La Terrazza, a significant part of their education was realising how their bosses' partnership worked. Watching Mario and Franco, many waiters gained valuable experience of the challenges which faced restaurant owners and managers. These skills stood them in good stead later, when they opened their own businesses. "Franco was a true gentleman," remembers Pasquale Lunghi.

> He was a professional in every sense of the word. A gem as a person and as a restaurateur. Mario was more volatile. He was wonderful because he was really good hearted. The only thing was that when he arrived at the restaurant, you wouldn't know if he was going to come in quietly or be blowing his top off. Every time he entered the restaurant he used to make you feel dizzy about something or other. That was his way of keeping you on your toes.

"Franco tasted the food every day," Mario Paggetti remembers,

> and every two hours he would go into the kitchen to listen and talk to the chef, while Mario focused on the customers and the front door. Mario didn't need to worry about the food. That was Franco's job. But anybody who came through the entrance, Mario would greet them by name and make them feel welcome.

"They were very professional, both of them," Mario Vollono, who later became La Terrazza manager, told me. "They were a good combination because of their very different styles."

Mario Cassandro, entirely fearless, not fazed by fame, grandeur or pretension, treated their regular customers as old friends, which, indeed, many of them became. He would welcome the film producers Cubby Broccoli and Harry Saltzman at the height of their James Bond fame, with a hug or a pat on the shoulder.

"I was astounded when I heard him say 'Hello, my friend' to Mr Broccoli," remembers Mario Vollono.

> I had never seen any restaurant manager do that before. Franco, however, was more old fashioned and correct. He would never do something like that. He would stand in front of the customers and pay attention as though he was still a headwaiter.

The overt friendliness between customers and staff was a great morale-booster. "After working in a slow, sedate hotel it was a shock when I first arrived," says Pasquale Lunghi. "La Terrazza had a fast pace and after two weeks all the customers coming into that room knew my name. It was wonderful to be known by name, not just be an anonymous servant."

Italians' love of children, their seemingly innate understanding of how to help them enjoy restaurants, came into its own at La Terrazza. At weekends, Mario and Franco started to run films in one of the new private dining rooms upstairs, so parents could leave their children there to enjoy a movie while they ate Sunday lunch below. Many of these children developed a lifelong passion for Italian food while they watched a film.

"What Mario and Franco did for the evolution of children's food, while looking after their clients' children, was staggering," remembers Carolyn Townshend.

> We would go to the Trat for the Sunday films, when my son was about two or three. I would arrive with him in my arms and he would be whisked away to spend lunchtime at the door greeting people with either Mario or Franco. They were so clever to have the Sunday lunch films upstairs, because it meant that we could all stay there for hours and we were so happy that the children were so well looked after.
>
> Five years later, when my son was about seven, I once took him to La Terrazza on my own, just the two of us and I suggested to him that since he was the man, he should be the one to pay the bill. So he asked Mario for the bill himself and when Mario brought it to the table, I secretly passed Vincenzo some money under the table and he went over to the desk and gave them the saucer with the cash on it. He stood there, about three feet high, waiting for his change.

Family life, though, was not so easy for the staff, always busy until last orders at 11.30 p.m. "My son grew up so fast and I didn't really know him," admits Pasquale Lunghi.

> I would get home maybe for an hour in the afternoon, but I didn't feel like talking, I didn't feel like doing anything. I was so tired I that I used to sit in the armchair with my son in my arms for an hour or so. I used to sleep for about twenty minutes and that was it. My wife put up with it. I came home about four thirty and then at six o'clock I had to be away back to work.

Some staff members found simple solutions. When Dante Betti came to Mario and Franco after a stint at Ad Lib nightclub, he was newly married. "I worked very long hours. But my wife managed to find a restaurant job as a receptionist. We had the same shifts and time off together. That's how we stuck together."

Others were not so lucky. "Some wives would be left at home in the evenings," one ex-husband says.

> But then their girlfriends, other married women or single friends, would call and say, "Oh you're stupid, why are you always sitting at home in that house, let's go and have a drink, let's go to a pub and enjoy ourselves and we'll be back home before our husbands finish work."

One thing would lead to another and many marriages were ruined by the pressure of the restaurant business.

*Mario and Franco celebrated the 1964 opening of their extension with a press call. Now they look every inch the prosperous business executives they had become. Photo: courtesy of Mario Cassandro*

## JUMPING ON THE TRATTORIA BANDWAGON

By the mid-sixties, the new generation of trattoria restaurants exemplified by La Terrazza, had left their competitors far behind: **Gennaro's Italian Restaurant, 44 Dean Street: The décor is drab fuss. Rather faded and tatty, dark and given to potted plants, the light comes from ghastly bunches of glass grapes, hung between beams. On the beams in both Italian and English are written meaningless proverbs, yellowing murals of Sorrento type and sub-Arno scenes complete the atmosphere; what is missing is the certainty that "I must be enjoying myself" which is the essential characteristic of the perpetually successful Terrazza. Summary: Super if you want to avoid your friends.**

QUENTIN CREWE'S RESTAURANT COLUMN, *QUEEN* MAGAZINE, AUGUST 1966

When the London Italian community saw Mario and Franco's success, some of its members were quick to follow their formula and, although none achieved similar fame, several of them contributed to the reputation of the quality and value for money of Italian restaurants and food, as well as the fun to be had on a trattoria evening.

Colombina D'Oro in Frith Street opened in the mid-1950s, with a chef proprietor still remembered warmly today by early student regulars, who recall that *la padrona* always charged them less than her main customers. Indeed she made out bills according to what she thought could be afforded and the more prosperous customers would end up paying for the table next to them as well as for their own party. Also as one customer remembers, she wouldn't serve her home-made grappa to anyone under thirty.

Trattoria Da Otello at 41 Dean Street was opened by another early pasta pioneer. Otello Scipioni asked Apicella to design his menu and paint a mural. Soon his restaurant appeared next to La Terrazza in the 1961 *Good Food Guide* as "one of the best." Later, he was to open a second, the Girasole in the Fulham Road. Trattoria Positano, also in Fulham Road, offered a very good value menu, with eight pasta dishes including *Spaghetti alle Cozze* and *Rigatoni all'Amatriciana* at 4/6d (12.5p). Their main courses such as *Pollo alla Cacciatora* were 10/6d (52.5p) and at these low prices it became popular with the young Chelsea crowd.

As La Terrazza's prices climbed, together with its popularity, other Italian restaurateurs stepped in to offer the most basic, genuine Italian food at prices affordable for London office staff, shoppers and residents. Budget

Italian restaurants sprang up in business areas like The City, Victoria and The Strand, as well as near the major shopping centres of Oxford Street, Kensington High Street and Knightsbridge.

Giulio Cornoli, who arrived in London in 1956, worked first as a waiter at Frank's, an old established Italian restaurant in Jermyn Street whose owner had changed the name from Franco's when he was registered as a wartime resident alien. When he realised the significance of Mario and Franco's growing popularity, Cornoli saw an opportunity to provide quick, inexpensive pasta-based meals for what he calls the secretary end of the market and opened the first of his Verbanella restaurants in June 1962, in Blandford Street, just behind Oxford Street. He offered basic main courses and occasionally more expensive and adventurous dishes such as *Cotechino con Lenticchie* – sausage-stuffed pig's foot with lentils. Verbanella quickly became popular with office workers, who could eat in under an hour, pay about half a crown (12p) for spaghetti and 5/- (25p) for main courses such as *Pollo Cacciatora* and *Ossobuco*. Soon Giulio opened a second, then a third branch of Verbanella, and, later, a fourth in Richmond, pitched slightly more up market, always taking into account the local budgets.

A major player in this market was, and still is, the Spaghetti House group. Although a Spaghetti House in Charlotte Street had existed since before the Second World War, the first of the current chain, owned by the Lavarini and Fraquelli brothers-in-law, provided Italian food at modest prices to office staff and shoppers in Goodge Street, from the mid-1950s.

But when it comes to a long run, the trattoria equivalent of *The Mousetrap* is San Lorenzo in Beauchamp Place, Knightsbridge.

On 18 October 1963, Mercedes Rizzini, the wife of the London correspondent of *Corriere della Sera*, was walking along Beauchamp Place, when she detected a familiar, but unexpected, aroma wafting from an open doorway. It was, she realised, garlic, odd in a street of antique shops. She sauntered through the door then down the stairs to see what was going on.

"*Buongiorno, signora,*" Mara Berni greeted her, looking up from stirring a pot in the tiny kitchen at the foot of the stairs.

"What are you doing? What is this?" the visitor asked.

"I am cooking," Mara said.

"Cooking what?"

"Risotto," Mara answered. "This is an Italian restaurant. We opened only yesterday."

The previous night they had only served two customers.

Mercedes Rizzini sat down in the tiny restaurant, ordered the risotto, which she seemed to enjoy immensely, and the next day, she brought her journalist husband for dinner. Mara and Lorenzo (her husband the waiter) served thirty-nine people at lunch and eighteen for dinner on the third day and over the next weeks the Rizzinis returned with colleagues and friends, so helping the fledgling Osteria San Lorenzo on its way.

The meeting of Lorenzo and Mara Berni is also part of London's Italian restaurant folklore. The film director Mario Zampi came to work in Britain in 1923 and, during the next thirty years, achieved the unusual feat of managing to understand British humour. In the 1950s he made his name with five enjoyable comedies with an Ealing Studios flavour. He is relevant to this story because, in 1960, he raised funds for one of the earliest London Italian Pizza restaurants, which he called Pizza Express, at 29 Wardour Street, on the corner of Rupert Court. It was close to a pub where the newly arrived Lorenzo, already with six years' experience as a steward on cruise liners, had found work behind the bar. He soon found his future wife, Mara Lasillier, working in what became La Romanella Pizza Express. (After Zampi died of a heart attack in 1963, the site was acquired by Peter Boizot, to become the first branch of his Pizza Express chain.)

Two years later, Lorenzo was manager at La Taverna Spaghetti Garden, in Kensington Grove and, married to Mara with their first child on the way, it seemed the moment to opt for independence. Lorenzo felt sure that a business in the upmarket Knightsbridge area would prosper. In those days, Beauchamp Place, not far from Harrods, was thronged with antique and couture shops; many wealthy people lived nearby.

Like Mario and Franco four years earlier, Lorenzo and Mara found a sympathetic bank manager, one of Lorenzo's customers at the Spaghetti Garden. When Lorenzo told him that he was planning to set up on his own in Knightsbridge, he was immediately offered support. "This kind of thing would never have happened in Italy for a new business and I was astonished when he offered to help us," Lorenzo remembers.

Client loyalty and friendship seem to have been there before San Lorenzo opened. Some of Lorenzo's lunchtime customers at the Spaghetti Garden were partners in a firm of architects and when they heard that he intended to start a business they immediately offered to do the drawings and apply for planning permission, *gratis*. Italians tend only to offer such generosity and support to their own families and closest friends and

Lorenzo and Mara were again astounded. Britain in the post-war era really was a land of huge opportunity for hardworking immigrants.

At first, the architects made the obvious suggestion of locating kitchens at the back, adjacent to the garden. But in a decision which would result in their restaurant being one of the very few in central London where it was possible to eat *al fresco*, Lorenzo was adamant that his customers should be able to sit outside. He was also determined to have the kitchen at the front, so, on arrival, customers would pass it, just like in a trattoria at home.

The pair had saved up a little over a thousand pounds and Lorenzo's bank manager lent them a further £1,500. This was barely enough to equip a restaurant, so everything was second hand; by the time Osteria San Lorenzo opened on 17 October 1963, Mara had had to borrow money from friends in order to stock up on olive oil and other imports.

In contrast to Apicella's white-dominated environments, the San Lorenzo tables were covered in wipe-clean plastic cloths, giving the impression of being in Mara's own kitchen and the staff wasn't uniformed. The result was untidy, unglamorous and unaffected and it was immediately patronized by workmen as well as the very chic – all tempted by the exceptional cuisine.

To begin with, San Lorenzo was hard to find. You had to go down a minuscule staircase, then round two sharp corners, to arrive at the kitchen door, from whence you could see, at the end of a small room, a door which led out into a garden shaded by a tall sycamore tree.

Mara's menu was quite different from that of La Terrazza. From the start, San Lorenzo offered unusual dishes such as Pigeon with Polenta, or Sea Bass, which was not the popular fish that it is today. Mara comes from Piedmont, where regional specialities include agnolotti, Bagna Cauda, Bollito Misto, gnocchi and risotto and these recipes very much influenced the menu from the earliest days. We ignorant British unwittingly sampled delicious northern Italian delicacies at San Lorenzo, completely unlike the southern-based food of the other popular trattorie.

With Italian and English customers, young and old, Lorenzo and Mara soon became accustomed to the idiosyncrasies of their regulars. "Mind the step," Mara said to the Duke and Duchess of Bedford, as she showed them through to the back. The very tall Duke promptly banged his head hard on the beam. Mara, accustomed to Italian aristocrats who tended to take themselves seriously, was astonished when the dazed Duke said, "Don't worry, there's nothing in there anyway."

Initially, there was no licence and as with so many other new restaurants, the customers had to bring their own wine, or alternatively, ask Lorenzo to run across to the pub for them.

"We'd only been open a few months," Mara remembers, "and on a warm evening, some customers were sitting outside in the garden. One of them, Clement Freud, asked with a twinkle, 'It's starting to rain. Do you charge corkage if I put up my umbrella?'"

"All the Italian movie directors came here," Lorenzo remembers:

> and I would know exactly what they would order and the way they ate, it was just like the films they were making. Antonioni, very complicated films and just little complicated food, little bit of this, some of that, all chopped up small, carrots, beans; Federico Fellini, his films were big and luscious and strong – he always ordered pasta and then a T-bone steak. Francesco Rosi, he was politically involved, very much of the left, so he always looked at his food as if he didn't care and, as for Luchino Visconti – he's the perfectionist – he always has an aperitif, then starter, first course, second course, sweet, coffee and liqueur. All perfectly organised, just like his films.

*It always felt like a family restaurant, because it was. Lorenzo and Mara Berni with their sons Paolo and Ghigo in their Osteria San Lorenzo. Photo: Courtesy of Lorenzo Berni*

When Sophia Loren visited the Osteria when filming *The Countess from Hong Kong* and was spotted by journalist fellow diners, the resulting newspaper diary items cemented the San Lorenzo reputation. "It was just a few weeks after we opened," Mara recalls, "Loren, just one woman at the long table with twelve men." She continues:

> In those days there was only white bread in the shops, so we used to get a man to make Italian bread specially for us and he used to bake SL, the restaurant's initials, onto each bread roll and loaf. So when Loren started to order takeaway dishes to be delivered to the set, she thought that we had had the bread made specially for her.

Within eighteen months, Quentin Crewe was raving about San Lorenzo in his *Queen* magazine column. "No one before," he wrote, "had so perfectly created in London the kind of backstreet trattoria which you would find in every Italian town." Crewe, who claimed he had seen the Italian ambassador in the Osteria, went on to chide himself that he was mad to tell his readers about such a wonderful authentic trattoria in the heart of Knightsbridge. Mara confirms his sighting.

> In the first days, the Italian ambassador used to come here and he had a very beautiful wife and six children. But he also had this lovely mistress – she also was beautiful– and on other days he would bring her. She had always the full make-up, with those huge false eyelashes girls wore then. One day I was looking at her and one of the false lashes dropped off into her soup in front of her – so, very quickly, she took off the other one, dropped it into the soup and ate them both.

Peter Sellers and his then wife Britt Ekland, who had held their wedding reception at Tiberio, were one of the first celebrity couples to visit San Lorenzo and it was they who memorably brought Princess Margaret and Lord Snowdon. As Ekland wrote later:

> At that time, it was a small place, literally a room with a tree that grew in the middle of it and you sat at long communal tables. The restaurant had an authentic Italian feel and look… it was just as if you were in Rome, rustic and very, very plain.

"There was an absolute craze for Italian restaurants, then," the actress continued:

> But the food wasn't the only thing that attracted us to San Lorenzo, it was very much to do with the zest of the owners. San Lorenzo is a family operation, Mara and Lorenzo Berni have always done everything they can to make you feel that you were part of the atmosphere. Mara would hug and kiss you, ask about the

children and show you pictures of her family and their house in Italy. The first thing my friends from LA do when they get off the plane is to head straight to Mara Berni because she's catered for high-profile people all her life. She's seen them start a career, like me, and been like a mother figure.

**SAN LORENZO BAGNA CAUDA**
**Lorenzo and Mara Berni's Recipe**

Over lunch at San Lorenzo in 2006, I asked Mara if I could use the upstairs mezzanine for Terry O'Neill to shoot the photograph of Mario and the surviving Pasta Pioneers. Her first question was, of course, what should she give them all to eat after the shoot? We settled on two great Piedmont specialities, *Bagna Cauda* and *Bollito Misto*, very suitable for a chilly April day.

*Bagna Cauda*, essentially a fondue of raw fresh vegetables, is one of the favourite starters at this celebrated restaurant.

Allow up to 400g of raw vegetables per person, using whatever is at its best. Usual ingredients are red or green or yellow peppers – often they serve all three – fennel, celery, radishes, cauliflower, fresh mushrooms, baby carrots, cucumber batons and chicory.

For the sauce, for four to six people: 10–12 fresh anchovy fillets, 250g fresh cream or crème fraiche, two or three cloves of garlic, 6 tablespoonsful of best quality olive oil, a handful of chopped walnuts, salt to taste.

Chop the anchovy fillets. Peel and crush the garlic. Heat the oil and add the garlic, being careful as it sautées, not to let it brown and then remove the garlic. Take the pan from the heat and add the anchovies, stirring well. Return the pan to the heat and continue cooking, stirring the mixture until the anchovies have dissolved into a paste. Now stir in the cream, allow it to warm through and add the walnuts.

Put the saucepan over a spirit lamp on the table – or pour the mixture into a bowl for the table. Mara uses Italian ones made especially for the purpose, which have a small candle burning below the earthenware bowl and which keep the mixture hot while guests dip their vegetables in.

## TREACHERY: MICHAEL CAINE'S TABLE, POSITANO ROOM, 1965

Michael Caine and his agent, Dennis Selinger, were finishing their meal at Caine's usual table downstairs in the Positano Room at La Terrazza when Alvaro drifted over. By November 1965, Caine, already a big star, was working on his new film, playing the Italian food-loving, espresso-drinking, Terrazza regular Harry Palmer in Len Deighton's *The Ipcress File*.

"Michael, may I have a word?" Alvaro asked. Four years after he had been promoted manager, Alvaro's name was synonymous with La Terrazza. He called regular customers by their Christian name, and had begun to feel that he could go it alone.

"Of course."

"I am opening a restaurant myself and I'm inviting just a few very good, very close friends for a party. I just want to ask you, I don't want to make a big event."

"Sure, sure. Yes, of course," replied Michael Caine, and gave Alvaro the address of his flat in Grosvenor Square. Selinger also hastened to offer his address.

Lauro Resta, one of Mario and Franco's regulars, who had done well in the plastics business, had asked Alvaro if he'd like his own restaurant. "I can't afford it," came the answer.

"Don't worry about money. If you want to do it, I can find that," said Resta. So Alvaro began to make his plans.

Throughout November, when Alvaro's particular customer friends such as the tailor, Doug Hayward, the photographers, Brian Duffy and Terry O'Neill, or the actor, Terence Stamp, appeared at La Terrazza, Alvaro had much the same message. "I'm opening my own place, I'm inviting some friends, Michael Caine is coming. Give me your address," he whispered, "and I can let you know where I will be."

Very soon, he had a list of the addresses and telephone numbers of most of the best of La Terrazza's clientele. They all seemed eager to know Alvaro's opening date.

With long hours and too much late-night drinking as he worked the room in the Gatto Nero, Franco was by this time suffering from a gastric ulcer. When it became acute, he checked himself in for tests at St George's Hospital at Hyde Park Corner, where the Lanesborough Hotel is now.

Several customers dropped by to visit him. Someone, keen to gossip and not stopping to think how bad news might affect Franco's condition, asked, "Do you know when Alvaro's going to open his own place?"

"Whaaaat? When? Where? How do you know?"

Aghast, Franco called Mario at the restaurant. Mario, stunned by the news, summoned Alvaro to the upstairs office. "Is this true?

"Yes, but..."

"Why you don't tell me you're going? Why must we find out from a friend?" Mario stormed. "Deceit! Sedition! Treachery! Dishonesty! Betrayal!"

For at least ten minutes Alvaro was loudly lectured on loyalty, duty, trust and friendship. Bravely, he protested that he was doing exactly what Mario and Franco had done a few years earlier. Like them, he simply intended to open his own place. Once calmer, Mario agreed on two months' notice and a parting date and, as Alvaro left the room, he hugged and kissed him and wished him good luck.

But Franco, fretting as he lay in his hospital bed, remained anxious. Alvaro had given his notice and would not be leaving until a month before his new place was scheduled to open. Franco worried that Alvaro would deliberately target the celebrity customers of the Positano Room. To what extent might his disloyalty stretch? Shouldn't they let him go at once?

*On the set of The Ipcress File, author Len Deighton shows Michael Caine how to crack an egg with one hand*

## EX-DIRECTORY: KING'S ROAD, 1966

By the time Alvaro went to look for a site, the social geography of London was quite different from what it had been when Mario had done the same thing. The King's Road, Chelsea, was becoming the centre of happening London.

"I could see an explosion was arriving," Alvaro says now.

> Something new was coming, every time I went down the King's Road. There was more happening there than in the West End. Soho was for the older generation, a continuation of the fifties and I was younger. The King's Road, the music, the fashion, was to me something fantastic, so I went down there to look and we found this place.

The place he found was the former Magic Carpet, a restaurant owned by Major Brampton and his ex-showgirl wife Poppet, a favourite haunt of Kim Philby, the spy. Egon Ronay wondered in his 1961 *Guide* if its murals of nudes had been designed to distract your attention from your plate.

Alvaro thought of christening his new restaurant Michelangelo. But Apicella, who did the design for a £600 fee, talked him out of it, saying it would give an old-fashioned, pre-Mario and Franco image. So "Alvaro" it was and in March, 1966, an invitation went out to about 300 "friends."

alvaro

is opening a little tiny house
of food orgies.
he would like you to come
and have a drink, a pizza bite,
and a look around.

the celebrations will take place
on friday 1st april
(honest, no fooling)
from 7 o'clock till down.

124, king's road, london sw3

My brother Robin and I, together with our girlfriends, arrived at the party quite early and stayed pretty late. (But not until *down*. Alvaro had spotted the error, but it was too late to change it.) I have read stories about that warm evening of 1 April 1966 and heard it described dozens of times and even though I was there myself, it is as hard to recount everything that happened as it is for a single soldier to give an account of a whole battle.

Alvaro was seldom without his famous smile, which made his face seem almost square. Because we were early, we were able to see inside. The first thing I noticed was that the room resembled La Terrazza. It had the same tiled floor, white walls and rustic chairs with woven rush seats. This was to be expected, as Apicella had designed it. There was, however, one original element, a group of seven small sepia family photographs on the wall. Presumably, these were of Alvaro's family. They gave the room an air of cosiness; it felt like a country trattoria.

As we recognised the familiar faces of staff as they passed round pizza and white wine, we realised that Alvaro had persuaded a manager and four or five waiters from La Terrazza to join him and we began to wonder how Mario and Franco would react. Alvaro had appropriated some of their best staff, all capable and ambitious, and it seemed more than likely they, too, would go on to open their own trattorie.

By 8 p.m., the party was spilling out into the street. My brother knew many of the other guests and there were quite a few well-known faces. Alvaro circulated, grinning delightedly, seemingly having lost the power to converse, he merely repeated over and over, "*Buona sera, buona sera*. Thank you for coming." By nine, there were more than three hundred people, most of them outside on the pavement. And predictably, the police turned up to move us off the road. At this moment, Mario and Franco arrived, noticeably increasing the confusion.

Some people thought because the restaurant looked like La Terrazza and Alvaro was there (and now Mario and Franco too had arrived), that this was a new Mario and Franco venture. But in fact the partners had come to show support to their former protégé, to show that they no longer felt hurt at the mode of his departure. They had no idea, until they stepped out of their taxi, that their waiters had planned to leave with Alvaro and they were horrified when they realised the extent of his poaching.

"When I saw Franco, I told him it was my night off," remembers Peppino Taboro. "But I gave my notice the next day and I started work at Alvaro's the following week."

Alvaro's original plan – "Just a small party, I don't want to make a big event" – had failed. Soon the police were having to push a huge crowd back from the road and it was impossible to move. Waiters, still calmly smiling, passed plates of pizza and bottles of wine over people's heads.

But Alvaro has a different version: "I invited a lot of people I knew face to face," he says. "But I didn't have the courage to invite the big stars,

*April 1966, "Alvaro started his restaurant with my staff, my menu, and my customers," said Franco Lagattolla. All of those staff subsequently left and did the same to Alvaro. The Alvaro brigade soon after opening day; left to right Mimmo Mattera (who went on to open Mimmo D'Ischia), Chef Peppino Amendola, Fabio Benet (Barbarella), Peppino Taboro (Mr Chow, Trattoria Conti & La Finezza), Franco Serpussi (Franco's), Sandro Tobi (Sale e Pepe, Signor Sassi & Sambuca) and in front, a suited Alvaro with unknown commis waiter.* *Photo: Brian Duffy*

because I thought they were too eminent – people like Cubby Broccoli and Antonioni. But on the night they all turned up, even Saltzman and Sean Connery, and the first thing they said was 'How dare you open your own restaurant and you don't invite us?'"

"That night was the first time that I realised I was becoming somebody – on the same level," he adds.

Alvaro's had sixteen tables, with 45 seats and room for about six more. In addition to the ex-Terrazza staff, manager Franco Serpussi, waiters Mimmo Mattera, Peppino Taboro, Fabio Benet and winewaiter Sandro Tobi, there were two commis waiters, a chef Peppino Amendola from Amalfi, a second chef, various kitchen porters and, of course, Alvaro's aunt Ida, who came in every day to make the pasta. "No Tuscan restaurant," Alvaro said, "is complete without a cat," and perhaps, feeling some guilt, or respect, he named the cat Terrazza. Alvaro's menu was more or less the same as at La Terrazza, but less expensive, with some new specialities which (especially Aunt Ida's freshly made pasta), had not been served in London restaurants before. Alvaro was always keen on staying ahead of the pack and when Tony Pirozzi, of the Italian suppliers, AliVini, brought a Wild Boar Prosciutto from Tuscany, he knew Alvaro would want to be the first to place an order. Prosciutto di Cinghiale was soon on Alvaro's menu at the high starter price of 18/6 (92p).

The night after the party, Alvaro expected a trickle of clients, but in fact there was a deluge. In those days, if you were invited to a restaurant opening, it was customary to return a few days later in order to show support, then give it a month to settle down. The idea of pre-opening dry runs had not yet begun. But the first night that Alvaro's was open, ninety customers were served and several dozen more had to be turned away.

It was unprecedented that a new restaurant should be full from its first evening and even more so that royal patronage arrived so quickly. Less than a week after the opening, Lord Snowdon and Princess Margaret brought friends for dinner. As Alvaro was taking their order, HRH spotted the American entertainer Sammy Davis Jr sitting at a table across the room. The Snowdons had seen Davis's show at the Palladium.

"I would love to meet Sammy Davis," said the Princess.

Alvaro went over to Davis's table. "Would you like to meet Princess Margaret?"

"What? Would I? Where is she!" He stood up and peered around the room.

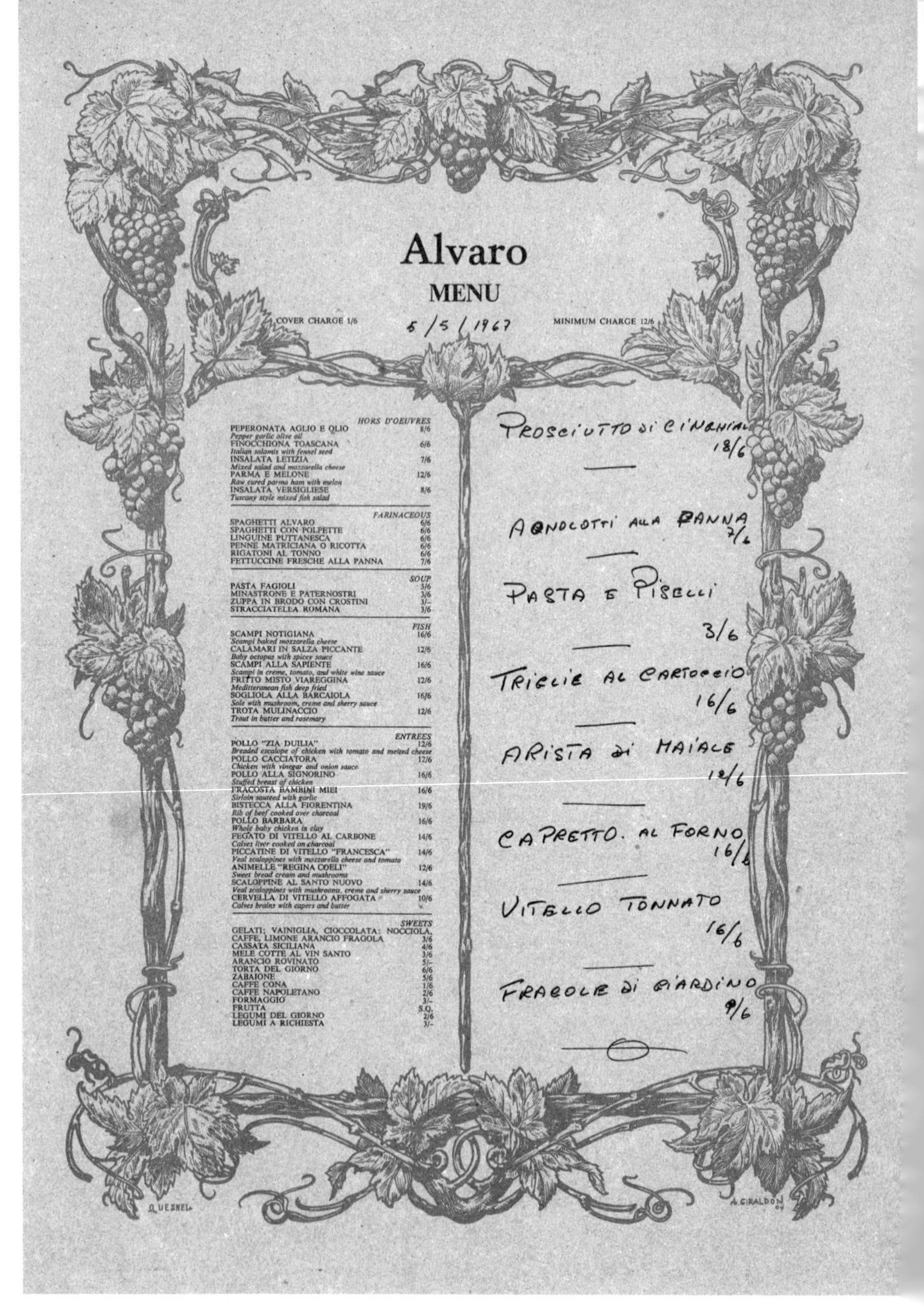

# Alvaro

## MENU

COVER CHARGE 1/6 — 5/5/1967 — MINIMUM CHARGE 12/6

*HORS D'OEUVRES*

| | |
|---|---|
| PEPERONATA AGLIO E OLIO<br>*Pepper garlic olive oil* | 8/6 |
| FINOCCHIONA TOASCANA<br>*Italian salamis with fennel seed* | 6/6 |
| INSALATA LETIZIA<br>*Mixed salad and mozzarella cheese* | 7/6 |
| PARMA E MELONE<br>*Raw cured parma ham with melon* | 12/6 |
| INSALATA VERSIGLIESE<br>*Tuscany style mixed fish salad* | 8/6 |

*FARINACEOUS*

| | |
|---|---|
| SPAGHETTI ALVARO | 6/6 |
| SPAGHETTI CON POLPETTE | 6/6 |
| LINGUINE PUTTANESCA | 6/6 |
| PENNE MATRICIANA O RICOTTA | 6/6 |
| RIGATONI AL TONNO | 6/6 |
| FETTUCCINE FRESCHE ALLA PANNA | 7/6 |

*SOUP*

| | |
|---|---|
| PASTA FAGIOLI | 3/6 |
| MINASTRONE E PATERNOSTRI | 3/6 |
| ZUPPA IN BRODO CON CROSTINI | 3/- |
| STRACCIATELLA ROMANA | 3/6 |

*FISH*

| | |
|---|---|
| SCAMPI NOTIGIANA<br>*Scampi baked mozzarella cheese* | 16/6 |
| CALAMARI IN SALZA PICCANTE<br>*Baby octopus with spicey sauce* | 12/6 |
| SCAMPI ALLA SAPIENTE<br>*Scampi in creme, tomato, and white wine sauce* | 16/6 |
| FRITTO MISTO VIAREGGINA<br>*Mediterranean fish deep fried* | 12/6 |
| SOGLIOLA ALLA BARCAIOLA<br>*Sole with mushroom, creme and sherry sauce* | 16/6 |
| TROTA MULINACCIO<br>*Trout in butter and rosemary* | 12/6 |

*ENTREES*

| | |
|---|---|
| POLLO "ZIA DUILIA"<br>*Breaded escalope of chicken with tomato and melted cheese* | 12/6 |
| POLLO CACCIATORA<br>*Chicken with vinegar and onion sauce* | 12/6 |
| POLLO ALLA SIGNORINO<br>*Stuffed breast of chicken* | 16/6 |
| FRACOSTA BAMBINI MIEI<br>*Sirloin sauteed with garlic* | 16/6 |
| BISTECCA ALLA FIORENTINA<br>*Rib of beef cooked over charcoal* | 19/6 |
| POLLO BARBARA<br>*Whole baby chicken in clay* | 16/6 |
| FEGATO DI VITELLO AL CARBONE<br>*Calves liver cooked on charcoal* | 14/6 |
| PICCATINE DI VITELLO "FRANCESCA"<br>*Veal scaloppines with mozzarella cheese and tomato* | 14/6 |
| ANIMELLE "REGINA COELI"<br>*Sweet bread cream and mushrooms* | 12/6 |
| SCALOPPINE AL SANTO NUOVO<br>*Veal scaloppines with mushrooms, creme and sherry sauce* | 14/6 |
| CERVELLA DI VITELLO AFFOGATA<br>*Calves brains with capers and butter* | 10/6 |

*SWEETS*

| | |
|---|---|
| GELATI; VAINIGLIA, CIOCCOLATA: NOCCIOLA, CAFFE, LIMONE ARANCIO FRAGOLA | 3/6 |
| CASSATA SICILIANA | 4/6 |
| MELE COTTE AL VIN SANTO | 3/6 |
| ARANCIO ROVINATO | 5/- |
| TORTA DEL GIORNO | 6/6 |
| ZABAIONE | 5/6 |
| CAFFE CONA | 1/6 |
| CAFFE NAPOLETANO | 2/6 |
| FORMAGGIO | 3/- |
| FRUTTA | S.Q. |
| LEGUMI DEL GIORNO | 2/6 |
| LEGUMI A RICHIESTA | 3/- |

| | |
|---|---|
| PROSCIUTTO DI CINGHIALE | 18/6 |
| AGNOLOTTI ALLA PANNA | 7/6 |
| PASTA E PISELLI | 3/6 |
| TRIGLIE AL CARTOCCIO | 16/6 |
| ARISTA DI MAIALE | 12/6 |
| CAPRETTO. AL FORNO | 16/6 |
| VITELLO TONNATO | 16/6 |
| FRAGOLE DI GIARDINO | 9/6 |

*Alvaro's menu, 5 May 1967. His Tuscan background had begun to show. The wild boar prosciutto was a first, and the capretto al forno (oven-roast kid with rosemary, garlic and thyme) brought real Tuscan food to the King's Road. Note also his Aunt Ida's freshly made fettucine.*

*A slender and confident Alvaro Maccioni, in his new restaurant, featured in The Sunday Times Magazine in 1966.*

Alvaro presented him, thanking his personal saint that, as she had been a regular at La Terrazza, he knew how to make the introduction.

"Your Royal Highness," he said. "May I present Mr Sammy Davis Junior?" Who was the more impressed, it was impossible to tell.

Within a month of the opening, Quentin Crewe visited Alvaro's for his column in *Queen* and his review appeared in the 8 June 1966 edition:

> **Alvaro's, 124 King's Road: Alvaro was manager of the Trattoria Terrazza and has now set up his own place in the Apicella trattoria style. The food is much as the others (although his aunt makes a special delicious pasta) but my bill was £3 12s for two including 25s for a flask of wine. He may be running at a loss but I don't think so. If not, it is a reminder that Italian food is basically cheap and other trattorias should remember the fact.**

All Alvaro's customers were of course contacts and friends from La Terrazza and many, like the Snowdons, appeared in the gossip columns every week. Alvaro quickly demonstrated some of the public relations and showmanship skills he had learnt from Mario. He offered a ten percent deduction to women who hosted a table. As Quentin Crewe observed, beautiful women are "unbelievably mean, meaner even than millionaires," so, every day at 1 p.m., Alvaro's was packed with some of the prettiest women in London, giving each other lunch. Then, he started to place people who he knew knew each other, at neighbouring tables. Thus everyone came to believe that Alvaro's was the place to be. Because he knew everyone in, and aspiring to, the scene, we all assumed that since we all knew him, we probably knew each other. So his restaurant was soon like a club – where everyone did know each other. Due to his client list, within a very short period, Alvaro was appearing in the gossip columns almost as frequently as his customers.

"The name Alvaro's is whispered from the studios of showbiz to the courts of Royalty," averred *London Life*,

> **but spoken sotto voce, away from the microphone or admiring crowd. For it means a passport to some sequestered place, an esoteric eating forum. It is in the King's Road, Chelsea, out of reach of the fashion-questing clutches of those who roam hopefully for the Mecca-of-the-moment.**

Soon, the *Evening Standard* broke the news, followed by *Queen* and *Vogue*, that Alvaro's, now the most popular table in town, had gone ex-directory. Within a few weeks, Alvaro had match books on the tables; embossed on them was his picture, a finger to his lips and the caption "Sshh! If you know who I am, don't say where I am." This, again, was Apicella's sense of humour at work. No restaurant had ever had the nerve to go ex-directory and *Queen* magazine, the monthly bible of the fashionable set, not only published Alvaro's menu, but got hold of, then published, a list of the 200 people who had Alvaro's telephone number.

Today, Alvaro denies credit for the idea – insists it was just a mistake. When, he says, he filled in the entry for the telephone directory, instead of putting the trading name of the restaurant, Alvaro's, he put the name of his registered company. "So when we opened, and people started to call directory enquiries for Alvaro's, they couldn't get the number. They said you should change the entry to Alvaro's, but by that time people had started to tell each other that we were ex-directory and it was too late."

My wife Felicity and her then husband, the newsreader Reggie Bosanquet, lived nearby in the King's Road. One evening, they were determined to get a table at Alvaro's, but didn't know anyone who had the phone number, and the trattoria wouldn't take bookings off the street. Felicity recalled that the site at 124 King's Road had previously been the Magic Carpet, so she looked it up in an old telephone book, dialled its number and immediately heard, "*Buona sera*, Alvaro." Of course, if you had the number, Alvaro's staff assumed you were in the in-crowd and accepted your booking.

Much later Alvaro would say that his was a Tuscan restaurant, not an Italian one. Today, looking at his first menu it's true there were dishes which are identifiable as being from his native Florence. But, in the sixties, we regular customers had little or no idea of the diverse regional cuisines which existed in Italy.

Tuscan or not, for my group of friends and friends of friends, Sunday night at Alvaro's became totally, definitely In – about as In as you could possibly be. We always ate out in groups in those days and I often found

*Alvaro enjoys the fruits of his success, outside 124 King's Road, 1967.*
*Photo: courtesy of Alvaro Maccioni*

myself part of a conglomeration of friends and acquaintances at a large round table on the last night of the weekend. Within a comparatively small space, but scattered round the sixteen or so tables, you would see a completely mixed crowd, actors, artists, photographers, journalists, musicians and the odd duke. Very often, the pop-singer-photographer-director, Mike Sarne, turned up to dine with his film industry friends. Sarne had an affair with Brigitte Bardot during filming *Two Weeks in September* and, although for a while it was asserted by the press and her agent that she had "vanished," they were often to be seen in Alvaro's.

"Twiggy used to go there quite a lot," remembers Carolyn Townshend, "I used to see her there with Justin (de Villeneuve), her manager. I remember her extraordinary, wonderful laugh. The hairdresser Vidal Sassoon and his rival Leonard were usually there too." There was Leslie Caron, world renowned as Gigi, just divorced from theatre director Peter Hall and accompanied by her soon-to-be husband, the producer Michael Laughlin; there was the Suzie Wong actress Tsai Chin and her brother, the artist and designer Michael Chow, with his enchanting girlfriend Patti Smith, or later, with the haughty model Grace Coddington. There was the composer John Barry with Jane Birkin or later, the stunning Polly Williams; Edina Ronay with Albert Finney, Doug Hayward and Esther Anderson, the beautiful Jamaican actress who would become Marlon Brando's mistress; there was the American expatriate film director Joseph Losey, who had directed that seminal Chelsea film *The Servant* and lived close by in Royal Avenue; sometimes he came in with his son Gavrick who was starting in TV commercials. Always, dotted round the tables, there were the big-name photographers like Lichfield, Bailey, Brian Duffy, Bob Freeman, Terry Donovan, often accompanied by spectacular models such as Tanya Mallett, Suzie Kinnear and Paulene Stone.

Another constant regular at Alvaro's was the TV actor and writer Rodney Bewes. Soon after he'd finished his long run in *The Likely Lads* TV series, he came in to the restaurant when a party which included Princess Margaret, was dining.

> **Half way through the meal I went to the loo and had a good look at HRH Princess M. She gave me a cross look for staring and I said, "Please forgive me for staring, your Royal Highness, but tomorrow is the day I must write to my mother and she will never forgive me if I don't tell her exactly what you were wearing." It was a black dress, sleeveless, with a black lacy bolero jacket over and pearls.**

**(4) ALVARO** **124 King's Road, S.W.3**
**Map 3** **01–589 6296**

**'Crowded with noisy second-rate talents, the photographers and the photographed.' 'All the nobodies who are supposed to be somebodies go there all the time, and it is fun watching them projecting.' Thus two experienced gastronomes; and several other members feel that the atmosphere is more that of an exclusive club than of an ordinary restaurant where all are treated alike. But the food, though overpriced, is usually good, especially if you keep to the simpler dishes such as pasta, stuffed courgettes and fritto misto di mare; the meat dishes and the attempts at haute cuisine italienne tend to be less successful. The restaurant has not divulged its food or wine prices.**

***Cl. Chr. Must book D. Meals* 12.30–3; 7–12. *Seats* 54. *Class B***

***App.* Simon Lanyon; B.H.; C.B.; D. J. Boyd.**

*The Good Food Guide people didn't really get the point when they suggested that what was wrong with Alvaro's was that it was like an exclusive club. It WAS an exclusive club.*

This incident was to give him the idea for his subsequent hit TV series, *Dear Mother, Love Albert*.

It was easy for outsiders to sneer at what Alvaro had achieved and several reviewers, while appreciative of the food, purported not to understand its popularity. "Crowded with noisy second rate talents, the photographers and the photographed," the 1968 *Good Food Guide to London* reported. "All of the nobodies who are supposed to be somebodies, go there all the time and it is fun watching them projecting." *Good Food Guide* members reported that they felt that the atmosphere was more that of an exclusive club than an ordinary restaurant where all are treated alike and of course, in a way, they were right. The *Guide* and most serious restaurant reviewers, with the exception of Quentin Crewe, missed the point of Alvaro's, when they reviewed only the food, without appreciating the rest of his creation. To echo Fats Waller, when asked to explain the nature of jazz, "If you had to ask, you'd never know."

"The rivalry between Alvaro's noisy but tiny restaurant and its prototype La Terrazza was quiet but intense during the first few months of operation," wrote Len Deighton later. "Friends were divided, protagonists of each establishment became quite bitter in their arguments."

Deighton had to leave England for a month to research a book and during his absence, both sides were convinced that he had gone over to the enemy. A few months after Alvaro's opened, a large group of Alvaro's old friends who had been, and mostly still were, Terrazza regulars, had a meal there. As Deighton remembered, there was exquisite pasta, cooked by Aunt Ida, chicken baked in clay, wine from Alvaro's father's home village, then coffee, grappa and cigars, all served with untiring and cheerful attentiveness.

When it got to 3.30 a.m., with none of the diners making a move, Ken Adam, sitting at the head of the long table, leant across to Alvaro and said, "You know, Alvaro, when we stay as late as this at the Trat… "

"Yes?" said Alvaro, expecting to hear a lavish compliment and thanks.

"…Mario or Franco normally sends over a free drink," Ken finished blandly.

## ALVARO'S INSALATA VERSIGLIESE

This refreshing seafood salad with a slight chilli edge, not unlike La Terrazza's Frank Sinatra salad, was a great favourite at Alvaro's. Prepare two hours in advance.

For six to eight people, you will need: 750 grams baby squid (calamari), 500 grams scampi, 300 grams peeled prawns, 200ml of good quality olive oil, the juice of two lemons, salt and pepper, one red chilli, 3 cloves of garlic and a handful of chopped parsley.

Clean the scampi and calamari and place into a pan of lightly boiling well-salted water. If you like you can add mussels or any other cooked shellfish as well. Simmer them together for twelve minutes and then put the saucepan immediately under the cold tap and let the water run through it until everything is cold right through.

Slice the calamari, not too small, sprinkle the crushed garlic and finely chopped chilli over them, then pour on the olive oil and the lemon juice.

Toss all the ingredients together until it is all properly dressed, leave in a cold place (but not in the fridge) for at least two hours.

Serve at room temperature with chopped parsley.

## A NEW MANAGER AT THE TRAT

A couple of days after Alvaro had given his notice, Mario Cassandro went over to Queen Street to have lunch at Tiberio with William Samengo Turner, a fellow Neapolitan. Mario was a little upset and the staff noticed. They guessed rightly that it was not only because he was fretting about Alvaro's defection and the manner of it, but also because now, he had to find a new manager for La Terrazza.

During lunch, Mario could talk of little else than staff problems, that is until Samengo Turner pointed to the Tiberio headwaiter who stood near their table. "You have a manager right in front of you," he consoled Mario. "Everyone likes him. He's always got a smile on his face. What more do you want?" Mario looked at his headwaiter and said, "When you finish at three o'clock, come to the office at La Terrazza; I want to talk to you."

Ten years earlier, Mario Vollono had quit his job as a station headwaiter at the Grand Hotel in Venice to come to England to the Savoy. Emerging from his train at Victoria Station, confident in a new coat, he had jumped into a taxi. "Savoy Hotel, please," he'd told the driver.

In Italy, hotel staff tend to be given accommodation, either in a staff block or on the hotel's top floor. He was expecting the same in England. As the cab arrived in front of the main entrance, the bell staff whisked away his suitcases, one containing street clothes, the other crammed with his uniforms; Vollono was impressed, though very scared he would be fired before even starting his new job, because he'd arrived at the wrong door. He approached the reception desk, then shyly explained his predicament. The receptionist called the general manager.

"So, Mr Vollono," the manager had said, then paused. "Welcome to the Savoy. Since you've arrived at the front door, you'd better enjoy a sample of Savoy hospitality for a few days. Until you get settled."

The incredulous, confused Vollono then found himself a guest of the Savoy for three days until, as he came down to earth, he was able to rent a room above a restaurant in Frith Street. He began as a waiter in the Savoy's Grill Room, was soon promoted to station headwaiter, then – because of his professionalism and charm – was given an important extra task, to look after the section where the hotel's directors ate.

"They were very difficult," he remembered. "Everybody was scared to serve them."

He had been working at the Savoy for nearly eight years when his former boss, Walter Orsi, by then the manager of Tiberio, contacted him and recommended him to Mario and Franco. Instead of the £24 a week he then earned ("more than a bus driver got," he remembers), Walter Orsi offered him £70 a week to come to Tiberio and, only two years later, following Mario and Samengo Turner's lunch, he became the new manager of La Terrazza. This was the most prestigious restaurant job in London. Soon after, Apicella asked Franco Lagattolla how things were going with the new manager. "We lost a good manager in Alvaro," Franco replied. "But we've found a better one."

Vollono was not entrepreneurial. He had no ambition to start his own business. But, as Mario and Franco expanded and weren't always in the restaurant, it helped the business that his Christian name was Mario. Hearing this, new customers often thought that he was the founder. When making a reservation, the caller often asked to speak to Franco or Mario and Vollono would say either "Franco is not available, but this is Mario, the manager. Can I help you?" or later, more courageously, "Yes, this is Mario."

After Alvaro's departure, Mario Cassandro wanted to forget him and move on. There were plenty of customers to go round, he felt, but Franco had seen so many of their best clients at Alvaro's opening party and continued to grumble that Alvaro had stolen staff from them, as well as targeting their showbiz regulars.

He complained to Adrian Bailey that he couldn't understand how Alvaro had managed to attract so many of their regulars.

> If we wanted to throw a party, a celebration and we wanted to invite you, Brian Duffy, Barry Driscoll, Len Deighton, Enzo, Cubby Broccoli, Saltzman, we couldn't do it, because we don't know where anybody lives. How is it possible that Alvaro creates an opening party, inviting every single celebrity and friend of ours? Where did the addresses come from?

"What do you mean when you say that Alvaro built up his business from scratch?" Franco continued. "We started from scratch. Lorenzo and Mara and Luigi Paglierani started from scratch. Alvaro started with my chefs, my waiters, my menu and even my customers."

Although La Terrazza's staff whispered about the number of clients that Alvaro had taken, there was, actually, no dent in La Terrazza's business. With the increasing popularity of trattorie, many of its customers just added the new Italian on the King's Road to their repertoire of restaurants. "Because I lived and worked near Sloane Square and often

*David Bailey's shot of his then wife Catherine Deneuve with Mario and Franco, at the height of their fame.*

was in the West End for the evening, I used Alvaro's for lunch and the Trat for client dinners," recalls Carolyn Townshend.

One young waiter, Valerio Calzolari, moved from Leoni's Quo Vadis to La Terrazza just as Mario Vollono became manager, and found that it was nothing like the gloomy place where he'd been working. At lunch and at dinner, La Terrazza was full every single day, seven days a week.

When *Time* published its memorable piece on swinging London, Mario and Franco's role in London's resurgence was absolutely clear.

> **The city that once had the worst dining out in the Western world now has a variety and a class of restaurants that rival New York or even Paris. The little restaurants of Soho are unpretentious but ever so In, beginning with the Trattoria Terrazza (especially its downstairs Positano Room). Tiberio's in Mayfair, with its band and dancing, draws the smart set for later dinners.** *Time, 15 April 1966.*

After the *Time* piece appeared, the transatlantic line to La Terrazza was almost permanently engaged, by Americans calling to request bookings downstairs. "I've read about the Positayno Room. Which one is the Positayno? I want a table in the Positayno Room," the receptionist heard, endlessly, every day.

In the expanded restaurant, Mario and Franco had christened all four rooms after little villages on the Neapolitan peninsula, dear to their hearts, – Positano, Amalfi, Maiori and Minori – but they had avoided putting the names up over each door.

Following Alvaro's telephone strategy, not only the *Time* piece but countless other newspaper and magazine articles had appeared, describing London's most famous restaurant and nearly all of them mentioned the Positano Room as being the one where celebrities were most likely to be found. Readers of these newspaper pieces would telephone from overseas, especially from New York and Hollywood and ask specifically for a table in the "Positayno" Room. Then, on arrival, they'd repeat time and time again, "I must have a table in the Positayno Room."

But unless the partners already knew them, it wasn't possible to satisfy them all without resorting to little white lies. "It's this one here," Franco or Mario would say, showing the customer to their table upstairs. "I can give you a table here in the Positano Room."

And for the next fifteen years, managed by Mario Vollono, La Terrazza would remain the most consistently popular restaurant in London, attracting both home-grown and international celebrities, as well as the entire spectrum of British art, business and professional worlds. (Over the years that he remained manager, Mario Vollono kept a notebook which contained his list of the regulars, their favourite tables and preferences; it is reproduced at the end of this book).

*By 1967, when this picture was commissioned by Jocelyn Stevens for Queen magazine, Mario was one of the recognised figures of the sixties establishment. (Back row, left to right) Lady Anne Tennant, racing driver Graham Hill, Mario Cassandro, sculptor Eduardo Paolozzi, The Marquess of Queensbury (then Professor of Ceramics at the RCA), comedian Ronnie Corbett and barrister-playwright John Mortimer, (Centre row, left to right) financier and retailer Charles Clore, Longleat safari park pioneer The Marquess of Bath, photographer-designer Cecil Beaton, bookmaker William Hill, writer Anthony Burgess, economist Sir Roy Harrod and cartoonist/designer Osbert Lancaster. (Front row, left to right) The Bishop of London, actress Joan Plowright, interior decorator David Mlinaric, philosopher A. J. Ayer, Conservative MP (and future home secretary) Reginald Maudling and writer-director-physician Dr Jonathan Miller.*

*Photo: Lichfield/Getty Images*

## 1967. THE FULHAM ROAD RUNS DOWN TO THE ARNO

*On a hot day as the sun shines in on Apicella's walls, you almost have the feeling that the Fulham Road is running down to the Arno, not the Thames.*

*THE TIMES*, 1967

Between them, Mario and Franco, Alvaro, and the Bernis at San Lorenzo had kept the new wave of Italian restaurants constantly in the press and in the forefront of restaurant fashion. By creating, however inadvertently, such a media stir about a small 35-seat restaurant and siting it in the King's Road, Alvaro had moved the centre of the developing "Trat scene," away from the West End and Mayfair.

Encouraged by Mario and Franco's success, another team came in on the act. Three Tuscans – Mino Parlanti, Sergio Galassi and Franco Buonaguidi – set out to copy La Terrazza's style, adopting a similar menu, the same designer and again, targeting many of the same customers.

Mino Parlanti and Sergio Galassi had both grown up and trained in Montecatini Terme, the spa town half an hour's distance from Florence and having arrived in London in the 1950s, they were determined one day to go into business together. Mino's first venture after ten years in the tail-coated environment of the Savoy, was at the Versailles, a Soho establishment with a French name and Italian waiters, but, in 1959, converted to an Italian menu. Across town, interesting Italian dishes were now to be had at the celebrated Alexander's restaurant at the corner of Markham Street and the King's Road, in the basement below Mary Quant's Bazaar boutique. Originally started by Mary and her husband Alexander Plunket-Greene, it was taken over by three Italians, one of whom was the chef Sergio Galassi. Sergio, who had trained at Florence's famous Oliviero restaurant, had already come to the attention of Egon Ronay's *Guide*, which noted "such new-found varieties as skewered scampi and bacon, flamed in brandy."

In 1962, Mino and Sergio teamed up with Otello Scipioni to open La Dolce Vita, in Frith Street. It soon attracted the smart young set, including Princess Margaret (she was everywhere), and was packed to the rafters every night. Over the next few years it remained popular and the downstairs premises, La Taverna, also offered dancing. Noisy and crowded, it had everything you'd expect of a pre-Apicella Italian nightspot in those days, complete with plaster bricks and mock beams.

Dinner cost 32/6 (£1.53) for three courses, which, given that it included live music and you could stay to 1 a.m., was very good value.

Mino Parlanti's next venture was beyond Soho, in the still slightly outré Fulham Road and there he was joined by his brother-in-law, Franco Buonaguidi, whose twin sister Franca was Parlanti's wife. Franco had originally come from Montecatini to London to train as an optician, but soon found himself washing dishes and helping out at Alexander's. So when Mino mentioned his plan, Franco jumped ship to go in with his brother-in-law and, with him on board, Il Porcellino opened in 1963, on the Fulham Road. Porcellino combined the traditional French-Italian food – Steak Diane and Veal Escalope – with a few new touches and a plainer, less fussy décor than usual; without Chianti bottles and fishing nets, but not yet up to Apicella standards.

Franco Buonaguidi acknowledges the debt the Porcellino owed to La Terrazza. "We knew about their *Pollo Sorpresa* and we had a version of it on the menu," he recalls. "Mario and Franco were the number one teachers for us in the next generation and there was tremendous interest in what they were doing."

By 1966, aware of Mario and Franco's and now Alvaro's great success and the resulting publicity, Parlanti and Buonaguidi guessed that old-style Italian restaurants were on their way out. Backing their hunch, they sold both Porcellino and La Dolce Vita and, within a few weeks, the two brothers-in-law and chef Sergio found a site at 64 Fulham Road. They invited the ubiquitous Apicella to design their restaurant and the resulting interior was in his familiar style: rustic chairs, arched ceilings, rough plaster walls and tiled floors.

Mino wanted to emphasise Tuscan country-style cooking, so they called their establishment not a restaurant or a trattoria, but a Borgo or "village," and named it after a patron saint of the Florentine region, San Frediano. Enzo also drew their distinctive logo, with the reversed letter И and helped to organise the opening party in the spring of 1967. He brought both Mandy Rice-Davies and Christine Keeler, among several hundred other people and the party, like Alvaro's, had spread into the street.

Several other restaurateurs admit that Enzo supplied them with a list of suitable target customers to invite to their openings, but none of them were sure how he had put it together, other than through his own very busy social life, which seems unlikely. One cannot imagine Enzo ever sitting down to make out a list.

Be that as it may, he categorised the key trendsetter customers, whom

*"Your crespoline are on the way" – the San Frediano brigade, Fulham Road, July 1967. (Front row, from second left) Chef-partner Sergio Galassi, head waiter Carlo Corsini, manager Carlo Esposito, Franco Buonaguidi in trademark black roll-neck sweater. Photo: Bryan Wharton*

he knew a restaurant must attract, as – models and their photographers – film and TV stars and starlets – producers, directors, theatre and show business types – commercial and other artists – journalists – and marketing, advertising and public relations people. The models and show business stars, he believed, make a good buzz, as often they know each other, while the journalists make the place better known. The public relations and advertising people are strictly customers but they eat out frequently and talk to many trendsetters. Enzo insisted that the best publicity was word of mouth and always advised his clients that if they didn't advertise in the media, they would more than make up for the lack of deliberate exposure by the creation of an air of snobbish exclusivity.

So, San Frediano began reasonably well after its traditional opening party. But it was not as packed out as Alvaro's had been. Only a few weeks later, an article about the restaurant appeared in the *Evening Standard* which astonished Franco and Mino. The journalist, it seems, had arrived at the San Frediano one evening at 7 p.m., just as they opened.

"He came in, had dinner, loved it and wrote an article entitled *See You at Seven,*" Franco Buonaguidi remembers. "The next day at seven o'clock, the restaurant was completely full." Franco was amazed at the extent to which the English followed what they read in the newspapers. "In Italy, it would have taken a year to build up such business," he marvels.

Mino became the new star. Good looking, charming, a touch grey-haired, his beautiful English accent seemed to encourage women to hope that he would be the one to come to take their order.

For me and many of my contemporaries, Saturday lunch at San Fred became our new routine. You would always see friends there and might join them to eat together, or merely go over and sit with them for a while. One couple, who were even more socially inclined than I was, would go separately to talk to other clients for so long that Mino would good-humouredly give their table to someone else and make them wait for another to become free.

The reviews were excellent. "San Frediano," said *The Times*,

> plays the smart Chelsea game, and its clientele is of the trend-setting type, but most remarkably its prices are less than two-thirds those of many of its peers. The menu is short with a number of unusual dishes, several of them Tuscan and the cooking is good; bean and pasta soup 3/6d, kidneys in white wine 9/6 and *Pollo Alla Diavola* 11/6, are all approved. The main dishes come garnished with decently cooked vegetables. It is a delightful self-assured restaurant with zippy service by waiters in jerseys and on a hot day as the sun shines in on Apicella's walls, you almost have the feeling that the Fulham Road is running down to the Arno not the Thames.

At San Frediano, value for money was key and the menus were pitched well below the prices being charged by La Terrazza and Alvaro's. Because of this, the clientele were generally younger. Over the next twenty years, as I passed into my thirties and forties, it seemed to me that half the population of middle-class West London dated there.

"I first met my husband one Saturday at San Fred's when a girlfriend brought him along to lunch," one early customer remembers, "and we came again on our first date. Nearly twenty years later we were still taking our children there."

Sergio's Tuscan menu offered more bean-based dishes and fewer tomato-based sauces than the Neapolitan Terrazza. The particularly popular specialities were the *Crespoline* (savoury pancakes) stuffed with spinach and the *Filetto di Manzo Sergio*, beef fillet with a dark wine sauce.

Unlike the chef-tycoons of the present era, Sergio Galassi was one of the few chefs in Italian restaurants who was also a partner. In the sixties, it

# San Frediano

~~MELONE DI STAGIONE 4/6~~
PIZZA PARTENOPEA 6/6
CULATELLO CON PERA 7/6
CARCIOFI A PIACERE 5/6 Charentais 9/6
LUMACHE PROVINCIALE 6/6
TAGLIATELLE ALLA CREMA 6/6
AVOCADO CON GAMBERETTI 6/6
SPAGHETTINI ALLE VONGOLE 6/6
MINESTRONE ALLA TOSCANA 3/6
CREMA SANFREDIANO 3/6

fish
CALAMARETTI LIVORNESE 9/6
SCAMPI VERSILIESE 15/6
FILETTI DI SOGLIOLA GIAN FRANCO 13/6
TROTELLA SPACCATA AI GAMBERETTI 10/6

meat
MEDAGLIONI DI MANZO SERGIO 13/6
Thin beef fillets, Sergio's sauce
SOVRANA DI CAPPONE MARESCIALLA 12/6
Capon's breast fried in butter with asparagus tips
SCALOPPINE ALL'UCCELLETTO 12/6
Veal small escalopes, white wine, tomato and garlic sauce
COSTATA FIORENTINA 21/-
Grilled T-bone steak
ROGNONCINI SAN FREDIANO 11/6
Calf's kidney in lemon, white wine and parsley sauce
PICCATINA AL MARSALA 12/6
Veal escalopines in marsala wine sauce
FEGATO ALLA SALVIA 11/6
Sauté calf liver, sage flavoured
POLLO ALLA DIAVOLA 12/6
Grilled half chicken with herbs in brandy sauce

vegetables
MELANZANE PARMIGIANA 3/6
ZUCCHINI PROVINCIALE 3/6
SPINACI IN FOGLIA SALTATI 2/6
FAGIOLINI AL BURRO 2/6
PISELLI FIORENTINA 2/6
CIPOLLE FRITTE 2/6
FUNGHI TRIFOLATI 3/6
INSALATE MISTE 3/6

RICOTTA CON CAFFE AL RUM 4/6
ZUPPA INGLESE MERINGATA 3/6
COPPA MARONITA ALLA PANNA 3/6
ARANCIO ALL'AURUM 4/6

PARMIGIANO E PERA 4/6
DOLCE LATTE — GROVIERA 3/6
BEL PAESE — CAMEMBERT

CAFFE 1/6

cover charge 1/6

Lunedi

Aperitivi 3/6

Cannelloni San Frediano 6/6
Crespoline Fiorentina 6/6
crêpes with ricotta cheese + spinach
Tonno e Fagioli 5/6
tuna fish, beans + onions
Carciofo all'Agro 5/6
artichoke
Pomodori e Peperoni 6/6
stuffed peppers + tomatoes

Pollo Mugello 11/6
chicken escalope with cheese + asparagus
Scaloppine Peperonata 12/6
veal with peppers
Scampi Livornese 15/6
scampi in tomato + garlic
Animelle al Marsala 11/6
sweetbread in marsala
Bistecca al Pepe 13/6
steak with pepper + brandy

Torta 3/6
Lampone 7/6
Gelati 3/6

Wine XXX 3/6

*Tuscan specialities such as Crespoline and Filletto di Manzo with Sergio's special sauce were features of the San Frediano menu.*

*Mino Parlanti at his Borgo San Frediano.*
*Having started at the Savoy in 1951, he built up an empire of trattorie*
*based on his native Tuscan cooking*
*and his own charming, relaxed style. Photo: courtesy of Mino Parlanti*

*Chef Sergio Galassi. At San Frediano, his food was loved*
*by customers and his stories by their children.*
*In retirement, his life ended in tragedy.*
*Photo: courtesy of Franco Buonaguidi*

**CRESPOLINE FIORENTINA**

**One of Sergio Galassi's specialities at San Frediano:**

For six people, you will need ricotta cheese, cooked leaf spinach, grated parmesan, chopped prosciutto, salt and pepper, béchamel with gruyère and parmesan and either fresh tomato sauce or a tin of tomatoes, crushed and reduced by half.

For each person, make one very thin pancake. In a bowl, mix fresh ricotta cheese, chopped leaf spinach, a little grated parmesan, some chopped prosciutto, salt and pepper, until properly combined.

Form a spoonful of the mixture into a roll between your hands, put this into the centre of the pancake and roll it up. Cut it half and put the two halves in a fireproof dish. Place all the halved and stuffed pancakes side by side and cover with a layer of the béchamel, adding in some gruyère and parmesan. Cover with the fresh tomato sauce or reduced tomatoes.

Sprinkle with more parmesan and bake in a hot oven for six to seven minutes or until the sauce is bubbling.

was always the managers whose names became recognised, never the chefs. Galassi had started work in hotels in 1936 at the age of fourteen, ending up in a German prison camp, during the Second World War, because he had refused to continue to fight any more after King Vittorio Emmanuele left Italy. At San Frediano, he became known for a beef fillet dish "with Sergio's sauce," so the customers grew familiar with his name. Then, they learnt to recognise his face, when, after they'd asked if they could meet the dish's creator, he became one of the first Italian chefs to emerge from the kitchen.

"It wasn't that he wanted to come upstairs," explained Mino Parlanti, "but he had problems with his heart, so, eventually, we decided he should stop putting in those long hot hours downstairs and come up to be with the customers."

Sergio was always popular and even though he couldn't speak English very well, he was loved by all the customers, especially by their children, who flocked to his chair by the bar where he would enchant them by telling stories, very seriously, with gestures and faces, but in Italian.

With Alvaro and San Frediano both going at full speed, Mino Parlanti and Alvaro Maccioni decided to join forces and take on Mario and Franco with the biggest investment in an Italian restaurant since the launch of Tiberio.

As a dry run for their partnership, they went sailing.

## COWES, ISLE OF WIGHT, AUGUST 1967

Alvaro and my brother Robin had become friends and in 1967 discussed the pros and cons of some sort of business partnership. Robin, a chartered accountant, had always been determined to be his own boss and had swiftly quit his first job as a financial manager to start his own business. He seemed to be able to persuade banks to lend him money on the strength of a tiny investment and a huge idea; bank managers, eager to catch on to the excitement of the sixties, seemed mesmerised by young entrepreneurs.

If Mario and Franco and now Alvaro could create glamorous and fashionable restaurants and transport the genre from the West End to the newly fashionable King's Road, Robin and his first partner, the artist and designer Michael Chow, could, they hazarded, do the same for hairdressing. In partnership with Chow's girlfriend, Patti Smith and her colleague Wendy Hawes, the four opened a unisex hairdressers, Smith & Hawes in Sloane Avenue. Chow's design featured white walls, white floors and white chairs. It instantly made every other hairdressing salon look old-fashioned and dowdy. Stories appeared in the media that its top stylist, Gary Craze (who went on to open Sweeny's), was earning more than £100 a week. This success encouraged Robin to look for another new venture.

Alvaro Maccioni, too, had started to think of his next restaurant and he and Robin often talked about possible future plans. Robin had a South Coast One Design boat, which he kept at Cowes and, in early June, he invited Alvaro to join us for a weekend. Alvaro had never sailed before, indeed he had hardly ever left London. But he took to sailing immediately. The fact that a restaurant was conceived on the Solent during a weekend on a boat seemed perfectly normal. With the distance of time, though, it has, for me, acquired a mystique utterly characteristic of the sixties.

As usual, as crew, I did all the hard work. Rob steered and Alvaro opened, then passed us, cans of chilled beer. As we cruised down the Solent towards Yarmouth, Robin explained that in two months' time it would be Cowes Week, the world's greatest yacht racing regatta.

Alvaro seemed fascinated. Ocean racing may well be, as the cynic said, like standing under a cold shower while tearing up fifty-pound notes. But Cowes, which for most of the year is a quiet provincial sailing port, becomes in Regatta week the social capital of the sailing world, a bit like Ascot-on-Sea. The difference is that here the owners of the contenders habitually pilot them. For one August week every year, Cowes is stuffed with money – money old and new, English money, Australian money, Irish, Dutch, American, Italian, French money, German money. Million-pound ocean-racing yachts converge on Cowes for the Admiral's Cup, the Fastnet Race and a dozen other cups for boats from twelve to 120 feet and more. The main harbour overflows with the world's sleekest, most glamorous sailing boats, their millionaire owners, immaculately groomed women and muscular crews.

Days, we explained to Alvaro, start at dawn during Cowes Week. And when dusk falls, all the yachtsmen celebrate into the small hours. As we enthused, Alvaro's magpie mind began to detect potential. "But where do they eat, all these beautiful people?" he asked. Having invented the phrase "beautiful people" in an interview, he reverted to it to describe any desirable customer.

Our answer was, that they didn't eat. Or if they did, not well. When we had arrived in Cowes the previous evening, our dinner had not been great. In fact no restaurant on the Isle of Wight was both accessible and good. The Royal Yacht Squadron was the world's most exclusive club. You certainly couldn't simply call and book dinner for eight. The Royal Corinthian, more amenable if you knew a member, was always fully booked weeks in advance. The Island Sailing Club had a buffet salad bar restaurant – very noisy and members only. Other than those, there were a few grill and chip bars and two or three small hotels with restaurants attached. Cowes had never had a decent restaurant (let alone a fashionable new trattoria) and was, Alvaro sensed as we talked, screaming out for a decent place where all the famished millionaire sailors and their spouses could be fed, given a good time and, importantly, separated from some of their spare change.

The upshot of Alvaro's first ocean excursion was that he and Robin decided that they'd open a restaurant together – just for the next Cowes Week. Naturally, they'd call it Alvaro in Cowes. There was, they thought, no sense in being there during the rest of the year when Isle of Wight regulars rarely ate out, so they would have to find an existing restaurant.

Number 60 High Street, Cowes, is, today, just another gift shop. But then, Tomalin's at Number 60 was a Café and Grill where the most expensive dish was a steak at 7/6d. (42p). Robin and I made an appointment to go and see its owner, Joe Tomalin. As we waited at our table, I checked the room and counted seats. There was a six-foot-long bar counter on the right of the door and fourteen tables – about fifty-five to sixty seats at a push.

"We were wondering if you're normally very busy here in the Café during Cowes Week?" Robin queried.

"Where are you from? Not the tax?"

"Not the tax. Just personal business. Between us."

"Well then. Cowes Week? It's our best time of the year," said Tomalin. "We're full from morning to night. For nine days solid. My wife takes on a couple of extra staff. It's good and busy. But it's very hard work. We hardly sit down for a minute."

"And I suppose you do very well out of it?"

"Of course. Business is good. It's the best week of the year."

"You net as much as five hundred pounds over the week?"

"Well, we do a lot of money, stands to reason. But look. What's it to you? If you're not from the tax, why're you asking me all these questions?"

"I was wondering if you and your wife would like to take a holiday this August?" Robin asked. "Rent the restaurant to us for nine days. It might make a nice change for you both. You'd make all the money you normally do, without having to do the work."

Eventually, a deal was done. Robin paid Joe Tomalin six hundred pounds, which was far more than the profit he would have made after working eighteen hours a day for the nine days of high season. So the place became ours and work started. We had less than two months to plan and when Tomalin closed, we'd have just two days to turn a cheap English grill café into the chicest thing Cowes had ever seen – a full-scale high-fashion "new" Italian trattoria.

By then, Alvaro knew everyone in the London Italian restaurant trade and already had in mind the staff he wanted. There were to be five in the kitchen and in the front, Alvaro himself plus four others. Robin also hired an extremely arresting, tall African-American barman, Bernard Boston, who could do the biz with flying vodka bottles. He and Alvaro started to devise the bar and wine list. My girlfriend, Annie Lambert, a beauty who was later to become an actress, was to be booker and greeter. A book-keeper, who worked regularly for Alvaro, agreed to take time out and handle buying, and customer bills.

My job was to make sure that captains, crews and their families had heard the word before we opened and then, that they'd come and spend their cash. If I succeeded, the place would be full. If not, we'd merely pick up a few passers-by.

Robin and I would be able to stay on his boat for a couple of nights, though access to a bath and clean clothes would be tricky. But all together, we'd be a team of nearly twenty. So it was back to the estate agents. Just off Cowes High Street, we were shown a huge unfurnished house with no fewer than seven bedrooms. We rented it for two weeks, which would allow for setting up and closing after the event.

I strode off to the Scout Shop on Buckingham Palace Road. It still exists, and today it is stocked with high-tech mountaineering gear, weatherproof boots and backpacks. Back then, it provided shorts and shirts, badges and canvas tents.

"We're making a summer expedition to the Isle of Wight," I explained. "I wonder if it's possible to rent a camp bed?" The shop assistant

*The restaurant postcard which invited Alvaro's regular customers to come to the Isle of Wight to eat Italian during the Regatta. Robin Sutherland (left) at the helm, with Alvaro (right) and Jonathan Abbott, on board Varthan, 1967.*

found two or three different models and explained how to assemble them.

"Great!" I said. "Can I have eighteen? I'll pick them up in five days."

During the four weeks preceding the opening, a giveaway postcard of Robin and Alvaro on the boat, captioned Alvaro says See you in Cowes, invited all the regulars to pitch up on the Isle of Wight for a week of fun and sailing. On the Thursday before we left, I set up a stunt to try and get publicity in the London media and alert all the gossip columnists and diary editors to a great story.

Supervised by Alvaro and dressed in "Alvaro in Cowes" T-shirts and the latest shorts from Mr Freedom, Annie Lambert and my flatmate's sister, the actress Polly Williams, plus several other photogenic girls, turned up to help the waiters load cases of spaghetti onto a truck parked on the pavement outside Alvaro's. Along with the pasta, we stashed the camp beds, blankets, dry goods, uniforms, glasses, tablecloths and linen, as well as pots, pans, crockery and cutlery – everything Alvaro knew we'd need.

Luckily, that day there wasn't much news. Several press agencies, the two London evening papers and a couple of the nationals sent reporters. Alvaro, Annie and the other girls did their stuff. The next day, after several pieces had appeared, the phone began to ring and diary editors smelt an ongoing story. Most of them, I thought, would send a reporter to Cowes Week to cover parties and dig for scandal and gossip. I fielded several calls asking for interviews with Alvaro.

"Since so many of my customers would be there on their boats," Alvaro told his interlocutors, "I decided to be there as well. I feel responsible for ensuring that my regulars get enough proper Italian food to eat and compete," he said.

At the beginning of August I took a week's holiday from my job in a public relations agency, to go to Cowes. Michael Chow's sister, the actress Tsai Chin, and her friend Elizabeth Harris (who had already been married to the actors Rex Harrison and Richard Harris and is now married to Jonathan Aitken), came down for the ride and to be part of the home team. Neither of them went anywhere near the yachts, but they both added an extra touch of glamour to Robin and Alvaro's host table and their presence provided more material for the gossip and diary columns.

When we opened for lunch on the first Saturday, nothing much happened. Passers-by paused to look at the menu which was pinned up outside. One couple came in and sat down. But when Alvaro handed them the same menu they had seen outside, they took one look at it and fled.

DAILY MAIL,

# The Swinging Scene hits sacred Cowes

**IT'S ALMOST blasphemy. But that revered yachting institution, sacred Cowes Week, is going all pop and mod and swinging this year. There is at least one psychedelic sail waiting for its owner to bend on to the mast of his Firefly dinghy.**

That hallowed home of sailing men, the Royal Yacht Squadron, which for years banned women in trousers, will admit mini-skirts this

a "retirement present" for the manager, Henry Van Thuyne, who has looked after visiting royalty, Mr Kosygin, Aristotle Onassis, Bing Crosby and a whole host of VIPs. But, says Van Thuyne firmly: "I'm not going. It's all a mistake."

I can no longer tolerate the tax situation."

Sir Andrew plans to move to a house he has bought in Devon. "It stands in 300 acres which I shall use for shooting and fishing, but I won't farm. I hate farming . . . I would be bound

# Alvaro, bringing Cowes a taste of Chelsea

TOMALIN'S is a chips-with-everything restaurant in Cowes High Street where one can eat well for about six bob.

Next week there will be some pretty glum faces among the regulars. Tomalin's becomes Alvaro's, and the cost of a meal will increase seven-fold.

Just "for fun" **Signor Alvaro Maccioni**, who owns the King's Road, Chelsea, restaurant, has paid **£600** to **Joe Tomalin** to take over his café during Cowes Week.

Mr. Tomalin, 55, who always makes that amount of profit serving chips with practically everything to the hungry **Regatta Week** thousands, will spend the time crewing.

At 6 a.m. today **35-year-old** Alvaro, with three chefs and six waitresses, will leave for Cowes with 20 cases of spaghetti, 10 Parma hams, 120 gallons of olive oil, and a lorry-load of Italian wines.

"I am not," he said firmly, "worried about profits. It is for fun."

DAILY EXPRESS

# Annie was still in party gear

**IT WAS simply a late party that caught the 21-y Annie Hole in her bell-bottom evening trousers and blouse, sauntering up the slipway as a crowd of entl set off for another day's racing.**

Annie, whose mother was married to composer Constant Lambert, works for *Vogue* and decided to spend her holiday working as a waitress during Cowes week.

She is one of the girls enrolled by Alvaro, the Chelsea restaurateur who took over a small restaurant in the High Street, where the patrons are used to good English food served with chips.

This was a venture that didn't start too well. Passers-by looked askance at Alvaro's Italian menu pinned up outside. One party strolled in at lunch-time on Saturday, sat down, read the menu and beat a hasty retreat.

No one else arrived and Alvaro said he was beginning to regret the whole enterprise.

But in the evening there was

DAILY MAIL

A few tables were filled. Robin and I sat in one corner with Annie, Tsai and Liz Harris. Alvaro fretted. He was beginning to think the whole thing was a waste of time and effort.

But in the evening it was a different story. As the *Daily Mail* put it, Alvaro in Cowes had suddenly become "the only place to eat in the island." There wasn't a table to be had and by the end of the first weekend, they reported, "one nautical mile of Spaghetti had been eaten there."

Alvaro's carefully planned eight-day restaurant plan went completely out of control. He and the team coped with lunch. But people came so late and stayed so long, that there was little chance for the kitchen to do much *mise en place* for the evening. The kitchen and front-of-house staff hadn't a hope of an afternoon break.

"We tried to do a split duty but we couldn't because of the late lunch," laughs Alvaro today. "People came and were still there in the early evening. We couldn't go away. We had to stay open the whole day through."

The telephone phone rang and rang.

"*Pronto*, Alvaro in Cowes, may I help you?"... "A table for six? At what time?"

"Eight bells."

Just a second, I'll see. Yes, I may be able to do it, yes. What name is it please?"

"Max Aitken."

"Yes, Sir Max." Alvaro was up to speed, as usual. After his first visit, Aitken, the sailing-mad owner of the *Daily Express*, who had a waterfront house just across the road, booked a table for every night of the week. That first evening there were never fewer than five people waiting to be seated and from then on, customers telephoned or came by to book up for the rest of the regatta.

We ran out of meat at about 11 p.m. on the second day and by closing time on the third day, we were out of the most quaffed wines. The kitchen staff were exhausted and Alvaro was reeling. He managed to acquire a modicum of fish, vegetables and dry goods locally. But then he had to send his lorry back to London (crossing the Solent), to bring back more pasta and meat.

"We – and especially you – can't go on like this," Robin told him. "We'll have to get more staff. More in the kitchen. More boys in front. And even more important, another manager. Someone senior to help you." Alvaro agreed. He told Robin that he knew just the person, Mino Parlanti.

Mino's San Frediano in the Fulham Road had opened a few months earlier. It was up and running smoothly and he felt he could leave his partners in charge. As soon as Alvaro called, he packed a bag and three hours later arrived at the hovercraft terminal in Southampton. Unfortunately, the last flight to the island was full and he would have to wait until morning. In normal circumstances, Mino spoke beautiful English, but for them, he put on the full *Italiano* act.

"But you got-ta put me on this-a ferry. Tonight, I'm-a-cooking for the Duca di Edinburgo. You see that a-big a-boat in the middle? That's-a the Royal Yacht. They wait for me. Please, you got-ta get me across."

It worked. He was ushered onto the hovercraft flight. I seem to remember that he had to stand next to the skipper in the cockpit, but it didn't faze him. He landed, found number 60 High Street, walked in, cheerfully greeted Alvaro and several of his own regular customers, picked up a pad and started to take an order. His only question was "What table number is this?"

As soon as extra front-of-house and kitchen staff had arrived, control was re-established, chaos was overcome, orders were delivered on time and, by the next day, and for the rest of the week, everything hummed. Crews and yacht owners came to eat and, within all the excitement, Max Aitken hosted a drinks party in his house across the road on the last evening of Cowes Week. Alvaro was his guest of honour.

Robin had put up the go-away money for the café proprietor and paid staff travel expenses and the rent on the empty house where we'd all dossed. His bank had provided the cash flow. Alvaro paid the staff wages and for all the basic ingredients. They had agreed on 50–50, but hadn't expected too much in terms of profits, calculating that the small room, even with three or four times a day turnover, wouldn't ever make them a fortune. The setting-up costs confirmed that and with the extra unplanned staff, travel and accommodation, it was hardly surprising that they netted circa £50 each.

But Alvaro was happy to have kept his name in the papers and his clients onside. "We had a lot of wonderful publicity," Alvaro recalls. Many of his new-found media friends would be very useful in the future. During this project, trust – beyond simple friendship – had grown between Alvaro and Robin. Subsequently they would become partners.

For me, that magical and memorable week remains a great sixties moment, my personal Isle of Wight Festival, not Hendrix or Dylan, but Alvaro in Cowes.

## CONQUEST OF KENSINGTON, 1967

While Alvaro was contemplating his Cowes venture and San Frediano consolidated itself on the Fulham Road, Mario and Franco were focused on a new goal.

"If you want to open more places," La Terrazza's accountant told Mario and Franco in 1967, "leave all the money in the business, show the maximum profit and then you'll be able to go public on the stock exchange." Revitalised by this prospect, Mario and Franco set out to double the size of their business.

One of their regulars, the stage and set designer Sean Kenny, had recently completed the re-design of Les Pies Qui Rient, a restaurant in Abingdon Road, off Kensington High Street. But Kenny had not been paid for the commission and, one day, while chatting in La Terrazza, he told Mario that he thought Les Pies was in trouble.

Mario made a few phone calls and discovered that Les Pies was owned by an Egyptian businessman (whose name is now lost to history). Having made a mid-afternoon appointment to meet him on site, Mario drove his new Lancia to Kensington High Street, turned left into Abingdon Road and parked outside the restaurant.

The Egyptian was waiting for him, sat him down and offered him a cup of coffee. Mario came straight to the point. "I understand you're not doing too well and you're thinking of selling the business? How much are you asking?"

"We are doing well," replied the owner. "Everybody comes here to this street, to this restaurant. Vidal Sassoon. People like that." He then named several celebrity Kensington residents, which was his first mistake – most of the people he mentioned were Mario's customers.

"But yes. I will sell. But for not less than fifty thousand."

"Sadly, I can only offer you twenty-five," Mario replied.

"Ridiculous," sniffed the Egyptian.

Mario knew that Les Pies was not doing well, so was not prepared to up his offer. He thanked his host politely, finished his coffee and left. He had, he told the Egyptian, to catch a plane to Italy that evening. When he returned ten days later, there'd been a phone call from the Egyptian asking for another meeting and this time, the deal was done. In December 1966, Mario and Franco bought the freehold of 2 Abingdon Road, including the restaurant as a going concern. It cost them £25,000.

Pasquale Lunghi was one of La Terrazza's four room-headwaiters and, one day, just as he was finishing his lunch shift, Mario and Franco called him up to the office. Franco sat him down and said abruptly, "We've just bought a restaurant for you."

Pasquale was stunned. "What do you mean? You've bought a restaurant for *me*?"

"Yes," Franco said, this time more gently. "We've bought this restaurant and we think it will suit you perfectly. It's smaller than La Terrazza, but you've had experience as a manager and you're ready for promotion."

Pasquale, still bemused, said he'd think about it. But Mario wasn't having any delay.

"What's there to think about? We offer you a job as a manager. You take it. You bloody fool."

So Pasquale did take it. He went up to Abingdon Road to see the site that afternoon and immediately he fell in love with it. Sean Kenny's design – with a big tree at the far end of the restaurant and a trellis with real plants on the upper balcony – made the room look as if you'd gone out to have lunch or dinner in a country garden. As it was their second "Trat," Mario and Franco decided to call it the Trattoo. They closed the site for two months to devise a bar area at the front and to upgrade the kitchen. Then came the extraordinary opening event.

This sort of thing had now become standard, but the Trattoo opening party cost Mario and Franco about £1500. More money than they had started out with at the beginning, seven years before. More than 500 of Mario and Franco's regular customers arrived and also, of course, Alvaro, which caused the habitual confusion among those guests who'd begun to think they'd finally made sense of the trattoria revolution. That night, the Trattoo brought the trattoria style to Kensington – and Kensington loved it.

"We never did anything really to promote it. We invited the old customers of La Terrazza and Tiberio, for the opening party. Then we left it at that," Pasquale remembers. "From the very first day, we had to refuse more people than we could accommodate."

Mario and Franco pitched the Trattoo as slightly more expensive than La Terrazza (over three pounds a head instead of the £2/15s (£2.75) which was the average at the Trat). It wasn't huge, with eighty or so seats and a more tranquil atmosphere. But the main reason for the higher prices was because in Kensington, the pace was more gentle. In contrast to the West

End where people ate before, during or after the theatre, before going on to a night club, customers at the Trattoo were, on the whole, older. They would spend a leisurely evening in the restaurant, starting in the bar, savouring a relaxed drink as they listened to Alan Clare playing piano. Then, after dining, they would return there.

"Not as frantic as La Terrazza," Pasquale recalls. "More like a place in the country. "

The reviews were excellent, especially in *The Times Saturday Review* which noted:

> **At the Trattoo in Kensington, Mario and Franco, these two gifted showmen, have once again created the kind of smart but informal modern ambience that attracts the fashionable set. Artists, producers, models and others sit amid an elegant summer house décor of real foliage and trellis work under a glass roof. The headwaiter, like many of his guests, wears a roll-neck sweater and you might just possibly imagine yourself in a private party on board some tycoon's yacht off the Cyclades. The chef and many others who work for this firm are from the Naples area and many of these dishes are certainly unusual.**

Egon Ronay was also a fan. "Pasquale, one of our favourite restaurant managers, presides, ministers, greets, smiles and tensely watches over your well-being at this cosy yet lively place," his 1968 *Guide* reported.

> **The atmosphere is right from the start, the little bar being well worth a visit if only for the piano music. Pasquale apart, the main asset is the staircase, tempting to any girl worth her mini-skirt to make a seemingly nonchalant entrance. Do try it for lunch, too, when it has the sunny relaxing character particularly conducive to business and other fields.**

What "other fields" Egon alluded to were, at the time, not easy to fathom.

As the sixties prosperity increased, dining out was more and more popular and affordable among Londoners and the network of new trattorie was exponentially growing. The opening of each new trattoria added hundreds more to the numbers who went out to eat in Italian restaurants every night. And, as when Alvaro's opened, La Terrazza lost none of their clients to the Trattoo; new customers came along and regulars of their other ventures added it to their repertoire of haunts.

Pasquale was joined at the Trattoo by Antonio Marson from La Terrazza and later by an assistant manager, Franco Pardini, a Tuscan who had trained as a chef and also had ambitions to own his own place.

"The food at the Trattoo was excellent and it was always busy, though they had some crazy neighbourhood customers," Franco Pardini remembers. "I once saw Oliver Reed drink a whole bottle of Sambuca in an hour. I had never seen anyone do that before."

The American actor, Robert Vaughn, was staying nearby, Pardini recalls, and at the time he was obsessed by the uniform he had to wear for the filming of *The Bridge at Remagen*.

> Vaughn would come for dinner in his Nazi uniform trousers and jackboots. Christopher Plummer was also with us almost every night. He usually came in the next morning as well to apologise for his behaviour the night before. Another regular, Spike Milligan, would sometimes bring his trumpet and play along with Alan Clare, our resident pianist.

The jazz pianist Alan Clare was a great friend of Spike Milligan and his evening slot was one of the reasons why the Trattoo was Milligan's favourite restaurant – whether for after-show dinners with colleagues like Peter Sellers and Eric Sykes, or with his friends such as publisher Jack Hobbs, or on more intimate occasions with his wife Paddy or one of his various girlfriends.

He had many meals there with his long-suffering manager Norma Farnes, who in *Spike: An Intimate Memoir* describes no fewer than twenty-two scenes at the Trattoo, which ranged from his standard reply to inebriate fellow diners who came up to him and asked, "Are you the comic? Go on, tell us a joke."

Spike: What do you do for a living?
Drunk: I'm a carpenter.
Spike: Make me a table.

to more dramatic, less amusing, encounters when Norma or Pasquale managed to soothe ragged tempers and nerves.

"After dinner at the Trattoo with Peter Sellers," Norma Farnes remembers,

> we went to the bar to listen to Alan, ordered more wine and Spike brought out his trumpet while Pete went to his car for his bongo drums. He and Spike were very, very good and Alan loved a session. Long after other diners had left, Pasquale, London's best restaurant manager at the time, would go home at one o'clock and give the keys to Peppino, our favourite waiter, with instructions to lock up when the music had finished.

The three of them were still playing their old favourites when they heard a tap at the door and the waiter went to open it.

"I was just passing and I heard the gig," said the man on the doorstep. "Can I join in?"

"Yeah, Daddy," Spike called. Then he and his fellow musicians watched in astonishment as the newcomer struggled through the door, lugging a double bass, to join them for a two-hour jam session. When they finally packed up at 3 a.m. and exited onto Abingdon Road, they watched in astonishment as their anonymous friend lashed his double bass to the roof of a Mini, explaining to them that he never left home without it.

Although the staff became used to the habits of their famous regulars, other celebrities were not so easy to handle. The battles between the hard-drinking actor Richard Harris and his wife Elizabeth gave Pasquale problems.

"Harris lived just around the corner," he remembers. "And when he

*Egon Ronay's favourite restaurant manager, the Tratoo's Pasquale Lunghi*

was in London he was with us every night, telling me, 'If my wife comes, don't let her in."

So when one evening Elizabeth arrived at the Trattoo with Christopher Plummer, Pasquale detained her in the bar and went downstairs to tell Harris.

"Your wife's here. What do you want me to do?" Eventually, they agreed that Elizabeth couldn't be banished, so Pasquale helped Richard Harris to escape through the back kitchen.

The photographers David Bailey and Brian Duffy, with Bailey's wife Catherine Deneuve, were also among Pasquale's constant regulars. "At about one every night I had to close up the Trattoo to go up to Tiberio to bank the money with theirs in the night safe," Pasquale recalls. "Duffy and Bailey were often still sitting over dinner with Catherine, ready to leave, but reluctant to end the evening. When I was about to go they'd ask, 'Haven't you finished work yet?'"

Pasquale would close up and all four would repair to Tiberio. The two photographers would order a bottle of champagne and continue, animatedly, to talk shop. Pasquale, who spoke much better French than Bailey, would dance with the French screen goddess to the music of Tiberio's house band.

**TAGLIERINI ALLA MARIO & FRANCO**
**A great favourite at Trattoo**

For three-four people, use about 300–350 grams of fresh taglierini, or if they are not available, linguine can be used. The thinner the pasta, the better.

For the sauce: 120 grams fresh squid, 4 medium scampi, 1 scallop, 30grams butter, 2 tablespoons brandy, one eighth of a teaspoon powdered saffron, 3 tablespoons sieved fresh tomato, quarter pint of double cream.

To make the sauce, chop the squid, scampi and scallop very finely and sauté them quickly in the butter. Add the brandy and set it alight. When the flames have died down, add the saffron and tomato. Stir, then add the cream. Heat the sauce without letting it boil.

Cook the pasta in plenty of rapidly boiling salted water. Drain the pasta well, put it onto a wide dish and pour the sauce over. Grind plenty of black pepper to taste.

## CAN YOU GET IN?

*"Are You one of the Beautiful People?*
*Simple Test: Can You Get in to the Dell'Aretusa?*

ANGUS MCGILL, LONDON *EVENING STANDARD*, SEPTEMBER 11, 1968

In the summer of 1966, *Queen* magazine had run a story about the 200 people who had access to Alvaro's unlisted phone number, whom he treated as though they were members of his own private club. This continued to fascinate the media and a year later, Alvaro decided to open a real club. It was to be bigger and more expensive than Alvaro's, not merely a restaurant. His original financial investor, Lauro Resta, offered to put up £30,000 and of course Alvaro had capital of his own now from the success of his restaurant.

For the design, Alvaro again consulted Enzo Apicella and, this time, he and Resta did something which Mario and Franco had never dared to do. They invited Enzo to become a partner in the new venture.

The site that they found was a garage on the King's Road, a few steps from Alvaro's and Apicella immediately started work on the conversion, his biggest project yet. His dream for the Club Dell'Aretusa was of a combined club-bar-restaurant-discotheque, in which he envisaged that Alvaro's "beautiful people" and like-minded others could drink, dine, dance – and even shop. There would be, he decided, boutiques, a cinema for private showings of new films and, of course, a kitchen which would provide the best Italian food in London, with chefs coming from all over Italy. To help run the Club, Alvaro invited Mino Parlanti of San Frediano to be a fourth partner. Soon, they were targeting Mario and Franco's staff to join them.

Long before opening day, the £85,000 budget had been massively exceeded and they desperately needed cash, so as to make sure the opening wasn't further delayed. Remembering the success of the Cowes episode, Alvaro then invited my brother Robin to invest in the club. Our grandfather had just left Rob and me each a small sum and we had agreed to pool it and invest together. But I was at work in the London office of an American public relations agency at the time and he was the one who decided what the investment should be. So now, as I later discovered, when he became a partner in something, I became one too.

Although none of the Aretusa partners confirm this, I seem to remember that it was owned by a holding company called ELMA

Restaurants (Enzo, Lauro, Mino, Alvaro) and Robin raised sufficient funds to make a loan to it, which would either turn into 15% of the profits and then shares of the business, or would be repaid with interest, given sufficient notice.

At the planning stage, the four partners decided to set up a formal committee structure which would give them a graceful excuse, plus a fallback position, when potential members that they didn't want requested to join. They were guided on this by Enzo Apicella, the best connected of the group, who, because of his nature, bachelor status and work, had in the dozen years he'd lived in England, penetrated far into London society and had many friends in different walks of life. He recommended that the committee should include representatives of all the creative professions and trades that were leading London's sixties renaissance. It would meet to vet all applications for membership and if applicants were known and liked by at least two committee members, they would be invited to join.

The committee members were mostly Alvaro's regulars – the artist Joe Tilson, Len Deighton, the artist and art editor Willie Landels of *Queen* magazine, the editor and cartoonist Mark Boxer, David Bailey, Alan Fletcher, the graphic designer, Alvaro's friend and mentor Laetitia Adam, Carolyn Townshend, Doug Hayward, the journalist Milton Shulman, the tycoon James Hanson and Patrick Lichfield. They would all meet once a month to sift through applications, then make their selection.

Invitations went out to Alvaro's "friends" for the opening party for the Aretusa, which was remarkably similar to the opening of Alvaro's, though on a much grander scale. The premises were only just ready in time and as Dante Betti remembers, there was nearly a disaster.

> As they opened the doors for the party, the decorators were walking out at the back and as people started to come in, one of them was Tom Jones, in his dinner suit. He must have leant against the wall and when he turned I saw that his jacket was all white. I quickly took it from him and promised to have it cleaned and returned to him the next day.

From that day onwards, the Aretusa became the latest social and media phenomenon, the most difficult and most desirable place to get into – one of the iconic London establishments of the sixties. The Aretusa immediately eclipsed Alvaro's and Mario and Franco's new Trattoo as the most talked-about restaurant in town. Alvaro's face was all over the magazines and newspapers.

*"I'm sorry, the terrace is already full, but I can give you a table here."*
*Alvaro in the Aretusa restaurant*
*– the place to be for Saturday lunch. Photo: collection Alvaro Maccioni*

"Are you one of the beautiful people?" demanded Angus McGill's double-page feature in the *Evening Standard*. Answer: "Simple test: Can you get in to the Dell'Aretusa?"

Not many people could. I never would have, if it hadn't been for the Cowes episode and all those Sunday nights at Alvaro's. Within a week or two, with 960 men and 660 women on its books, the membership list was full. According to the *Evening Standard*, the Aretusa had "the world's most distinguished waiting list. If you aren't a member already, forget it!"

So, by mid-summer 1968, Saturday at the Aretusa was one of the most coveted stages upon which the trendies could strut, see and be seen. Imagine it…

A Saturday afternoon: I arrive soon after one o'clock. In keeping with Enzo's strategy of exclusivity, there was no neon, no large sign, only a pair of polished glass doors before me. I'm greeted by Tony the doorman, resplendent in his chic grey multi-buttoned uniform. If I'd owned a Rolls, he would have parked it (he was saving his tips to open a supermarket). The King's Road, still thought of as louche, had not yet become used to the idea of a place with a doorman. The local residents in Markham Square opposite are, I realise, uneasy about Tony parking ostentatious cars outside their homes.

I pass through the glass doors, to enter a cool white, arched corridor; terracotta floor tiles underfoot. On our left is the reception desk and the secretary – a well-bred English girl who, I think, was called Allegra – knows all the members' faces. If you are not on her list, or your name has not been given as a member's guest, Tony will show you out again. As I stroll down, on my left, just in case my date is late, is a standard red telephone box, but instead of the usual royal coat of arms, it announces itself as "*Telefono*." Ahead of us is the door to the discotheque – perhaps a little dance another time, after dinner – and before me are two small boutiques: one offers ceramic tiles, the other belongs to Browns, the new fashionable clothes shop. Just right for a spot of light shopping later on.

Then I turn right into Apicella's vast domed bar, unfurnished except for three huge, black leather sofas and supervised by three white-coated acolytes; one of them is Alvaro's cousin Piero. I order a Nastro Azzuro, and, before it is too busy, I can admire Apicella's plain white décor, as it fills with members in the latest rainbow fashions.

After my beer, it's one-thirty, my date is on time after all and we go upstairs to the restaurant, which, some still say, is Apicella's masterpiece. In his simple but sophisticated style, it features a huge mirror and a clock whose hands never moved – one of those touches which in spite of having so many recognisable common features, give each of the premises he designed such individuality. Three rows of gleaming white tables stretch to the far wall and, on the right, are sliding glass doors, which open onto a massive terrace which leads back, above the entrance corridor, towards the King's Road. A pleasurable, leisurely lunch stretches ahead.

Whenever Apicella started work on a design for a new trattoria, café or restaurant, his partners or clients found that they got more than they bargained for in some areas, less in others.

Apicella continued to refuse to draw proper plans and would simply walk round the area, then round the whole site, then proceed to make a few notes on the back of an envelope – or on the tablecloth if he was eating at the time. He would then try to explain what he intended. Somehow, the result was nearly always phenomenally successful.

"Enzo brought in completely new, fresh thinking to restaurant and interior design," says a contemporary designer, Zeev Aram. "Posters, big cartoons; he would just draw something on the wall and it would be perfect."

"Enzo always knew how to think sideways," one of his other clients remembers. "Because he had such a good sense of humour, you never knew how serious he was about anything. Everything was done as though it was so easy. Just a gesture, as if no tremendous thought has gone into it. It just happened… and always, the design on the back of an envelope."

"He had such good insight and could always see the intrinsic merit in a space," Aram told me. "Enzo opened the door for people to see that there was another way of doing a restaurant."

"The Apicella characteristics are all there at the Aretusa, but used with more severity than before," was the verdict of one contemporary design magazine. "The bar is almost ecclesiastical and the restaurant on the first floor, with its wide terrace, is extremely pretty and on a fine summer's day it will be ravishing." It was indeed ravishing.

On that Saturday, as we walk out into the sunlight, we can hear a buzz from the terrace area, which, for special occasions, had room for a long, long table: Carolyn Townshend has booked it for fourteen, for her client Sammy Davis Jr's birthday lunch. Just as we take our seats, Davis walks out onto the terrace. As Alvaro turns towards him, Davis jumps onto the table and starts to sing *O Sole Mio!*

A photographer who has been lurking in the street opposite the Aretusa has seen him enter and within half an hour, the King's Road is swamped with fans and photographers from all over the world trying to get pictures. Eventually, Davis walks the length of the terrace and rewards them with a wave.

We fellow guests watch the commotion, and as the restaurant manager Mimmo Mattera takes our order, we can see several familiar faces at other tables, including the showbusiness columnist Peter Evans.

"The Aretusa finally shattered all the old social barriers," wrote Evans later, "lords, layabouts, artists, playboys, politicians, models, actors and assorted bon vivants competed for the best tables and a personal greeting from Alvaro himself. Mixing the customers provided the atmosphere for all."

So the mix of Aretusa member-customers that we most likely saw that

Saturday lunch could have included actors Michael Caine and Terence Stamp, the model Twiggy sitting quietly while her manager, Justin de Villeneuve, toured the room; a couple of peers – skirt-chasing baronet Sir William Pigott-Brown with two tall blondes, and Michael Pearson, the heir to Lord Cowdray, with his new film production partner; Willie Robertson, insurance broker to the Rock 'n' Roll business, in his characteristic red trousers; the actress-singer Anita Harris and several other girls, with pale faces and dark fringes, who look very like her clones; the runaway teenage heiress Jayne Harries with her new husband, the hairdresser Gavin Hodge and, over in the far corner, Doug Hayward and his great mates Philip Kingsley and Terry O'Neill. On another table there could have been business tycoons like James Hanson and Gordon White, plotting new industrial dynasties.

At the window table by the sliding door which opens to the terrace might well have been the singer-songwriter Peter Sarstedt and his friend and manager, Chris Peers, an inveterate Alvaro's and Terrazza regular. Sarstedt's hit composition *Where do you go to, my lovely?* would stay at Number One in the pop charts for sixteen weeks the following year and on the B side of his subsequent record, *Frozen Orange Juice*, there was a little song which I've often thought must have come to him one melancholy evening in the club. "I sit here at the table in the corner, hoping that

someone will take a chance on me*," he sings. The song is called *Aretusa Loser.*

Watching everyone and picking up material for next week's columns, there would surely have been several journalists, often the diary columnist rivals Ross Benson of the *Daily Express* or Nigel Dempster of the *Daily Mail*, the *Evening Standard's* star columnist Angus McGill, or their diarist Paul Callan. Many gossip stories of the sixties had their genesis in the Aretusa. One instance of this was when, sitting at a table against the far wall where she was lunching with Peter Evans, the actress Viviane Ventura scribbled an admiring note to send over to the table of King Hussein of Jordan. She had, she wrote, always admired him and what he had achieved; then she added her telephone number. His Majesty called a few days later, then sent his car for her. According to Nigel Dempster, his "large personally inscribed colour photograph occupied pride of place on her bedside table for most of the seventies."

Dining at the Aretusa, it was impossible not to star-gaze, especially because, in another change from English tradition, the more famous a client, the more prominent his or her table. Gone were the days of stars being ushered to a discreet booth. "The most intimate corners of any fashionable restaurant were reserved for the anonymous supporting players only," wrote Peter Evans.

> Privacy was for the poor and ugly. Restaurants lit by candles became passé. Now it was bright lights.

After a long and leisurely lunch – followed by the pain of an expensive bill, far more than one paid across the road at Alvaro's, or next door at Trattoria Don Luigi – one could dawdle at the Browns boutique downstairs, say a fraternal goodbye to Tony on the door and head off into the King's Road Saturday afternoon crowd. A few hours later, one could return and start all over again, staying up in the discotheque until 3 a.m.

Lauro Resta took care of finance, Mino Parlanti and Alvaro were in charge of restaurant purchasing and admin and Apicella was, supposedly, responsible for the bar and the discotheque. But Enzo was unsure of his duties, beyond greeting his friends, as the barman was in charge of stock and Dante (the manager in the discotheque) was very experienced. Although Apicella's role was never clearly defined, it was, for his partners, inordinately useful to have someone of his taste and influence to think about and protect the club's image. Enzo's ideas were ubiquitous, not limited to bar or design.

> The chef Vittorio was Sicilian and I said to him one day, 'Why don't you make that famous Sicilian dish, the one with Aubergine and chocolate?' They put it on as a starter and it was a disaster. We only sold two portions, so we put it on the menu as a dessert and people went mad, they love it, they said fantastic, you must tell us, what you put in this?

It was Bailey and his fellow photographer, Brian Duffy, who were responsible for bringing the East End villains, the Kray twins, whom Bailey had photographed, to the Aretusa.

"Ronnie Kray rather fancied Bailey," Duffy remembers, "and he would often call up and invite him and me down to the East End. At that time we owed them for a couple of times they'd hosted us. So in order to clear the air, we thought we'd invite the twins to our part of London." Which, of course, at that time, could only be one place. "We'll take you to a great new club, the Aretusa," Duffy told Ronnie Kray on the phone.

"Where's that?"

"The King's Road, Chelsea."

There was a silence.

"We don't like the Chelsea law."

"Never mind. Come over, it's a great place."

Bailey brought his then girlfriend, the model Penelope Tree, and Duffy brought Samantha Bond, a model he'd been working with. They hoped that Ronnie would drop all this stuff about fancying Bailey when he saw him with Penelope.

The photographers planned to arrive early, before the Krays appeared, but, as they walked in, Dante came up urgently and stopped them by the red telephone box.

"Mr Duffy, Mr Bailey. There are people here who say that they're your guests." And there in the bar sat the Kray twins, with their notorious bodyguard Ginger Ernie. Most people in the room had recognised them and, although it was full, the room was surprisingly quiet.

"Hello, David, Brian. What you having?" a twin greeted them.

Duffy and Bailey had planned to drink little and avoid trouble. But hardly before they'd greeted their guests, a bottle of Courvoisier appeared on the table.

"It's still only quarter to nine," Duffy remembers thinking. "And we're drinking brandy on an empty stomach."

It was like walking on eggshells. The Krays had very little

conversation. But the photographers and their dates did their best to keep things going. Once upstairs in the restaurant, the Krays ordered steaks and as the meal progressed there was a little more small talk. Alvaro came over to say hello, but didn't stay to chat.

Just as they were about to finish their meal, Duffy stiffened as he heard an unmistakeable, richly accented Irish voice behind him.

"They're nothing but a couple of punch-up artists. A pair of tea-leaves," said Richard Harris, who was sitting just two tables away.

Duffy upped the conversation, in the hope that the twins hadn't heard. Then, there was a moment of silence. Ronnie showed no sign of having heard anything, but he was glaring at Duffy.

"Brian, you're Irish, aren't you?" he said slowly.

"Yes. Oh yes. Well, yes, I suppose I am," Duffy stuttered.

"Is he a friend of yours?"

"No, no, no, I've never met him," Duffy replied, his face ash-white. Ginger Ernie seemed to be baring his teeth, waiting for the word to attack.

Ronnie continued to chew. As soon as they'd finished eating, Bailey and Duffy knew they had to end the evening quickly. It's our shout, they thought, and it's getting out of hand. They shepherded their guests to the Bar, where Bailey, pleading a headache, beckoned to Apicella and said,

"Enzo, I'm really tired. We're going now. Our guests can stay on."

Enzo's eyebrows shot up. "No, no," he said. "Get them out. They came in with you. You signed them in, and they must leave with you."

Bailey and Duffy ushered their companions to the door, where several cars awaited them. A few days later, the Krays were arrested and subsequently jailed for murder.

Another instance of Enzo earning his keep was an evening when a beautiful blonde woman with a very familiar face was shown into the bar by the receptionist to sit alone, seemingly a guest waiting to meet her date. Alvaro's cousin Piero, the head barman, knew she wasn't a member, so he decided not to serve her until her host arrived. In those days, so many girls had long blonde hair, pouting lips and wore little shift dresses that none of the staff recognised this newcomer, until Enzo went over to her.

"Miss Bardot?" he asked. "May I order you a drink?"

There were many familiar faces among the Aretusa's staff. One of the first that Mino and Alvaro had hired, with an offer of higher wages and less hectic hours, was Mimmo Mattera, one of the five who had abandoned La Terrazza for Alvaro's eighteen months earlier. Mimmo had subsequently gone back to his old bosses at the Trattoo, rising to the post of assistant manager. But now he returned to Alvaro at Aretusa. Dante Betti, one of La Terrazza's room managers, who had earlier worked at the Ad Lib discotheque, came to run the Aretusa discotheque. "Many members were my previous customers from one place or another," says Dante. "All the same people who used to come to Ad Lib came also to La Terrazza and vice versa. They went from one to the other. When they arrived, they just said, 'Hello, Dante, how are you?'"

Several other chefs and restaurant staff had been recruited by Alvaro from his former employers, and one bit of poaching was especially irksome to Mario and Franco. Alvaro and Mino realised that their chef, who had been imported directly from Italy, was not up to the job. While Alvaro was absent, Mino contacted Tiberio's chef and with large sums of money, persuaded him to defect to the Aretusa. Returning to London, Alvaro was more than upset, because this had ruined his forecast for the wages bill; more worrying was the thought of his old bosses' fury. Up in their Romilly Street office, Mario and Franco were indeed livid. Mario ranted and shouted and Franco seethed quietly. But there was nothing they could do.

As the word spread, there was a steady stream of membership applications, but the planned system of screening prospective members never really functioned. The whole committee seldom turned up, so it was farcical that each new applicant had to be known to at least two of its members. "Those who did turn up would look at a few applications and postpone many decisions or let people in anyway," Carolyn Townshend recalls. "We'd sit around for an hour and then drift off. Although James Hanson was supposed to be chairman, he was always busy and couldn't make it. So the meetings never had any guidance and nothing really ever got done."

As a result, after about eight months, Enzo's friends would ask him – who were those new people at the table over there? Since he didn't know them, this, to Enzo, meant that the Aretusa had lost its exclusivity and would soon die. He decided get more active with the admissions committee and as this issue came to a head, he had a major row with his partners.

"At our next meeting, we passed ten people for membership. But we turned down eighty," Apicella remembers. "My three partners said we have to accept the other people, we need the money. At that time the membership was £11. So I said, do you want to destroy the club for eight hundred pounds?" Apicella resigned as a partner, leaving with a cheque for £5,000 in addition to his £2,000 design fee.

The designer, however, continued to drop in frequently. "Enzo probably spent more money and time in the club as a paying customer than he did when he was in charge of the bar," observed a former member.

Sometimes Alvaro was inordinately obsessive. Zeev Aram, who imported Italian furniture for his showroom next door, lunched at the Aretusa almost every day. In summer he would sit on the terrace and pretend he was on holiday in Italy. One afternoon when he'd finished eating, Alvaro came over to ask what he thought of the coffee.

"Nothing much."

"Yes, I know." Alvaro responded. "But from now on I am going to have the coffee roasted in Italy. I am going to buy it direct, so now it will be Colombian beans, roasted and packed in Italy." Ten days later Alvaro again approached Zeev. "How's the coffee now?"

"Much better."

"OK," Alvaro said. "The machine is Italian, the guy is Italian, the coffee is Italian and it's still not right."

Three weeks later Alvaro again asked. "How's the coffee now?"

"Mmm, OK, better than three weeks ago. It's OK." Alvaro, still not satisfied, replied, "It's better than three weeks ago. But it's still not very good, not like in Italy, is it?"

Zeev answered, "No. It's not like it is in Italy."

*Roger Moore and Linda Thorson join Eamonn Andrews for dinner at Aretusa – a piece from Woman's Own magazine, 1968.*

"Mr Aram," Alvaro said, "the coffee is from Italy. The guy is from Italy, the machine is from Italy and now also the coffee water is from Italy."

"You imported the water as well?"

"I give up," Alvaro said. "It must be the atmosphere."

It wasn't easy for the Aretusa to make a profit, despite its glamour. Even without Alvaro's obsession with quality, with its original building costs and its sheer size – more than 50 staff – bar, reception, discotheque, restaurant and kitchen – it was open seven days a week from midday to three in the morning – there were some uncertain times at the beginning. A few months after the opening, Robin told me that he had discovered that as well as ELMA Restaurants (the company in which we had invested), a separate company called LEMA Foods seemed to exist. As far as Robin could gather, LEMA's sole function and responsibility appeared to be to buy food and wine from the usual suppliers and then sell it to the Alvaro restaurant and the Aretusa Club at prices which would ensure that the Aretusa restaurant company, ELMA, where our interest lay, made no profits at all. This seemed treacherous and I expected a plausible explanation or a huge row. Neither happened, the money was paid back and the Aretusa lived on through the late sixties – the flagship of the King's Road, with Alvaro on the quarterdeck.

Life for Alvaro and his wife Letizia Maccioni had changed beyond recognition from the days when he'd slept on the floor in a shared room in Victoria. Alvaro had become used to the queue of journalists wanting to interview him about his success at the heart of the swinging King's Road. Although sometimes he was overwhelmed by his celebrity, he kept his head down, worked hard at the details of the business and at heart remained a professional restaurateur, focused on his family, on getting things right and on keeping the food that he served authentically Italian.

Letizia, originally from Syracuse, had joined her husband in London in 1960. By 1968 they had three children, Alessandro, Marietta and Alphonso, and had moved to a Tudor-style house in an elegant street in Streatham, a popular suburb for many expatriate Italians. Outside the front door – whenever Alvaro got home from his long hours – was a yellow Lotus Elan Plus Two and the first thing the couple did to their new house was to knock down several interior walls and install Italianate arches. As a prosperous businessman with a moustache to match, Alvaro decided to make his own wine in his cellar, from Italian grapes that he bought at Covent Garden.

## BREAKING OUT ALL OVER

### Mario and Franco Feed Fleet Street, Float in the City, Acquire in Chelsea, Go French in Fulham and Struggle in Edgware Road

As many new ingredients became available, Mario and Franco realised that their menus could expand and grow. One day their new Terrazza head chef, Osvaldo Antoniazzi, suggested that maybe they should think about adding some quails with polenta.

Franco was nervous. "I love it. But will the customers? Do you reckon we'll sell any?"

Osvaldo said he'd make the polenta and they got hold of enough quail for a few portions. On the first day that he produced the new dish, the actor Laurence Harvey, who came to La Terrazza once a week, ordered it, and within a short time, it was regularly on the menu and was appreciated.

It wasn't easy working in La Terrazza's heated, pressurised environment. When one day, two of Osvaldo's three senior sous-chefs were sick, Osvaldo had to prepare 280 lunches without them. By the time he'd finished, he remembers, his skin was "wetter than the inside of his mouth." As the last dish left the kitchen, Mario and Franco came in to thank him and gave him a cash bonus plus two bottles of champagne. Their sensitivity to the pressure of a successful business and to their staff's efforts to overcome problems was something Osvaldo has never forgotten.

Mario still lost his temper under pressure and, a year or so later, a kitchen crisis turned into a fierce row. Mario called Osvaldo a son of a *putana*. Osvaldo took a swing at him. It was, Mario later acknowledged, an echo of his own scrap with Lord Scott at Hatchett's years before and once again there could be only one winner. Osvaldo was out.

Less than ten years after opening their first restaurant, Mario and Franco were now being recognised as leaders in Britain's catering industry. In January 1968, the *Sunday Times Magazine* called for the launch of an academy of gastronomy to "guide and encourage and give status to the food industry." The editors organised a photography shoot to which they summoned all those whom they judged to have the drive, authority and prestige to make it happen, including food and wine writers and leading restaurateurs. Mario and Franco and six others – the Café Royal's Charles Beaufort, Bill Lacy, chef of the Empress, Madame Prunier of the eponymous fish restaurant in St James's, Albert and Michel Roux of

Le Gavroche and Nick Clarke of Nick's Diner – were selected.

It was at this point that Mario and Franco finalised preparations for the flotation of their company Mario and Franco Restaurants Ltd on the London Stock Exchange. In late 1967 they had invited their solicitor David Napley to join the company as its chairman. Jim Long would be chief accountant. Now all they needed was one more restaurant, to increase their turnover sufficiently to attract investors.

Their former Hatchett's colleague Antonio Pizzala and his two brothers owned the moderately successful Pizzala restaurant in Chancery Lane and Mario and Franco knew they wanted to retire to their native Como. After a short, convivial meeting, the deal went swiftly through and, with Enzo's assistance, the restaurant was swiftly converted into the 90-seat Terrazza-Est, always affectionately known as "Trat-Est."

Their trusted Pasquale Lunghi was sent from the Trattoo for a week to help managers Mario Bariosco and Luigi Destro train staff to Mario and Franco's standards and teach them about the central kitchen buying system. Franco believed that Terrazza-Est – their first city restaurant – should be a little different from the others. An hour before they were due to open, as Pasquale was supervising the arrangements for the first lunch service, Franco called him. "Pasquale, have you remembered Melba toast?" he insisted. "You've got to have Melba toast on the tables. We're in the City now and City people like Melba toast. I must have Melba toast on the tables."

"Franco," Pasquale replied, "by tomorrow, you will have Melba toast on the table."

"I want it on today!" was the answer.

"Listen. It's physically impossible today. It's impossible to get the bread to do the Melba toast. Impossible to slice it thinly enough in time. We've only got twenty minutes."

"No!" Franco, by now, was shouting. Normally, it was Mario who shouted and Franco who remained calm.

"Don't tell me, what can and cannot be done; I tell you I want Melba toast NOW."

Pasquale started laughing. "Franco," he said, "why don't you take a few days' holiday?"

When, later, Franco turned up at the restaurant, Pasquale thought his boss would kill him. Instead, though, Franco was laughing.

"Today, you are right. But tomorrow we will have Melba toast on the table. Tomorrow. You be ready."

Now, all the Fleet Street journalists who had rushed to Soho at lunchtime could meet their contacts a few yards up the road and for many, especially the new breed of successful young women editors such as Joyce Hopkirk, Eve Pollard and Lesley Ebbetts, Terrazza-Est provided a welcome alternative to sitting at the back of the long-established Fleet Street El Vino's, where only men were allowed to stand at the bar.

The restaurant became a home from home for Lesley Ebbetts, the *Daily Mirror* fashion editor, as she tried to succeed in a highly pressurised job and keep up with the public and private lives of colleagues in a period of highly dramatic cut-throat journalism. "The Trat-Est was probably the most long suffering, constantly accommodating restaurant you could have wished for as a newspaper man or woman at that time," she says.

> You may have been first hired in the office, but it was at the Trat-Est where you were given a fabulous lunch by your boss and then told to go home and never speak to any member of staff again. It was where many people were wooed "over the road" by a series of lunches and at the same time it became the place for a catch-up lunch with friends and rivals from other papers, so much easier and more discreet there than at the pub.

Many notorious Fleet Street affairs began at the Terrazza-Est and the participants seemed able to conduct them openly at Mario and Franco's tables, Lesley remembers:

> At the Trat-Est, anyone watching you was either at it as well, with their own secret affair too, or they came from an accepting clique of people who all worked and played hard together and who guarded your secret. It wasn't "back street" if it was conducted over dinner at Trat-Est.

From La Terrazza, Mario and Franco already knew many of their journalist customers. They made sure that Fleet Street's eccentricities – late bookings, late arrivals, unpredictable shrinking or burgeoning numbers of guests – were always accommodated.

With four establishments on the go, Mario and Franco were ready to float the company on the stock market. David Napley had identified a city broker to handle the public launch. Mario and Franco's ideas, that they talked about on a daily basis, but had never before formalised, were translated into city-speak for their flotation prospectus. "While the activities of the group had been so far confined to central London," potential investors learnt, the directors "were satisfied that the organization with its centralized controls was now capable of supporting expansion outside the capital and intended to take advantage of any suitable opportunity which occurred."

The company's plans included opening Terrazza branches in Manchester, Birmingham, Liverpool and Leeds. Mario and Franco gambled that their concept would be just as successful as it had been in the capital.

It was time to meet the media – but this time on a formal basis. Mario, Franco and Napley held their first press conference at Terrazza-Est, adjacent to the City. In this skilful public relations move, they would also introduce major business and city editors – nearly all, in those days, based in Fleet Street – to their new place. There was a full turnout of editors and their deputies – Mario and Franco were such familiar names and so many City types wanted to meet them and see how they coped with a more formal environment than Mayfair, Kensington or Soho.

Napley made a brief, introductory chairman's speech. The company was announcing profits for 1967–68 of £125,000 on a turnover of £694,000, a mouth-watering pre-tax profit margin of 18%. With the flotation impending, everything he was permitted to say about the company's performance was in the prospectus.

Then, Mario and Franco took questions. "What's the secret of your success?" asked *The Guardian's* representative, their friend William Davis. Mario and Napley turned to Franco. They had anticipated this one.

"Simple," claimed Franco. "We keep emotion in the restaurants and the cold-bloodedness in the office."

"How do your different places retain their individuality?" asked the *Daily Mail* reporter. "And how will this be maintained?"

"Each restaurant has a different menu and each its individual atmosphere. The managers play an important part in this. We are there every day, but we can't be everywhere all the time. And although each restaurant is very much a separate unit, we're great believers in central control when necessary," said Mario.

"What makes your business different?" enquired the *Financial Times*. Mario started to answer. "We are entirely Italian. The whole restaurant, the whole business is Italian. Our food, the dishes and plates, the wines, the décor, the furnishings, the staff, everything is Italian. "

Franco jumped in. "With our increased buying power, regular shipments of fresh sardines, clams and even fresh anchovies are now coming to us from Naples."

*David Napley in the chair at Mario and Franco Restaurants Ltd's press conference, with Franco Lagattolla and Luigi Paglierani. The media wanted to know how they could maintain standards as they grew.*

"They are in the sea at seven in the morning," said Mario. "And on our tables at ten the same evening."

The *Investors Chronicle* raised its hand. "As you grow, how will you ensure you have enough of the right type of staff?"

"It's a hard question," admitted Mario.

> We now have 400 staff in five restaurants. Finding and training our staff is a problem every day. Many of our people have left to open their own trattorie. But we are very good employers, we pay our people well and we have a good reputation, so we get many applications.

"But", he continued,

> It's not just people leaving to start their own business. The cooks and waiters go outside after lunch, It's sunny, it's beautiful, they suddenly think of Italy and they miss their mothers and wives. They take off for a month or two, they leave us stranded. They come back and we forgive them, but oh, it makes life difficult. They're good boys, but who knows? Right now there are probably two more Marios and Francos who dream of opening their own restaurant.

In the subsequent reportage the effective combination of Mario and Franco's personalities was noted. "Lagattolla," it was said in one broadsheet, "is shy and soft spoken, seemingly hiding behind his tinted glasses," while Mario came across as "dapper and ebullient."

William Davis, one of Mario and Franco's long-standing regular customers, observed how good they had been at listening to advice, noting that their banker had, right from the beginning, helped them get onto their feet and their solicitor would now make sure they kept them on the ground.

> Mario is restless and flamboyant. He charms the customers, organizes publicity and keeps an eye open for new opportunities. He is temperamental and much more inclined to take chances than his partner. Franco keeps the staff on their toes and frets constantly about the food and service. He has the knack of walking into a place and instantly sensing what is wrong.

For a while, some speculated that anyone who had been a regular customer at any of the restaurants would be entitled to priority shares, but this turned out not to be the case. The City people didn't have Mario's flair for public relations. Some columnists predicted that this might result in a lack of support for the share issue. But the outcome was generally favourable and in the final days before flotation, several city editors advised their readers that Mario and Franco Restaurants Ltd would make a better investment than the partners' long-time Old Compton Street neighbour and rival, Wheelers, whose proprietors were also contemplating going public at the time.

Eventually 600,000 two shilling (10p) shares, representing some forty per cent of the equity, were sold, making both Mario and Franco millionaires. They had also given shares to several of their key employees and of these, their five most important staff members, Walter Orsi at Tiberio, Mario Vollono at La Terrazza and Pasquale Lunghi at the Trattoo, Angelo Cavaliere the head chef of the Tiberio and Mrs Emily Neal, responsible for office administration, were made "Special Directors" of the company.

Soon after the flotation, Mario and Franco also discovered that shareholders reacted very differently from restaurant customers. With help from Spike Milligan, they made a Christmas record, a plastic 45 rpm disc which was sent out together with a greeting card, to all customers and shareholders. Each restaurant manager recorded his own message from his restaurant and his staff, including Mario Vollono who declaimed, "Happy Christmas, this is Mario – not *the* Mario. I wish I was. But I'm *this* Mario." All the messages were accompanied by Italian Christmas music. Mario and Franco felt extremely pleased with themselves, until a Scottish investor wrote indignantly, "How dare you misuse shareholders' money in this way?"

The partners' home lives were now heading in very different directions. Mario's marriage had ended. One evening in the mid-sixties, Mary decided she had had enough of life with a man who was never home and she asked him to move out of their house in Sydenham. Earlier, he had taken a flat in Porchester Place near Marble Arch and, given that for several years he had hardly seen his wife for more than five minutes at a time, the formal end of their marriage didn't significantly change his lifestyle. For a while, his private life had been a series of unrewarding relationships and, following the flotation, behaving like the millionaire he now was, he ordered a Maserati and flew to Italy to pick it up from the factory.

Franco and Sara, meanwhile, had become more settled and whenever he had a free evening, there were dinner parties at their new house in Dulwich – often with Italian friends such as Germano Facetti, the artist Gianetto Coppola and, of course, Enzo Apicella. Nick, Franco's elder son – now a successful surgeon – remembers that, in those years, his father's joy was a new Jaguar XJ12, while his mother lavished love and care on her new Lancia Fulvia.

"Although he knew it was better for me to walk the four hundred yards home from school," Nick recalls, "Franco used to come and pick me up from the gates in his Jag and after his favourite lunch of mother's steak and kidney pie, we would set off to watch Crystal Palace. Dad was very proud of having his own parking space next to the directors' cars."

Zeev Aram's King's Road showroom, fifty metres up the King's Road from the Aretusa, was next door to Luigi Paglierani's Don Luigi trattoria and Aram would often lunch there. In 1967 Luigi's business partner had returned to Italy and he missed the company of his close colleague.

"Luigi used come and sit with me, just to chat," Aram says.

> He was always the formal headwaiter type, he didn't have the style of Alvaro or Mario. He didn't handle customers so well, or become such friends with them. He always used to call me "Mr Aram" every time I came to the restaurant and even when I said, "For heaven's sake, you know me so well," he said, "I am so sorry, *mi scusi*, Mr Aram."

One day Aram was lunching alone at Don Luigi, when he saw Mario Cassandro enter.

"What are you doing here? Do you eat here too?" Mario laughed.

"My showroom is just next door," Aram said. "And I can't be in your place all the time. Anyway, what are you doing down here?"

The next day Luigi told Zeev, "Mario wants me to join the group."

Mario had seen that his old friend was feeling lonely and, with his eyes and his ears open, realised the contribution that Luigi could make. They, now, could help him.

The group agreed to buy Don Luigi and, as soon as their old colleague sold his trattoria to the company, he joined it as administrative director. Paglierani's arrival took a great deal of weight from the partners' shoulders. He would handle details such as employee benefits, food costs, furnishing and replacements as well as personnel and administration matters. This left them able to focus on the front line – able to visit each of the properties twice a day. A senior Terrazza room manager moved to Don Luigi to help integrate Luigi's team into their management and buying arrangements. Now, Mario and Franco owned a restaurant directly opposite Alvaro and a few doors down from the Aretusa. It was not long before they alighted on yet another opportunity.

There were several French bistros in Chelsea in the sixties, far more

*Mario (centre), with longtime Terrazza regulars journalist Peter Evans (left) and photographer David Bailey; their Goodbye Baby and Amen, a farewell hymn to the sixties, recognised Mario and Franco's influence on Britain's restaurant culture. Photo: Kelvin Brodie, Sunday Times*

than there are today – another indication of how Italian has taken over as the principal foreign influence on British cooking. The best in Chelsea at that time was Bernard and Jean Jacques's restaurant Le Français on the Fulham Road – where Lucio Altana's Lucio is now. But Le Français was too old-fashioned, formal and haughty for the young Chelsea clientele; waiters would sniff and look down their noses at you if you asked them to explain one of the dishes.

Mario and Franco felt that perhaps there was room in Chelsea for quality French food in a smart, but informal environment. Could there be a solution in applying Italian management, style and atmosphere to a French restaurant? Also, this was an opportunity to score a few points over Alvaro. What was the French for "trattoria"?

And so, a few months after the flotation, Mario and Franco astonished their public by going French. They bought Rupert's, a failing business in Park Walk, close to Le Français, invested £15,000 on an Apicella refurbishment and reopened it as a French restaurant. To celebrate their new partner, Luigi Paglierani, they named it Les Trois Amis.

John Junor, in the *Daily Express*, called it the best and most beautiful French restaurant in London. It certainly stood out from all the fussy, curtained and chandeliered French restaurant interiors. Enzo, once again, had produced a remarkable design – simple, clean and functional. Les Trois Amis was laid out over two floors. The ground floor was a bar where customers waited for their tables; a circular staircase connected it to a large room below. This was a long basement, with ceiling spots and hanging lamps as at Tiberio and La Terrazza, providing pools of light on each table. Enzo lit the spiral staircases slightly more brightly than the room below, so that whenever anyone walked down the stairs, those already seated would look up at them. The sea of faces turned up towards you made you instinctively turn round to see which celebrity was following behind you.

Franco was the partner most likely to be found at Les Trois Amis, probably because, as he was most concerned with the food quality and remembering his training at the Savoy and Mirabelle, he badly wanted to be able to beat the French at their own game. The menu featured *Beignets Soufflés de Moules* and *Boudin Noir aux Pommes* but the main thing I remember about Les Trois Amis was their incredible Marseilles fish soup. The first time I ordered it as a starter, it was so good, I cancelled my main course and asked for a second portion. Growing up on school fish lunches and not yet having been to the south of France, I had no idea just how delicious real Provençal fish soup could be. When I told him how much I liked it, Franco said that the best French food was naturally to be had in Provence, essentially because having been a Roman province, it was really part of Italy.

"For example, *Salade Niçoise* is not French food at all," Franco insisted. "In truth really, it's an Italian dish. It's called *Insalata alla Nizzarda.*" And that was how it always appeared on their menu. The food, however, was the one of very few things there that were French. Finding a group of his waiters idly gossiping in Italian at the waiters' station nearby, I heard Franco hiss, "*Parlez Français, porca la Madonna!*"

But Les Trois Amis didn't work out. Mario's insistent desire to grow and expand had not, for once, been held back by Franco's caution. By setting out to deliver something with which they were not completely familiar, they made their first big mistake. The partners eventually decided it was not doing well enough to keep open – or, as the announcement explained, it "was not on strategy for their expansion plans."

The site was put on the market in 1971 (this would prove another opportunity for Enzo Apicella), while a little further up the Fulham Road, unperturbed, Restaurant Le Français stayed open for another decade.

The next opportunity for Mario and Franco was a Sardinian trattoria in the Edgware Road. Le Nuraghe (named after the giant prehistoric stone dolmens which dot the island's landscape) had been designed by Apicella, but the young Sardinian lawyer who had provided its capital was now anxious to sell. The company bought it and within a few weeks it reopened as Terrazza-West. For a while, the simple Mario and Franco formula increased business, as their regulars turned up to see what the place was like. But Mario and Franco hadn't really done their homework and, although the comedian Ronnie Barker and other TV stars who worked in the nearby studios, frequented it, there weren't enough of the partners' usual sort of customers prepared to flock to that part of London. They turned the problem over to Pasquale Lunghi.

"I took over at Trat-Est while I was still manager at the Trattoo," remembers Pasquale,

> and I found it was doing absolutely zero. I used to jump in the car and go there from the Trattoo at lunchtime and twice during the evening. After four months, it was beginning to get better, we had our best month, but then my assistant manager at Trattoo went on holiday, so I couldn't go there any more and when I went back about two months later Trat-West was on its knees again. I said forget it. My baby was the Trattoo and I wanted to look after it, first and foremost. I told Mario and Franco they must find a new manager there and I would go back to my own job.

Mario and Franco then found Romano Romoli, who rose to the challenge. Slowly, over the next five years, Romano built up the business into a success which lasted more than a decade.

## CUSTOMER, DESIGNER, NOW RESTAURATEUR TOO

Just as Enzo was departing the Aretusa, an Italian friend he had worked with earlier was planning to open a new restaurant on the Fulham Road. Apicella, still the unmarried, freelance boulevardier, realised that it was time to attempt to metamorphose from designer and advisor to serious restaurateur and businessman.

Enzo had been busy. His recent work included the Trattoria Parioli in Crawford Street and two restaurants for his friend Angelo Colla from Bari, the Santa Lucia in Rupert Street and, in a cool basement in Albemarle Street, Trattoria Angelo, decorated as an Italian courtyard with white stucco walls, latticed shutters, tiles and arches.

His latest commission had been one of his largest. The Morelli brothers commissioned Enzo to conjure up a giant late-night club-restaurant, Barracuda, in Baker Street. He fixed for everyone on his usual list to be invited and off we went to the opening night. Once again the same look pertained – rough white walls, tiled floor, downlights over the tables.

"A restaurant, to be successful, must have atmosphere and atmosphere is created by people who know each other," Enzo says. "To know each other means they would go to the same restaurants often, sometimes every day – and to go often means they will be bored with the decor if it isn't white." He believed that as no play is complete without an audience, the décor in his restaurants was not finished until the customers arrived; it cannot be denied that they looked their best when crowded.

"Many designers," Apicella avers, "create a restaurant as if it were somebody's peaceful dining room, forgetting that homes are occupied by only a few people except when there is a party, But if it's going to thrive, a restaurant must have a party every night."

The Apicella style had evolved from myriad observations of diverse, often apparently irreconcilable details. Working in television as a set designer had taught Enzo a great deal about lighting and the idea of spotlights and downlights had come to him when one evening, walking along Piccadilly, he had stopped in front of a shop lit in a way he had never seen before. He discovered that what he was looking at was a display lamp, hitherto only used in retail and, with his typical lateral jump, immediately thought, "Why not in restaurants?" He had a seldom-fallible feeling for what – perhaps a feature or a light or a striking curve – would make a room or a whole restaurant come alive. He was determined that customers would remember their visit for the total experience, not merely the meal.

"A restaurant should never be so awe-inspiring or overpowering," he pontificated, "that customers feel they must only come on special occasions." He believed that while white walls and tablecloths were bound to make a room brighter, colour should emanate from the guests and the food. In almost every case, his most conspicuous trademark, pendant downlights over the tables, created pools of dark between them, contributing to intimacy, while at the same time enhancing the general view across the room, accentuating glinting glasses, seductive food, flowers and faces. It was astonishing to see how he did it, almost anew, for every commission.

Anyone who went to one of Apicella's restaurants would always notice the lavatories, especially those in the opulent Tiberio or at Alvaro's La Famiglia which still exist. Even in the Pizza Express chain, he paid particular attention not only to perfecting the interior but also to ensuring that customers visiting the washrooms found that the standard of design was on a par with that in front of house.

Elsewhere he had come up with inspired features, such as hanging Alvaro's framed family photographs on the walls, which immediately gave the room an intimate feeling; he had invented the distinctive reversed И of the San Frediano chain's logo and put the red British *telefono* box in the Aretusa lobby. Another original Apicella touch was the use of the rustic chair, with its woven rush seat, actually designed by Vico Magistretti, which has a very square, idiosyncratically Italian peasant look. It was copied in various colours by many others, but always instantly told of his influence. He was also credited with introducing what soon became another visual cliché for the trattorie – the eighteen-inch peppermill, named "Rubirosa" after the legendary equipment of the 1950s playboy.

There was always a clear distinction between Apicella's work and that of a surveyor or architect. For him, architects are merely mathematicians who must be kept well away from designing interiors. "Eighty per cent of architects are criminals," he often says. "The architect thinks he can do anything, including interior decoration and that is very bad. Architecture is structure. Architects know about mathematics. I don't want to know anything about the mathematics."

> He always recommended his clients should avoid music in restaurants. In Italy it's frowned upon. Nothing to do with volume, but everything to do with the kind of music that's played. Usually, the rhythm's wrong for the current mood.

> Many restaurants play pop or jazz because, it is supposed, it makes people eat faster, so they leave the place faster and can be replaced by new customers. But jazz has its place in a drinking ambience, where you want to be stimulated. It's wrong to play music in an atmosphere where you are going to have a relaxing, enjoyable meal, and you want to talk.

He also knew exactly how a restaurant should market itself, though again, he would never have committed such a plan to paper. His feeling was that the designer must primarily create breathing space for the customers, who are the finishing touch to his décor. Once a trattoria opened, he knew how to manipulate customers to then make a new restaurant fashionable.

Now Apicella was ready to do it for himself, with a colleague who was prepared to come up with all the investment funds and to do most of the work – just to have him as a 50–50 partner in his new restaurant.

Walter Mariti arrived in London in 1958 and his first years were a whirl of different restaurant jobs. In 1961, he was a station headwaiter at the Savoy Grill, where his colleagues included Mario Vollono and all the senior team who would later move on to Tiberio. Mariti had read about the success of Mario and Franco, knew many of their employees and clients and had become determined to open his own trattoria.

By 1963, he had found a suitable site in the Old Brompton Road and had obtained promises of bank funding. At this stage, though, he wasn't sure how to approach the question of design. He had never been to La Terrazza. But, late one evening, Mariti dropped in on his way home. He took a look around, was impressed with what he saw and suddenly found himself chatting to Apicella – as usual one of the last to leave. The two became friendly and, impressed with his vision, Walter asked Enzo down to Kensington and invited him to design his new trattoria – to be called Pontevecchio. Immediately, Enzo offered to do it for nothing – or for a few pounds' worth of signed restaurant bills – a typically generous gesture.

Mariti remembers that, in fact, Apicella did far more than just the design. "Enzo was more than a friend to me, he was like an older brother, he helped me get started, he brought his friends and advised me on how to make the place known."

Another kindness made a great deal of difference to Mariti. A few days before the Pontevecchio opened in June 1963, when he was perched high on a ladder with a pot of paint, a passer-by knocked on the window, asked what was going on and when the new restaurant would be open. It was the Terrazza regular, William Davis, in those days the city editor of the *Evening Standard*. When he'd first peered in and seen the décor, he thought he had stumbled on a new Mario and Franco.

After a brief conversation with Walter, and appraised of the new enterprise, he decided to dine at Pontevecchio, booked a table and arrived for dinner on the second night. He gave it a very good review, which attracted a horde of customers and gave a great boost to the fledgling business. With Mariti's Tuscan background, the food at the Pontevecchio offered yet more different Italian regional specialities, alongside La Terrazza's (mostly) Neapolitan cooking and the northern Italian fare to be found at San Lorenzo. Although the Old Brompton Road was not a busy lunchtime venue except at weekends, within a month of opening, Pontevecchio was full every night and, taking advantage of the wide pavement before it, Walter soon obtained planning permission to add a dozen tables outside.

The Pontevecchio was the first tennis trattoria. Following an evening visit by the Wimbledon greats Roy Emerson and Fred Stolle, word soon spread among pro players who arrived for the pre-Wimbledon Tournament at nearby Queen's Club. Here, it became swiftly clear, was an ideal local haunt where they could meet and relax either before or after a big game. Throughout the London tennis championships over the next twenty years, Pontevecchio was always full of well-known players and their entourages and, on summer evenings before Wimbledon, there were often no fewer than four former champions, with coaches and friends, seated at one vast table.

With the Pontevecchio now hugely successful, Walter decided to expand and, in 1968, just as Apicella was leaving the Aretusa, he asked Enzo to be his partner. Walter would handle the business and the running of the new restaurant and Enzo's contribution would be the design and marketing. Due to Enzo's contacts and personality, he would, it was hoped, immediately create a stir of publicity and interest.

The two joined forces to open a spectacular new restaurant which would, they felt sure, become the centre of media and "Trat Scene" attention. They would compete directly with both Mario and Franco as well as with their neighbours Alvaro's and San Frediano and they would take customers and staff from all.

The site was the former Il Porcellino, at the corner of the Fulham Road and Sydney Place. It metamorphosed into a conspicuous, white-painted landmark building and a light, graceful, sunny restaurant, with vast arched windows, a roof terrace upstairs and a spacious bar – much bigger than the usual Chelsea restaurant bar – in the basement. For six windows which gave onto the Fulham Road, Enzo had Venetian blinds made in wood, (previously they had only been available in plastic or metal), an elegant solution to the problem of covering such large windows at night.

With Carlo Calabrese as manager, Orson Welles's daughter Beatrice checking the coats, Tony from the Aretusa downstairs in the bar and with a Tuscan chef, Meridiana immediately became the most popular middle-market restaurant in Chelsea. Later Enzo persuaded Angelo Cavaliere, previously of Tiberio, to join them as chef and the food gained an excellent reputation, with a large hors d'oeuvre table and several quirky asides, such as papaya with crab, or Apicella's own favourite – asparagus with parmesan and fried eggs.

The Meridiana was popular with a wide range of clients – actors and the film crowd, magazine owners and editors with their current companions, denizens of upper Chelsea, business people coming west from Mayfair, shoppers up from the country, stars and new faces from the sporting world (especially tennis players who had followed Walter Mariti from Pontevecchio), and even on one memorable night, a group of six Royal Navy ratings, brought in by Francis Bacon who had picked them up further down the Fulham Road.

### ASPARAGUS AND FRIED EGGS, PARMESAN STYLE

**Apicella's recipe, always very popular at the Meridiana:**

For four people: Steam about 1 kilo/2lbs of fresh asparagus *al dente*. Put them in an oven dish previously smeared with butter, with the tips of the asparagus pointing the same way in slightly overlapping rows.

Add some salt and a generous sprinkling of parmesan cheese, bake for about ten minutes until the cheese is golden. Divide the asparagus into four portions and place each portion in a preheated dish.

Fry one or two eggs for each portion (Enzo recommends that they are underdone) and place them over the asparagus tips. Grind salt and black pepper over the eggs and serve immediately. Eat with your hands, dipping the asparagus in the eggs.

*Enzo Apicella's design for the original frontage of Walter Mariti's trattoria Pontevecchio in Old Brompton Road. Later, Walter obtained planning permission to put tables on the pavement outside. Photo: courtesy Walter Mariti*

*Twenty years later, Walter Mariti with his manager Tony Farina at Pontevecchio in 1983. Note Apicella's metal tube downlighters, which could be carefully moved to be centred over each table. Photo: courtesy Walter Mariti*

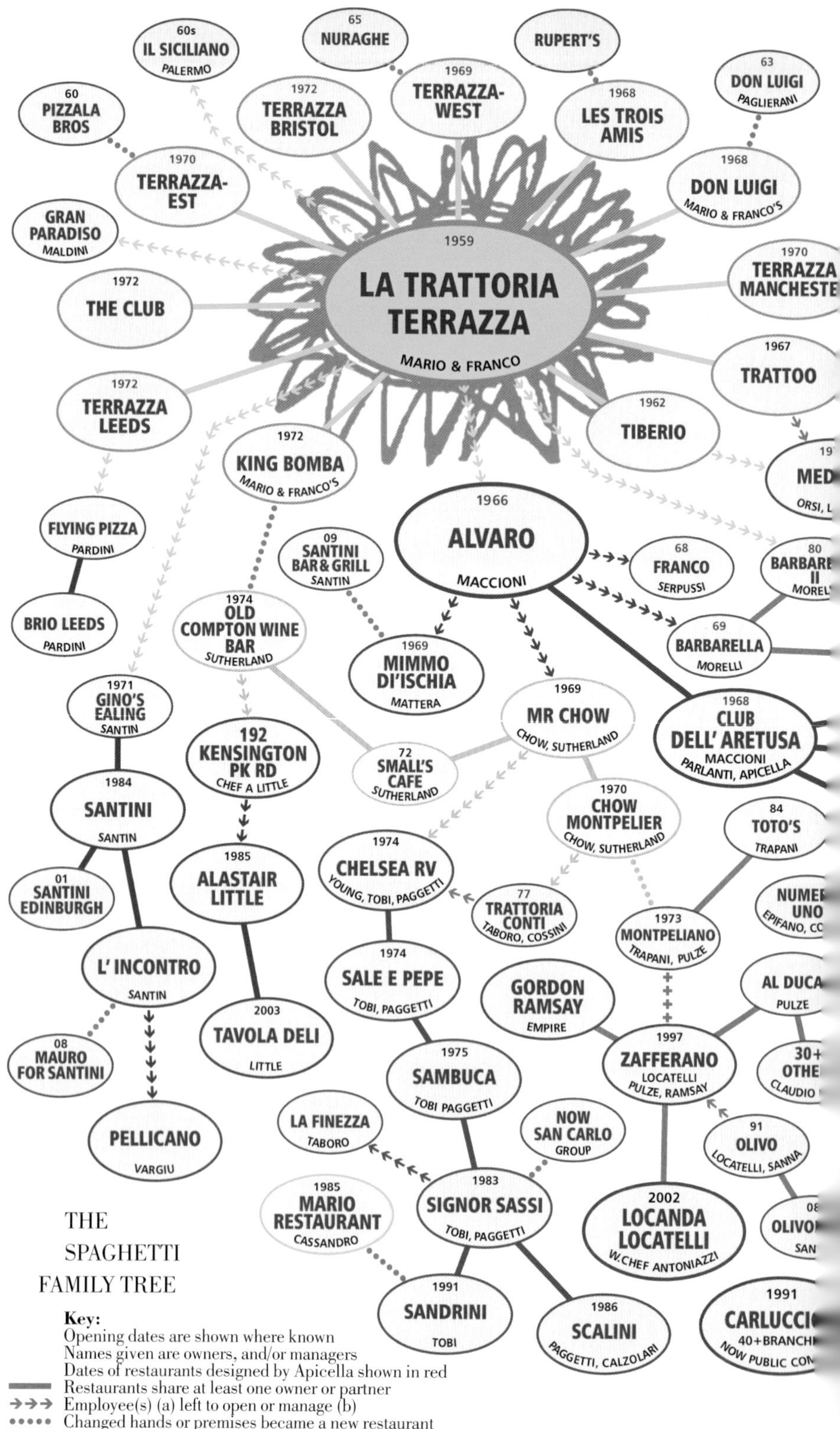


**Key:**
Opening dates are shown where known
Names given are owners, and/or managers
Dates of restaurants designed by Apicella shown in red
▬ Restaurants share at least one owner or partner
→→→ Employee(s) (a) left to open or manage (b)
••••• Changed hands or premises became a new restaurant
+ + + Business relationship e.g. supplier

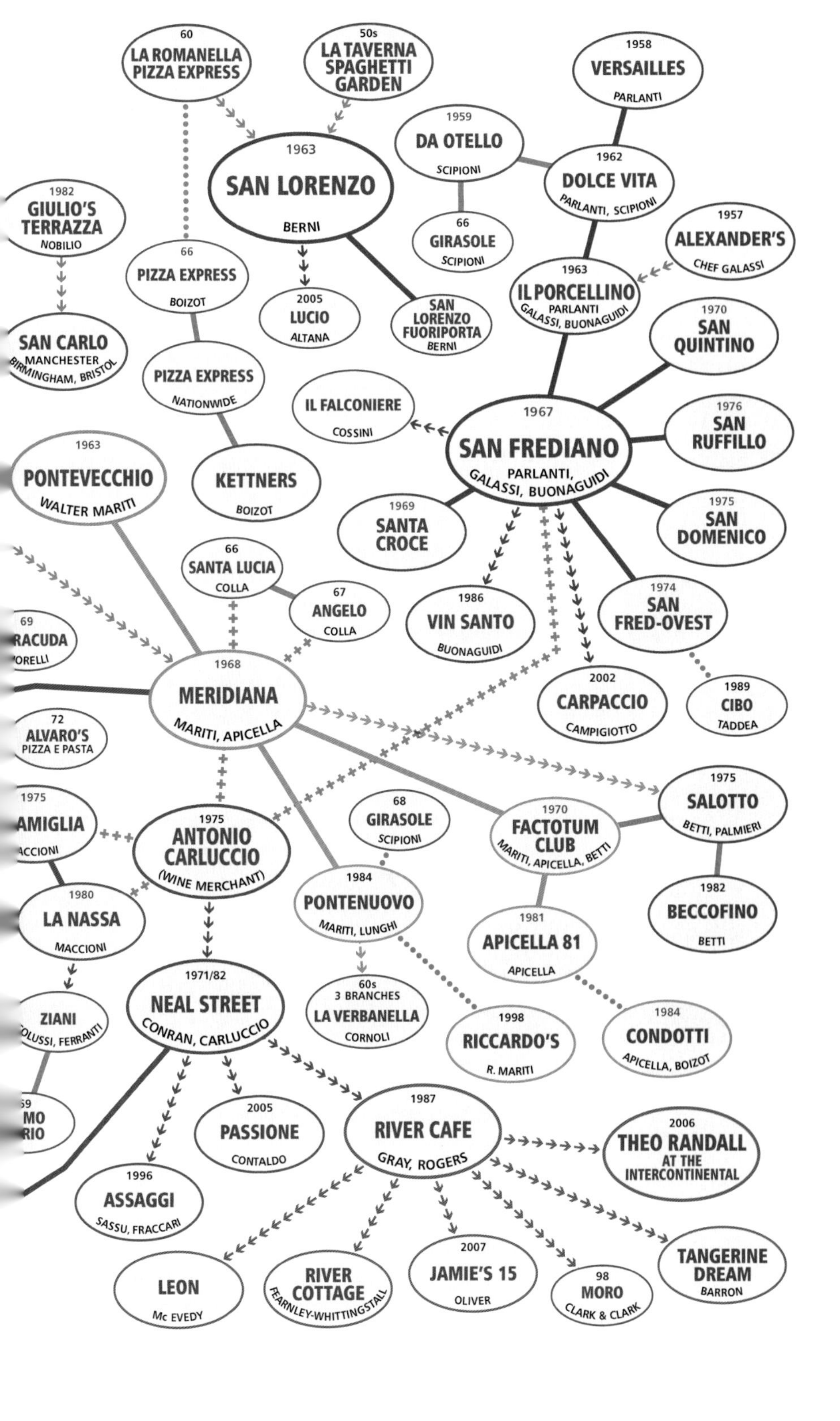

60 LA ROMANELLA PIZZA EXPRESS
50s LA TAVERNA SPAGHETTI GARDEN
1958 VERSAILLES PARLANTI
1959 DA OTELLO SCIPIONI
1963 SAN LORENZO BERNI
1962 DOLCE VITA PARLANTI, SCIPIONI
1982 GIULIO'S TERRAZZA NOBILIO
66 GIRASOLE SCIPIONI
1957 ALEXANDER'S CHEF GALASSI
66 PIZZA EXPRESS BOIZOT
2005 LUCIO ALTANA
SAN LORENZO FUORIPORTA BERNI
1963 IL PORCELLINO PARLANTI GALASSI, BUONAGUIDI
SAN CARLO MANCHESTER BIRMINGHAM, BRISTOL
PIZZA EXPRESS NATIONWIDE
1970 SAN QUINTINO
IL FALCONIERE COSSINI
1967 SAN FREDIANO PARLANTI, GALASSI, BUONAGUIDI
1976 SAN RUFFILLO
1963 PONTEVECCHIO WALTER MARITI
KETTNERS BOIZOT
1969 SANTA CROCE
1975 SAN DOMENICO
66 SANTA LUCIA COLLA
67 ANGELO COLLA
1986 VIN SANTO BUONAGUIDI
1974 SAN FRED-OVEST
1968 MERIDIANA MARITI, APICELLA
2002 CARPACCIO CAMPIGIOTTO
1989 CIBO TADDEA
72 ALVARO'S PIZZA E PASTA
1975 SALOTTO BETTI, PALMIERI
68 GIRASOLE SCIPIONI
1975 ANTONIO CARLUCCIO (WINE MERCHANT)
1970 FACTOTUM CLUB MARITI, APICELLA, BETTI
1984 PONTENUOVO MARITI, LUNGHI
1980 LA NASSA MACCIONI
1982 BECCOFINO BETTI
1981 APICELLA 81 APICELLA
1971/82 NEAL STREET CONRAN, CARLUCCIO
60s 3 BRANCHES LA VERBANELLA CORNOLI
1998 RICCARDO'S R. MARITI
1984 CONDOTTI APICELLA, BOIZOT
ZIANI
2005 PASSIONE CONTALDO
1987 RIVER CAFE GRAY, ROGERS
2006 THEO RANDALL AT THE INTERCONTINENTAL
1996 ASSAGGI SASSU, FRACCARI
LEON Mc EVEDY
RIVER COTTAGE FEARNLEY-WHITTINGSTALL
2007 JAMIE'S 15 OLIVER
98 MORO CLARK & CLARK
TANGERINE DREAM BARRON

*More like a many-decked yacht sailing down the Fulham Road – Apicella and Walter Mariti's Meridiana restaurant, with arches and roof terrace.*

*Feeling a little waxy? Enzo Apicella helps his double to read the paper. Lynn Kramer's wax dummy fooled many people who would stop to speak to it as they went in to eat at Meridiana. Photo: Lynn Kramer/Morgan Rees-Williams*

On a whim, Apicella commissioned a life-size, seated, waxwork dummy of himself from the ex-Madame Tussaud's sculptor Lynn Kramer. This figure, dressed in one of Enzo's corduroy jackets, was seated at a table near the Meridiana entrance, apparently reading that day's newspaper. Janet Ibbotson, who owned a clothes shop across the road, much favoured by post-prandial Meridiana customers, recalls:

> From my window, I could see the Enzo figure sitting at the table. It was terrifyingly realistic. People would walk in to the restaurant and always stop and say hello to what they thought was the real Enzo and then, after a few seconds, put their hands to their mouth in horror or laughter when they understood.

In 1970, while Mario and Franco were planning their first venture without his participation, Enzo announced that he and Walter were now planning to open a club.

"The King's Road is not exclusive enough, it is becoming too much like Oxford Street," Enzo pronounced, in a mild dig at his former partners.

He and Walter approached Dante Betti, the manager of the Aretusa, who, to Alvaro's chagrin, defected to become manager-partner of Enzo's new club. Apicella and Mariti bought Mario and Franco's now defunct Les

Trois Amis, which was quickly transformed into the Factotum Club – Enzo had designed it as Les Trois Amis, so changed very little. Finally, with two businesses, Apicella was not merely a restaurant designer but a real restaurateur. Soon, there was a Maserati outside his door.

At Factotum, Enzo experimented with another eccentric business idea. In those days licensing laws still required that wine bottles be removed from tables when permitted hours ended, giving customers half an hour to finish their glasses. This, over the years, had led to some ludicrous rule-bending, whereby, if customers arrived a few minutes before the end of the licensed hours – often at 11 p.m. – a waiter would pour out a full bottle into five or six glasses in order to comply with the outdated edict. At the same time, in a club, a completely different rule applied; providing the customer was a member, drinking could continue until well past midnight. So Factotum became a club; but the membership fee, in contrast to the 11 guineas (£11.55) a year charged by the Aretusa, was just one (old) penny (about 0.4 new pence).

Dante Betti remembers that this ruse instantaneously appealed:

> Ten days after we opened, Sir James (later Lord) Hanson, his partner Gordon (later Lord) White and David Niven Jr visited and on the way out, Hanson said, "Nice place you have, Dante, I hear you have a club licence. Send me fifty membership applications."

Dante thought he'd misunderstood him.

"Excuse me, Sir James, did you say five or fifty?"

"Fifty. Are you deaf? Send me fifty forms."

Dante sent him the forms and in a matter of ten days they were all returned, completed. The word got round and Factotum was on its way.

## THE TREE SPREADS ITS BRANCHES

Towards the end of the sixties, as trattoria food and culture grew more and more popular in London and, indeed, throughout the whole country, no fewer than five of the original Terrazza waiters who had, all together, defected to Alvaro's, decided individually to leave him and to open their own businesses, thus further spreading the branches of the trattoria network.

The first to leave was Franco Serpussi, who acquired premises on the Old Brompton Road, only 75 metres from the by now well-known Pontevecchio and opened Franco – a confusing name for a restaurant if there ever was one. Its main distinction was the round window, only recently replaced, which Apicella installed. We all went along to the opening party, then revisited once or twice. But probably because of its more famous neighbour, it did not last long. Serpussi sold up and left for Sardinia; his trattoria is one shoot of the family tree which did not thrive.

The second ex-Terrazza waiter to abandon Alvaro's was Sandro Tobi, who turned out to be one of the most successful businessmen of them all. Born in Eritrea of Italian emigrant parents, Sandro had arrived in London in the 1950s, but, after a brief and unhappy period at the Coq d'Or, had left the country. He returned to Britain in 1963 and worked as a waiter at La Terrazza, moving to Alvaro's in 1966, as the wine waiter. Dark, compact and neat, not given to smiling, Sandro had a dry sense of humour which endeared him to customers. Three years after Alvaro's success, Sandro and his friend Peppino Taboro, another ex-Terrazza employee, were asked to help launch a new restaurant.

This was to be the exception which proved the trattoria rule – a place which had aspects of the classic Apicella design, where you would find smiling Italian waiters. But instead of a trattoria menu, one found classic Peking and Northern Chinese food. Mr Chow at 151 Knightsbridge was, in fact, the first Chinese trattoria. Born of the partnership between the designer Michael Chow, the son of China's greatest classical opera singer and my brother Robin, the Mr Chow concept restaurant was a gamble – the result of a hunch that a restaurant offering one of the world's great cuisines could succeed at the highest level if it were presented in a modern Western environment where it could be enjoyed, then understood, by the London restaurant-going public.

Before Mr Chow opened in February 1969, a good Cantonese or

Peking meal could only be found in one of very few Soho restaurants or in the East End. But in those days, no fun was to be had in Chinese restaurants. As Michael was fond of explaining, the Chinese are so sophisticated that their fleeting smiles couldn't be spotted by the uninitiated. This, he believed, led to misunderstandings. So he opted for Italian waiters – men who would know how to make their fellow-European customers feel welcome. At first, customers were never quite sure if they were going to dine in a Chinese restaurant with Italian waiters, or in an Italian restaurant with Chinese food.

With Alvaro's blessing, Sandro Tobi left to become manager at Mr Chow. Soon he was joined by the fourth Alvaro's defection, everyone's favourite waiter, Peppino Taboro. Eventually, when Michael Chow and Robin Sutherland decided to launch Mr Chow's Montpelier Grill – this time Italian in both food and staff – Peppino managed it.

Sandro Tobi left Mr Chow in 1974 to start his own empire, joining with Mr Young of the Soho and Richmond Rendezvous Chinese restaurant group, to create the Chelsea Rendezvous, in Sydney Street, a direct replica of Mr Chow. While getting the Rendezvous off the ground, Sandro also began a separate business, in partnership with Mario Paggetti (yet another former Terrazza waiter, the one who had spilt garlic butter on Bruce Forsyth). They found premises in Pavilion Road, in Knightsbridge, and opened Sale e Pepe, adopting the Mario and Franco formula, a similar southern Italian design, with a very Terrazza-ish menu.

It transpired that Sandro's Chinese partner, Mr Young, had, for several years, neglected to pay his company's VAT bill and the entire Rendezvous empire (Sandro had nothing to do with the other Rendezvous branches) closed down and Young vanished; some said he went back to Taiwan with a suitcase full of cash, leaving the Chelsea Rendezvous staff high and dry.

However soon afterwards, Sandro and Mario Paggetti managed to open a second eatery, Sambuca, which became popular with customers of the department store Peter Jones in Sloane Square and, in 1983, a third venture, on Knightsbridge Green, called Signor Campari (which after a complaint from the pink drink company's lawyers, metamorphosed into Signor Sassi). As a businessman, Sandro was proving a worthy heir to Mario and Franco.

Fabio Benet, the youngest of the group which left La Terrazza with Alvaro, was approached by the Morelli brothers, owners of the Barracuda and the Alpino Group of pizza restaurants, to become manager-partner of

Barbarella, a restaurant-nightclub on the Fulham Road, near Stamford Bridge football ground.

The final deserter from Alvaro, Mimmo Mattera, was the one who, perhaps, made the most long-term personal impact. He had already worked in four influential Italian restaurants – La Terrazza, Alvaro, Trattoo and the Aretusa. He proved that Belgravia, too, could be persuaded to fall in love with Italian food.

Mimmo first surfaced at La Terrazza as a waiter in May 1964, in the Positano Room. He was one of the original team of waiters at Alvaro's, then re-appeared as assistant manager to Pasquale Lunghi, at the Trattoo, where he made some very valuable contacts. In 1968, Alvaro invited him back as manager of the Aretusa's dining room.

As surely as rivers flow downstream, Mimmo Mattera soon opened his own place; his chance came when the couple who had owned the newsagent's and provision store opposite the Trattoo agreed to back him. He decided on a site in the Fulham Road, but, just as he was about to sign the lease, Alvaro discovered that he was planning to leave. So Mimmo was obliged to bring forward his departure. However, his investor partner fell ill and he was out of work for nearly seven months, trying to pick up the pieces – even taking a temporary job at old-fashioned Leoni's Quo Vadis, which still plodded on in Dean Street. "It was," he recalls, "the worst three months of my life."

But with Mario and Franco, Pasquale, Enzo and Alvaro as his tutors, Mimmo had already learnt a great deal about public relations. Every day, between shifts, he would rush to the King's Road, and walk up and down, in the hope of meeting some of his former customer acquaintances from Alvaro and the Aretusa. I remember running into him and, even before we could exchange greetings, he blurted out,

"I'm going to open my own place, just you wait and see."

By Christmas 1969, he had obtained 2000 addresses (from Enzo? from the Aretusa Club?) and sent 2000 postcards of himself dressed as Father Christmas, conveying the message that soon he'd have his own restaurant, Mimmo d'Ischia. And inevitably, this came to pass; not long after, Mimmo d'Ischia opened on Elizabeth Street with the by now traditional massive party, its guest list based on Enzo's contacts; it did well from day one. Predictably, too, he had poached his chef, Michaele Frangiamore, from Mario and Franco. He threw off his manager's white jacket and reinvented himself as a hunky-macho seventies male, with a huge medallion and shirt unbuttoned to the navel.

One of Mimmo d'Ischia's long-standing favourite dishes was spare ribs, which remained on the menu for four decades and always seemed to me to be an odd example of the daily fare of an island in the Bay of Naples. Mimmo always refuses to divulge his "secret" recipe, but, actually, it was on the menu at Trattoo when he worked there. Like so many other restaurant entrepreneurs, he took to his next place what he had learnt in the previous one. A Trattoo insider reveals that the recipe was borrowed from the staff at Mr Chow down the road; it involved buying the ribs from Sainsbury's, marinating them in soya, chilli and brown sugar for 48 hours and then roasting them, very slowly, in the oven.

In spite of all these desertions, Mario and Franco were still the leaders of a growing pack. But they now had to compete with no fewer than seven former employees, all running independent restaurants across town; all having appropriated their designer, their menu and their format.

"No other city in the world, not even New York or Paris, has such a variety of restaurants as London," boasted the *Good Food Guide* in 1969. "New Italian restaurants are spreading rapidly into the outer suburbs these days." The *Guide* listed more than 60 Italian restaurants in London and felt that Britain would be very much the poorer without them.

> **While the quality is as good as in most Italian cities, the food is filling and appetising and good value for money, although rarely distinguished and this qualification applied just as much to the quieter older places as to the newer Trattorie.**

In 1970, in the *Evening Standard*, Quentin Crewe suggested that no two people had ever had so dramatic an impact on London's eating habits as Mario and Franco. Crewe had spotted early on what he called a process of parthenogenesis, whereby

> **headwaiters, waiters and even kitchen boys from La Terrazza split off to found their own places, faithfully modelled on the original design by the indefatigable Enzo Apicella.**

A typical example was Trattoria Conti, in Leicester; running it was the familiar Peppino Taboro, who had been with Mario and Franco, then Alvaro, managed Mr Chow's Montpelier, before leaving for the provinces to start up on his own. His partner, who Crewe would also have recognised, was Carlo Corsini, formerly the manager at San Frediano. The experience when dining at Trattoria Conti, Crewe noted, "gave one an eerie feeling of bi-location." Sadly Leicester wasn't ready for Trattoria Conti. Taboro and Corsini cut their losses and moved back to the London circuit.

Crewe also realised that a side effect of the trattoria revolution was that some of them no longer offered cheap, easy-going alternatives to formal eating out. Many had become "expensive, pretentious, snobbish restaurants," denying the original premise. Crewe singled out three of the most popular restaurants, all closely influenced by Mario and Franco, which had maintained standards. He recommended the San Frediano in Fulham Road "which really keeps its prices down while still experimenting with unexpected dishes," Mimmo Mattera's Mimmo d'Ischia in Elizabeth Street, "probably Enzo's most truly Italian creation," which offered a perfect Italian meal and Don Luigi, in the King's Road (now owned by Mario and Franco), "still a simple good restaurant."

The 1970 *Egon Ronay Guide* also focused on the Italians – more than thirty were listed in London alone; all of Mario and Franco's establishments, plus Alvaro's and the new Mimmo d'Ischia were given a star and there was a complimentary review of San Frediano, now into its third year:

> **one of the more hopeful additions to London's bustling trattorie, also to the dwindling number of places where the food satisfies but the prices do not ruin you... The noise is great but the place exudes friendliness.**

Outside London, other new Italian restaurateurs were following the money. Ronay noted that the "ever-growing network" of Italian restaurants had extended its feelers to stockbroker belt Weybridge, where Casa Romana, a simply decorated, roadside restaurant, flourished. In Casa Romana, the *Guide* noted, Roberto Ballerini had created a "congenial restaurant offering authentic Italian dishes."

Looking back at the period, Elizabeth David remembered that London seemed in entirety to have succumbed to everything Italian. The sixties were, she wrote (in her introduction to the revised 1987 Penguin edition of *Italian Food*), "the height of Italy-fever, of Italian fashion, Italian knitwear, Italian furniture, Enzo Apicella's Italian trattorie – in short of anything Italian from Parma Ham to Ferragamo shoes."

## A PAIR OF TYCOONS

Two years after the public flotation, Mario and Franco Restaurants Ltd owned seven restaurants, employed 450 staff and fed more than 1600 people every day.

As the company's operations expanded and became more complex, Jim Long, its finance director, was responsible for most of the financial management, but Mario and Franco still felt the pressure of running a public company.

Mario admitted that it was hard to adjust to having gone public.

> At first we had only been concerned with our own risks for success or failure, but suddenly now we had much more wide responsibility. We felt like professional gamblers who had suddenly become family men and now we had all those shareholders to worry about.

Mario and Franco had begun to look beyond Britain, although Franco, characteristically, worried that it was all happening too fast. They visited New York, but decided against opening there; mainly, they said, because they found they could not source real buffalo mozzarella. Mario also says that they tentatively explored possibilities in Capri, Paris and a German city, though nothing ever came of this particular fantasy.

Franco, especially, was particularly anxious about the problems of coping with spread over distance as well as over-popularity and the consequent pressure. Hurried service and loss of personality would be the inevitable result. He was, of course, right. More and more competition appeared, not only from former employees, but also from many others, as the craze for fresh Italian food and cool, tiled interiors fuelled ambition.

There was one diversification which worked extremely well. Mario took advantage of the growing craze for ceramic tiling, like that which had been specially imported for the floor of La Terrazza, He set up a new company, Domus, which became the UK agency for major Italian ceramic manufacturers. From the office above La Terrazza, he built up a thriving business – selling ceramic tiles to hotels and restaurants throughout Britain. So now, at the very least, when their employees left and started their own business, designed by Apicella, there was still a certain amount of profit from the new British appetite for Italian food.

Mario and Franco together faced the problems that all businessmen find at the stage between running a successful business at a personal level, when they know all their customers and staff, and becoming a company bent on corporate development. At this point, it was imperative that they should spend less time in the kitchens and restaurants, with their employees and customers, and more time in the office and the boardroom. This, though, they were determined not to do.

Luigi Paglierani had begun to make a significant contribution to Mario and Franco Restaurants Ltd, enabling the duo to continue to visit each

*Mario and Franco, now tycoons, in the upstairs office at Romilly Street. The former waiters were now running an empire which fed more than 1600 people a day, but when they argued and stopped speaking to each other for a day or so, their secretary, Pat Copeland, had to run between them, passing messages down the corridor.*

restaurant twice a day. They maintained their success by doing what they did best – dealing with people at the coalface. Mario, due to his extraordinary ability to remember names and faces, even out of context, was at his best when touring the room, making each and every table feel that here sat his most important customers and how flattered and lucky he and his staff felt that they had chosen to come to eat in their establishment that day.

"Even when Mario and Franco's empire had stretched to half a dozen places," a Trattoo regular said:

> Mario was still able to go to around all the tables, greeting friends and new customers alike, but without making anyone feel he was in a hurry.
>
> He would always wave to another group and say hello across the room, before starting to chat with the guests at the table in front of him, so that then when he moved on, to speak another table, it seemed a natural break, as a host at a party.

Now that air freight was commonplace, Franco could be sure of a more secure supply of fresh and imported ingredients. Fresh anchovies from France, real buffalo milk mozzarella and calamari from Italy were now coming in by air, and increasing demand from Italian delicatessens meant that it was much easier for importers to provide fresh supplies.

At last, Mario and Franco's contribution to the transformation of British dining out was acknowledged by the catering industry, which, in those days, was mostly obsessed by Charles Forte's growing empire and by the motorway service areas. *The Caterer* magazine, noting the growth of Italian trattorie, reminded its readers that, while in 1952 the *Good Food Guide* had listed only three Italian restaurants, by 1969 there were 60 listed, including all of the Mario and Franco chain. Professionals especially, *Caterer*'s editor stressed, should sit up and take notice; he then drew attention to the fact that Tiberio was one of the very few establishments which had earned the *Good Food Guide*'s class C for "strikingly individual cooking, the work of an artist."

Franco had begun to feel that he could relax away from the business. Pasquale Lunghi and he had become good friends and, since they were both Crystal Palace supporters, on Saturdays together with their families they would meet at the football ground. But back at the office, or in one of their restaurants, it was a different story. Mario took most problems in his stride, occasionally losing his temper, yelling and screaming, then quickly reverting to his normal bonhomie. Franco seldom lost control, he bottled it in and, by 1970, increasingly lived on his nerves. Neither partner took proper breaks or holidays and Franco continued to suffer from gastric problems. Pasquale noticed that Franco constantly worried about anything and everything and was, as Quentin Crewe had observed, "as privately melancholy as Mario was extrovert." Whenever Pasquale or another member of the staff came to ask him a question and found him apparently daydreaming, it would transpire that he was actually away working on a particular problem – the correct way to hang the beef, or a quest for a new supplier of grissini sticks.

"If we were to move that chest a bit to the left," he'd say, "and that station forward a little, we could fit in another table over there in that corner."

Several of the staff remember how fanatical Franco had become about fresh ingredients. Although most Italian cooks would keep a delicious pasta and bean soup for at least two days, allowing it to become richer and more flavoursome, Franco would insist that everything – sauces, barely matured soups and stews – must be totally fresh and at the end of each day, he would make sure the remainders were thrown out. As one Terrazza headwaiter remembered,

> Franco was always was very particular and very meticulous. At first we used Bifulco, the butcher on the corner of Old Compton Street. But they were too expensive. When we moved to another supplier, Franco wasn't happy with their meat at first, because it was never hanged long enough. Mario would get the people into the restaurant, then it was up to Franco to give them the best he could.

By now, Franco's stomach gave him a constant, burning pain, which sometimes made eating difficult and didn't help his mood. He had become tired of having to be "on" all the time and, often, having inspected the kitchens and made the rounds of lunchtime customers, he would spend the next hour and a half next door in Gaston Berlemont's French pub; this did him no good at all.

"When Franco had spent lunchtime in the French next door, he would come back in to La Terrazza at past three o'clock," said one colleague,

> and because I knew his habits, I would try to push him to have some food in his stomach, I tried to take care of him. He was such a nice person. But Franco would say, "I don't feel hungry. Well, OK. Give me a couple of fried eggs and some chips on the side." And then he would get upset if the fried potatoes were not all the same size.

## OFF TO THE COUNTRY

### Terrazza Manchester, Terrazza Bristol, Terrazza Leeds

Having promised their shareholders that the group would expand, Mario managed to convince Franco that in order to keep the stock market happy and maintain their growth, new restaurants, as near as possible copies of the original Terrazza, must be opened across Britain. But, beyond London, neither partner really knew the country; they had been to New York, N.Y., more often than York, Yorks.

Mario Vollono (who had managed the original Terrazza for five years) had noticed that among their regulars were large numbers of out-of-town businessmen who, on their weekly or monthly visits, would always book well ahead, to make sure of a good table. Many of them came from the major conurbations of Bristol, Manchester and Leeds.

So it seemed logical that the group's development outside London should start with La Terrazza Manchester, on the corner of Charlotte and Nicholas streets, and it opened in September, 1970. Giulio Nobilio began there as a young wine waiter and after Mario and Franco had sacked three separate managers in the first six months, he became the group's youngest manager, at the age of twenty-four.

In Manchester, however, Mario and Franco could no longer rely on an unlimited supply of Italian cooks and waiters. Straight out of catering college, seventeen-year-old Peter Spencer arrived from an agency to start working as a commis chef and soon discovered that he was part of a team which included Swedish and Spanish, as well as Italian, staff.

"Nothing at catering college had prepared me for working in an Italian kitchen, with a chef like that," Spencer remembered.

> To call it volatile would be an understatement, there were screaming matches every day between the Italians in the kitchen and the Spanish out in front, knives and choppers were wielded and there was terrible language.
>
> It was a real apprenticeship. Everything, including pasta and soups, was made fresh every day from scratch and there was non-stop preparation work. Somehow we managed to do forty lunches and eighty covers every evening.

Even without Mario's and Franco's presence – to supervise staff and charm customers – La Terrazza Manchester quickly became the most fashionable spot in town. Many fans of the London restaurant who for whatever reason, found themselves in Manchester, now had a recognisable and reliable name they could call for a restaurant booking and locals soon heard on the grapevine that at La Terrazza, they could be sure to eat alongside the actors and actresses who were appearing at city-centre theatres, or recording at the Granada television studios.

Spencer remembers that when, freed from the kitchen, he was sent upstairs to work in the salad bar, he would see stars (in town that week) ordering *Petto di Pollo Sorpresa* or Veal Nodino. Although he remembers identifying singers like Andy Williams or Lulu, who was a London Terrazza regular, the customer who most impressed him was the Manchester United manager, Sir Matt Busby.

In 1972, Mario and Franco asked Giulio Nobilio to move to manage a new Terrazza Bristol. Although it began slowly, it was decided, soon after it opened, to go ahead with the next expansion – in Leeds. Mario, Franco and Luigi Paglierani went up to reconnoitre, identified a site in Greek Street near the city centre and decided to press on.

Franco Pardini had left Pasquale's Trattoo in Abingdon Road a couple of years earlier, to start, then build up his own place, Franco's Bussola. One night in 1972, he was dining at the Trattoo, celebrating the sale of his restaurant to a catering group.

Just as he finished his meal, Mario strolled in for his evening visit.

"Ciao, Franco, what you doing here?" Mario punched his old colleague on the shoulder, then moved round to kiss Franco Pardini's American wife.

"I've sold the Bussola; I'm a free man," Pardini grinned.

"Wonderful news. Congratulations," Mario said as he shook Pardini's hand and turned to the nearest waiter. "Hey – Tony – a grappa for Franco. He's celebrating." Mario sat with them for a time and then went to tour the room, while Pardini and his wife enjoyed their digestifs. Suddenly Mario appeared back at their table.

"What you doing next week?" he said.

"Nothing much. One or two appointments. Why?"

Mario grabbed Franco Pardini by both wrists. "You wanna help run our new restaurant for us?

"What you saying? What new restaurant?"

"What about it? In Leeds."

"Leeds?" said Pardini. "Where's Leeds?"

After Mario, persuasive as usual, had convinced him to go up and take a look, Pardini drove up to Yorkshire, and fell in love with the countryside. "The dales are just like Tuscany," he says. He agreed to be Terrazza Leeds assistant manager, sold his flat in London, moved his family to the north and the restaurant opened in November, 1972. The first manager was Mario Bariosco, a veteran of Trattoo and Trat-Est, while a Terrazza sous-chef, Franco Vinci, became the chef. The company's eight other managers were all invited up to Leeds to its inaugural party for 300 guests.

However, Mario and Franco soon realised that the Yorkshire businessmen who enjoyed paying sixteen shillings (80p) for a delicious *Saltimbocca alla Romana* or eighteen shillings (90p) for a *Fracosta alla Pizzaiola* in London, were less keen to be asked to pay the same prices in

Leeds. Whereas in London, dining out had become an any-night-of-the-week activity, in Yorkshire this was still a weekend treat. The restaurant was full to bursting every Friday and Saturday night, but otherwise it was rarely busy. "They had misjudged the market," Pardini remembers.

After a year, Franco Pardini, like many other members of Mario and Franco staff before him (and dozens later), saw his chance and took it. The Leeds Terrazza, he understood, was pitched too upmarket for the majority of customers, so he quit his post and, in 1974, opened The Flying Pizza, which offered pasta and a few other daily specials. It was exactly what the local community needed and became the favourite place for Leeds society to see and be seen – any and every night of the week. Pardini, a larger than life character and lover of language, poetry and song, was in his element and, at the centre of his fashionable establishment, became the best-known Italian host in the region.

In a way, his departure helped the Leeds Terrazza to get on its feet, as Yorkshiremen who enjoyed his flying pizzas, cautiously began to make steps upmarket to the more sophisticated Italian food at La Terrazza, and under a new manager, Pino Cecere, the Mario and Franco Leeds operation became a success.

Late in 1972, back in London, Mario and Franco, as well as many of their loyal customers, suffered a blow. Two of their most senior managers, both "Special Directors," decided that they, too, would take a gamble and hazard a restaurant of their own. Walter Orsi had been running Tiberio for ten years, while Pasquale Lunghi had been a waiter at La Terrazza since 1964 and manager of the Trattoo since 1966. All those late nights sitting over a coffee and grappa in Tiberio after closing had given them plenty of opportunity to plot their future.

They gave in their notice and went into business together, at Medusa in Kensington Church Street. Given their training and their knowledge of the company's operations, their suppliers and customers, Orsi and Lunghi felt assured of a fair wind. "Cream walls maintain orthodox trattoria style," reported the *Egon Ronay Guide*, "but deep carpets and chairs and an attractive piano bar add a particular sophistication." So Mario and Franco were now in competition with yet another copy and, of the 1968 "Special Directors" of Mario and Franco Restaurants Ltd, only Mario Vollono at La Terrazza remained.

Soon after Medusa opened, the 1973 recession started to bite. The

British economy slowed, and there was a general cutback in dining out. This affected the whole catering industry, but particularly new restaurants seeking to establish their names. This was made worse by what Pasquale called "very unhappy Irish people throwing bombs in restaurants" (the bombing of Walton's in Walton Street, SW3). Although Pasquale and his partner were paying themselves a decent wage, their business was not thriving and, after two and a half years, they contemplated selling it and moving on, secure that if the worst came to the worst, they could always go back to waitering.

Then one day, an Indian came into Medusa and asked if he could talk to them in private. Without preamble, he came straight to the point.

"I want to buy your restaurant," he said. The two partners stayed poker-faced.

"Well," said Pasquale, as if weighing up the proposition, "the restaurant is not on the market. But, for the right price, everything is for sale, my mother included."

A deal was swiftly concluded. It wasn't until later that Pasquale and Walter discovered the background.

They were told that the mysterious Indian had, in fact, been the accountant of a large restaurant group. Apparently, he had discovered that his employers were skimming off cash from the takings and hiding it in a safe. One evening he had appropriated the safe keys, emptied it and vanished with its contents, knowing that it would be impossible to report him to the police, since what he had taken was, in entirety, owed to the Inland Revenue.

## FISH & CHIPS IN SOHO, DANCING IN BELGRAVIA

The King Bomba delicatessen in Old Compton Street in Soho was named after King Ferdinand II of Sicily, whose navy's shelling of the inhabitants of Messina in 1848, even after they had surrendered, earned him the nickname *Re Bomba*. The deli had existed for ever, at any rate for several decades. It was there that Mario and Franco had often enjoyed free lunches as they were fitting out La Terrazza.

Now, its elderly *padrone*, Eugenio, was ready to retire and of course Mario and Franco were the first to be told the news. The partners decided they could – and would – take advantage of the empty premises to offer an Italian take on the ultra-British fare of fish and chips. Since this was not exactly Apicella's Neapolitan style, they asked their friends Willie Landels and Zeev Aram to design them a suitable ambiance.

When Landels and Aram came to the offices above La Terrazza to discuss the design, Franco only wanted to talk about the price of the fish and chips.

"It should be expensive fish and chips," he insisted. Aram and Landels demurred.

"This is a contradiction. It should not be expensive fish when you have Wheelers next door," they sensibly advised.

"I'd do it an injustice if I were to call it a fish and chip shop," Quentin Crewe reported when Mario and Franco's King Bomba opened, "for it is a most elegantly decorated affair." It extended over two floors, with a long green bar flanked with high stools as well as a large marble-topped table on the ground floor; downstairs there were beech-wood tables. It all looked shiny, efficient and stylish, with a metal-topped counter and white tiled floor. The food was simple – oysters, pizza, hamburgers, fried fish and chips. "The quality is perfect, the cooking will no doubt be too, when they have had a little more practice at such foreign dishes," judged Crewe.

Alas, King Bomba failed within less than two years. In retrospect, this was because Mario and Franco had lost focus and this calls into question whether they were by this time still functioning as interactive partners. Why would the operators of the most successful Italian restaurants in London want to open a fish and chip shop? The answer was, because the site was there. Mario certainly liked the idea of owning another place right behind their head office. But, for him, fish and chips was not good enough. He also wanted to provide pizza and Franco wanted to charge the same prices for fish and chips as he did for a fish course at La Terrazza.

Eventually in 1973, Mario and Franco sold King Bomba to my brother Robin and instead of Mario and Franco's King Bomba Fish and Chip Restaurant it became the Old Compton Wine Bar.

The next phase of Mario and Franco's expansion was to be their version of the Aretusa Club. They were determined not to make the same membership mistakes as Alvaro and Mino had on the King's Road. The Club, as it was simply called, was in the Halkin Arcade, near Belgrave Square, and once again was a departure from the trattoria concept. For the first time, Mario and Franco ran into local opposition. Although they never intended that The Club would specifically be a "nightclub," it was

*Design Journal, 1971. Mario and Franco's King Bomba didn't last long; the site was bought by Robin Sutherland, and became the Old Compton Wine bar, where the author was the first chef, succeeded in 1976 by Alastair Little.*

# Interiors

### Fish and chip sandwich

King Bomba, Mario and Franco's latest London restaurant, has just opened at 37 Old Compton Street, W1, where Zeev Aram & Associates have converted a wine store and delicatessen into a three tier eating house specialising in fish and chips. The eating house is in what used to be a very dilapidated nineteenth century terraced building, whose exterior has been spruced up by painting the brickwork white and providing a new, ground floor frontage. This consists of a bronze tinted window, curved at one end, and a bronze, armour plate glass door, which leads straight into the ground floor restaurant. There is also a separate entrance to the floors above the restaurant, which at present are used as changing rooms for the staff.

Inside, the building has been strengthened by the insertion of a

new ground floor, supported on steel columns which rise from the basement and alleviate the loading on the side walls. The ground floor has a green stove enamelled sheet steel bar counter with a marble top running from front to back, behind which is the main area for serving drinks and a fish frier. There is also a service lift connecting the other floors. On the other side of the counter are bar stools and other stools around marble topped tables which have green stove enamelled tubular steel bases. The whole area is tiled, and has white or stainless steel clad walls, except for the rear wall which has a bronze tinted mirror to create an illusion of space. Black metal panels cover the services in the ceiling.

At the front of the ground floor is a spiral staircase connecting the basement and first floor restaurants. Both floors seat 30 people each.

One of the main problems of King Bomba is the building's confined and awkward space. Hence the kitchen has had to be sited at the rear of the ground floor and public lavatories at the back of the basement, while under-pavement cellars have been used for wine and linen storage. The owners' brief also required a versatile restaurant providing speedy service for customers in a hurry, where people will eat for under £1 per head at lunchtime or in the interval between leaving work and going to the cinema.

The conversion was carried out by Mario and Franco's own company, Thornton Contracts Ltd.

perceived as such by the council planners and by local residents. Associating Mario and Franco's project with the wave of discotheques which were springing up all over London, Belgravians were afraid of noise and raucous late-night excursions which, they felt, would "inevitably accompany" the arrival of a "nightclub." They complained that they would be forced to listen to car doors throughout the small hours.

However Mario was confident that those fears were unfounded.

"The club will be perfectly soundproof," he told protesters.

As it turned out, there was no problem. Far from being a discotheque, the club was a staid establishment with little soul or atmosphere, certainly no riotous clientele or deafening music.

When it opened in 1972, its decor was a complete breakaway from the formula of white walls, tiled floors, arches and light filtering through blinds. Mario and Franco brought in the architect Antonio Malarasi from Rome, who created what was then described as an urban and sophisticated 1930s look, but which, in retrospect, seems to have been the epitome of early seventies grunge. There was a stainless steel dance floor and the walls were various shades of brown becoming gradually lighter until the top stripe was cream and the ceiling was covered with dark brown felt. There were tables tucked into small alcoves, banquette seats covered in canvas and leather upholstered chairs upon which clients' bottoms slid uncomfortably. It didn't look remotely Italian and it was totally different from everything that Mario and Franco had done before.

In addition to the upmarket set living in Chelsea and Belgravia, regular customers from all Mario and Franco's other restaurants were invited to join, and, so as not to create too much of a cliquey atmosphere, they deliberately targeted a wide spread of potential members.

The Club was out of sync with the formula which had made Mario and Franco so successful. But, without being a great success, it made money and contributed to the company's profit. I don't think that either Mario or Franco enjoyed owning it. It had nothing in common with their Neapolitan roots and provided them with management headaches without the joys and highs which come from seeing a room buzzing with energy and pleasure.

"Every time Franco arrived in the bar, I had to give him a very large whisky," a former manager told me:

> He would stand with his back to the room, take a few sips, walk around to see what was happening, give some instructions here and there, then come back, finish his whisky and leave.

## PIZZA COMES IN, AND ALVARO SELLS OUT

What Mario and Franco and their successors were doing for British consumption of pasta and polenta, a new successful chain was now doing for pizza. Like most Italian food, in whatever inauthentic guise, pizza had existed in London well before the sixties. Research suggests that Olivelli's, which opened in 1934 in Store Street, off the Tottenham Court Road, was one of the first establishments to offer the real thing.

However, it took a talented entrepreneur, in the mould of Mario and Franco, to make pizza as fashionable a dish as pollo sorpresa. When Peter Boizot tasted his first pizza in Florence just after the Second World War, he vowed that one day he would start a business which would bring the delights of this Italian version of fast food to the UK. Later, back in London, he realised that for pizza to be worth its name, it would have to taste like the pizza he had enjoyed in its homeland. For that, he needed a special oven which could reach the necessary high temperatures. So he imported one, together with a cook to operate it and, having bought the site of Mario Zampi's La Romanella-Pizza Express in Wardour Street, his first Pizza Express opened in 1966. After a slow start, during which Boizot had to give away slices to persuade passers-by to try a first taste, business grew. So he opened a second, designed by Apicella, in Coptic Street, opposite the British Museum. His simple stroke of genius was the importation of the oven, which ensured enough heat to achieve the correct light, crisp base, and as a result, a network of branches spread across London and throughout the country over the next thirty years, initially on a franchise system, then returning to central ownership. Determined that an inexpensive meal should not mean unattractive surroundings, Boizot later engaged Apicella to redesign the entire organisation and as the chain developed into a real brand, more than eighty Pizza Express outlets eventually received his treatment.

Alvaro Maccioni soon jumped onto Boizot's bandwagon. Three years after opening the Aretusa, he and his partners sold the Alvaro together with the Aretusa Club to a mass catering concern whose directors had decided to move into the pizza market and needed a figurehead. Taking advantage of the new craze, Alvaro and the Golden Egg Group opened a chain called Alvaro's Pizza e Pasta, starting in style with a huge restaurant in the Haymarket. A similar frenzy had occurred in New York several years before, and the pundit Egon Ronay noticed that something was afoot. "The Pizza craze has hit London," he said in his *Evening News* column in 1971, "and London's catering scene will never be the same again."

> In the sixties we were saturated by trattorie and now, the Italian invasion had spread even to the Park Lane Hotel world. Last week I reported on the first Italian incursion into smart West End clubs and the other end of the scale, mass catering, is now due to be Italianised too.

Alvaro Maccioni's first Pizza e Pasta was, at the very least, daring. The Haymarket site was expensive and vast; but, backed by Golden Egg, he was able to open eighteen outlets in the next two years.

Unsurprisingly, the man who had coddled royalty, of both blue-blood and Rock 'n' Roll varieties, was temperamentally not suited to bringing pizza to the masses. If anyone could get in to Alvaro's, where in the Pizza e Pasta chain was his cachet?

Mass catering was not Alvaro's forte.

*Peter Boizot, pizza and jazz enthusiast and occasional Liberal candidate, outside the Coptic Street Pizza Express.*

## MAYHEM AT MERIDIANA

Soon after the sale of his Medusa restaurant to the Indian, Pasquale Lunghi got a call from Walter Mariti and within a week found himself the new manager of the Meridiana on the Fulham Road. It was a massive challenge, for the restaurant was huge, on three floors, with more than 130 seats and forty staff. Both Meridiana and Factotum, the restaurants created by the Mariti and Apicella partnership, were now successful – with elegant designs, above average food, competent and well-trained staff and, often, great fun.

With two of his own restaurants up and running, Apicella the artist was less than happy in his new role as a business man. Temperamentally unsuited to routine and business detail, his relationship with Mariti began to sour. Enzo wasn't the type to sustain an everyday business relationship, and, by this time, Walter was a highly experienced professional.

Gradually, the staff's loyalty split between the two bosses – the witty, irrepressible, passionate, creative artist and the professional restaurant businessman. Apicella and Mariti's feud became one of the longest-running gossip stories in the London media. Although usually full, Mariti's restaurants would never have become so fashionable and successful over so many years if Apicella had not been involved at the beginning. But without Walter's skill they wouldn't have prospered. Apicella did, though, rather over-rate his contribution to management. Sometimes he needed to be reminded that there were other elements in a restaurant's success beyond his design and ideas.

Mario and Franco had always been wholly aware of what he had done for them and how complementary his role had been to theirs; they saw him quite objectively. "People are always telling us what a great debt we owe to Enzo, for the way he designed our restaurants and the way he introduced so many ideas and customers," Franco Lagattolla recalled. "But, also, they forget that Enzo owed a lot to us too. We couldn't have got where we are without him, nor he without us. It works both ways."

When Pasquale Lunghi started at Meridiana, he soon found that almost every member of the Meridiana's large staff was either in Enzo Apicella's camp or in Walter Mariti's, and the two sides quarrelled. He immediately fired the ringleader mischief-makers.

"Walter treated Enzo like a brother," one former Meridiana waiter told me. "Walter put in all the money and Enzo designed it. But Enzo owned 50%, even though he hadn't put in any investment." As another insider put it:

> Enzo was not really interested in the details of the business. In fact, Enzo was not normally interested in any details at all. But when he decided he did want to know what was going on, he found he couldn't understand the accounts, which quite naturally infuriated him and it also infuriated Walter since it meant he had to spend time trying to explain everything over and over again.

Yet another long-time employee explained how the relationship fell apart.

> Enzo was always very generous to his friends, but he took liberties with his partner. He used to come to the restaurant with a big entourage, on a big table and they were all eating without paying. He was always the one to foot the bill, because he was that sort of a man; they were in his restaurant, he would take the bill.

To begin with, when Apicella was bringing in new customers and Walter was there taking their orders, all was well, but:

> after a while it became too much and Walter didn't like it. They would fight, they'd start arguing and shouting across the room at each other in front of a restaurant full of people.
>
> I think it was more Walter being annoyed with Enzo. Enzo wasn't the type to get annoyed about anything. He wouldn't give a damn as long as he could come in there and have his lunch and his dinner and change the car every two years. He got the house in Chelsea and the firm used to pay his mortgage. As long as he had a few pounds in his pocket and a credit card, he wasn't bothered about anything.

There was nothing in those aspects of Enzo's character that Mario and Franco could not have told Mariti years before. Of course, Walter was more than aware of Enzo's talents and connections. Latterly, he realised that while Enzo's design and his contacts would prove valuable, Enzo the flâneur would be more suited to free lunches rather than doing his share of the hard graft of running a restaurant.

At one point, between them, Apicella and Mariti ran three restaurants, Pontevecchio, Meridiana and Factotum – from a single office. One business was Walter's alone, while the other two were partnerships. How would the butcher or the dry goods suppliers split up their invoices? This, former staff believe, was what led to the rows. There were violently opposed factions and because so many journalists, such as Paul Callan of the *Evening Standard*, were regular customers, the bickering was exposed in gossip columns.

Not before time, the pair decided to break up and they put the restaurant on the market for £900,000. Although the Queen's cousin, the photographer Patrick Lichfield, made a speculative bid, there were no other takers. So Enzo committed himself to buying Walter out for £500,000 (not a bad deal for half the business). Having originally acquired the site on a nineteen-year lease, they had subsequently bought the freehold, which meant that the property alone was immediately worth £450,000. Apicella raised a bank loan to cover the cost of the buyout.

"The feuding partnership between restaurateurs Walter Mariti and Enzo Apicella is finished," the *Evening Standard* informed the Meridiana's customers.

In order to repay the loan, Enzo again relied on his creative genius. He launched a co-operative scheme, inviting customers to buy a share in the restaurant. He offered 1,100 £500 shares and the further temptation of a beautiful share certificate which he personally designed. This, he insisted, would be a valuable work of art, particularly because each customer would be allowed to buy only one example. Sadly there were very few takers. However, as always when he applied himself, he eventually found professional backers.

"Italian friends are putting up the money," he finally announced. The place, he promised, would stay exactly the same and no one would be sacked. Apicella's new partner, Roberto Bassanini, was an experienced Italian hotelier. Even so, three years later, still struggling financially, Apicella gave up the ghost and Meridiana's freehold was sold for £800,000.

Walter Mariti bought Otello Scipioni's Girasole with some of his capital. It was opposite the Queen's Elm pub about four hundred yards away from Meridiana; he reopened as Ponte Nuovo in 1984, with Pasquale Lunghi as his partner-manager. He also bought a new BMW and a yacht berthed in the south of France, so although my wife and I and our friends started going to Ponte Nuovo most weekends for Saturday lunch, we rarely saw him. Yet again, Pasquale was a superlative manager. (When I reminded him that this was the fifth restaurant he had worked in where I'd been a regular customer, we began one of the conversations which led to this book twenty years later.)

"Enzo and I were more than friends," Walter said later. "Enzo was a genius, but he is an artist and it was not a sensible idea for him to become involved in the business side. He would have wanted to pay all the staff at least three times more than we could afford. It was wonderful when he did good public relations and I did the business."

Apicella, however, has less fond memories of his former partner. He refused to attend the Terry O'Neill "Pasta Pioneers" photo shoot if Walter was to be invited. "The problem with restaurants today is that they are all opened by ex-chefs or ex-waiters," he complained in a magazine interview not long after the sale of the business.

"What did he expect?" Mariti pondered when he read the article. "Pharmacists?"

*Apicella lectures the author on correct Italian dress, at the Meridiana, 1979.*

## THE BEGINNING OF THE END

In the spring of 1973, Mario and Franco's overall business was doing well. "Mario and Franco Restaurants," said the *Evening Standard* in March 1973, "today reports half-year profits of £118,585 against £99,069 last time. Underlying the improvement was a 29% increase in turnover to £956,639. The interim dividend stays put at 20%. Chairman Mr David Napley says he is well satisfied with progress at the new restaurant opened in November."

But after the two failed initiatives – Les Trois Amis and King Bomba – and La Terrazza Bristol also losing money – all was clearly not well between the two partners.

In the days when Mario and Franco were building their empire, their different personalities complemented each other perfectly. But now, these same characteristics seemed to push them apart. Mario wanted to continue to expand, whereas Franco, less adventurous, insisted that everything had to be perfect before they could dive into new projects. Growth for Mario meant more income, more to pass on to his children. But Franco believed that without firm foundations, growth would put more and more pressure on their ability to deliver quality and consistency – and as always, he felt responsible for quality. He also felt that, increasingly, he was overshadowed by Mario. Instead of their former equal prominence, Mario was always the one who was quoted in the press and seen as the external face of the business – Mario, rather than the two of them, had been invited to judge a National Restaurant Planning Competition award. "There was an article in the paper about them and they spelt Franco's name wrong. Franco was furious. He went berserk," remembers a close colleague.

After one occasion when Mario fought vociferously with his partner, they didn't speak to each other for several weeks. This was the Rome restaurant debacle.

As those who have never emigrated can only imagine, there is nothing an émigré loves more than to be a hero in his home country and, in Mario's case, he wanted to be a hero in its capital, Rome. For a while, this was on the cards. During a visit in 1973, the partners were offered a prime site in a fashionable area and, dreaming of how he and Franco would make their triumphant entry to the eternal city with Mario and Franco's Terrazza Romana, Mario shook hands on a deal. Where Mario came from, a handshake signified a deal.

However, back in London, having discussed the initiative with Sara, Franco changed his mind. He decided he wanted absolutely nothing to do with it. Sara was troubled by the amount of travel and absence that would be involved. Franco refused to get on the plane to go back to Rome and complete the deal. Nothing Mario could say would convince him. This episode became to both of them more than just a deal that fell through – Mario's honour was now at stake. His reputation in his home country would be as nothing if it became known that he had shaken hands on a deal and then reneged on it. He never forgave Franco for forcing him to break his word. This alone, though, doesn't explain why, six years later, Franco so much hated the mention of Mario's name that he vetoed any mention of his erstwhile partner in his memoir and cookbook, *The Recipes That Made a Million.*

## ALMOST THE END

Five years after Mario and Franco had gone public, it was rumoured that there was a bidder keen to acquire the majority of the company's shares and, after a week of media speculation, it emerged that Spillers, the giant petfoods company, was the contender.

It has always been assumed that this bid initiated in the boardroom of Spillers, that the board members decided on expansion and that they and their advisers selected Mario and Franco Restaurants Ltd as a prime target. But in fact, this was far from the truth. Mario and Franco had realised that, as their personal relationship had broken down, their business partnership had gone as far as it possibly could. They met with David Napley, their chairman and, together with the increasingly successful and prominent lawyer, agreed that he would seek a buyer for the business.

The decision that Mario and Franco had reluctantly arrived at was a million miles from what they'd imagined when they had decided to become a public company. "I always dreamt that one day my sons would take over the business," Mario recalls. This was truly the end of a dream.

The Spillers group was one of David Napley's corporate clients and its directors were interested in broadening their business base and, too, in the cachet which Mario and Franco's names would bring. So, with the consent of both partners, as well as that of the other shareholders, the Spillers acquisition went through. And as soon as the company's individual restaurants became units of a huge group, everything started to go wrong.

The Spillers board in general had little experience of catering and one director, Harry Colbourne, a former artillery officer who evidently had none, became responsible for its new subsidiary. For the first time since they'd left the Mirabelle, the duo had to report to a boss. "Colbourne was stiff, military, and formal," says former Terrazza Leeds manager, Pino Cecere, "as unlike Mario and Franco as anyone could possibly be." Not unnaturally, they lost their passion for the business to which they had devoted a crucial part of their lives. Staff and customers, from then on, rarely saw them in the restaurants.

Spillers appointed a Swiss general manager to run the group on a day to day basis and for Mario Vollono, who'd continued as the manager of La Terrazza, life became harder. Previously, Mario and Franco were always available, but after the new boss took over, they put in fewer and fewer appearances and the sort of decisions that they'd made together with him, were left entirely in his hands.

"Mario would call me on the phone," remembers Vollono, and ask 'Mario, everything alright?' And before I could answer, he'd say, 'OK, see you tomorrow.' And tomorrow would be the same story."

Mario Cassandro soon clashed with his new parent company. Spillers managers lacked his magic touch with customers and expected accountants to run what, in his mind, remained his restaurants. Colbourne – who the staff referred to as Harry the Horse – had been given the task of finding new responsibilities for Mario and Franco. Months passed and he had still not decided who would do what. This disturbed Franco deeply and was driving Mario mad. One day Mario invited Colbourne to lunch at La Terrazza and, as they ate, he grew more and more agitated.

Eventually, in front of all the usual lunchtime regulars, Mario lost it completely.

"Why can't you make a fucking decision?" he shouted at the top of his voice, grabbing the unfortunate Colbourne by his tie. "Make a fucking decision or I'll fucking well fucking strangle you!" Silence ensued. Clearly, Mario didn't understand his new bosses, and the feeling was mutual.

At a meeting convened to discuss the struggling Bristol Terrazza, there were about fifteen Spillers executives sitting round the table. Mario suggested that, since the restaurant was losing money and so many directors seemed to be going round and spending shareholders' money lunching on expenses wherever and whenever, surely they should spend it in the group's own restaurants? He proposed that the chairman should tell them that, as of tomorrow, all Spillers executives had to conduct their business lunches in the group's restaurants. "Stop them racking up expenses in other people's places," he urged.

"Oh yes. Excellent idea. Thank you, Mr Cassandro," replied the conference's chairman. "I will write and tell them tomorrow."

"Write? Tomorrow?" Mario swelled, even more furious. "Forget about the letter writing. Don't hide behind letters. Lift the phone. Get onto them. Tell them straight away. Now!"

Silence followed. This sort of behaviour was unheard of in the City of London. Very soon afterwards, Mario was banned by Spillers from going anywhere near La Terrazza. In spite of the directors' business lunches and the manager Giulio Nobile's efforts, La Terrazza Bristol was never in profit and the recession didn't help. It closed in 1974.

## THE END

In mid-1974, it emerged in the press that Mario and Franco were no longer speaking to each other. The break-up of their relationship had been a long, gradual process, which Mario will still not talk about – even thirty-five years later. But it seems clear that what had initially bound them together and made them successful had finally led to their separation.

"These two eminently civilised men who for so long enjoyed such mutual regard cannot now bring themselves to talk to each other," informed the London *Evening Standard*. For their friends and long-time customers, who realised how dependent each was on the other and how much we had come to depend on them, it was a matter of much sadness. It almost felt like bereavement.

"I'm sure I couldn't have built up the organisation without Franco," Mario told the *Evening Standard* reporter. "And I don't think he could have without me."

The fact that, once again, it was Mario rather than his partner who was quoted in the newspapers, added to their alienation. Mario was right that neither of them could have done it without the other, nor without Apicella, but the manner in which this was expressed was, for Franco, the final straw.

Having to report to a new boss had exacerbated the tension between Mario and Franco. Mario, hating the corporate environment, soon contrived to create so much mayhem that the Spillers board was forced to fire him. He accepted a compensation payment of £85,000 and left for Rome, so avoiding the, by now, exorbitantly punitive UK tax regime.

After Mario's departure, Franco was made managing director of the group, reporting directly to Harry Colbourne, with Luigi Paglierani continuing as administrative director. But soon Franco, too, found he disliked corporate life as much as Mario had and still only forty-three years old, he decided to retire. However, when he gave in his notice, he was offered no compensation and, understandably, felt even more resentful. Mario's behaviour had led to his being able to clean up, while he, having done the honourable thing, came away with nothing.

For the next six years, with his investments providing a healthy income, Mario lived in Italy in the manner of many of his former customers and clients. He went where impulse took him and he had sufficient funds to enable his son Piero, who had stayed on in London, to develop their ceramic tile company Domus, which had grown into a market leader. Symptomatic of Mario's lifestyle is the following anecdote: one summer in the late seventies, he was invited by an aristocratic Italian family to join them for a week on their yacht on the Sardinian Costa Smeralda. After the cruise, having driven from the port to the airport, his host asked if he could give Mario a lift back to Milan in his private plane.

"That would be *molto gentile*, so very kind," said Mario, "But I'm catching a plane down to see my brother in Napoli. Drop me at the terminal."

"No, no," said his host's wife. "We've got our own plane waiting; we'll drop you off in Napoli."

As they circled above Naples, before turning onto the final approach, Mario, sitting next to his host with a glass of champagne in his hand, gazing down at his home town through the Gulfstream's window, remembered his determined younger self who had left Naples broke, in 1947, in search of his fortune. Now, coming home in a private jet, he found himself whispering under his breath to his long-dead mother, "If only you could see me now..."

After six years, Mario realised that he felt more of a foreigner in Naples and Rome than he had in London. So he decided to return to Britain and in 1985, he reappeared on the London restaurant scene, to open Mario Restaurant in the Brompton Road which, with its chic glass frontage and pavement seating, was reasonably successful. But eventually, seventy-one years old, even Mario had finally to concede that it was time to call it a day.

"When I realised I couldn't hear well enough to take the orders any more, it was time to go," he says. In 1991, he sold Mario Restaurant to Sandro Tobi, one of his former Terrazza waiters, who by this time had an empire of his own.

Franco left the Spillers group a few months after Mario. Free at last to do what he pleased, he vacillated between writing and travelling. First, though, he had an appointment with his accountant, who advised him to leave the UK for a couple of years. Italy wasn't an option. Even though he treasured and respected his parents' love for their native south, he never really felt at home there and he worried that in Italy he, like Mario, would be regarded as a foreigner. He tried Ireland for a few months, then changed his mind and, still undecided, bought a small flat in Le Touquet – Sara and the children stayed on in London and commuted to see him.

Their treasured family life was fragmented for the next three years, but the wealth which the share sale had brought him enabled Franco's boys to grow up in a secure environment – an entirely different milieu to that of his childhood. They both settled into Dulwich College prep school and Franco planned that they would go on to join its senior school.

But after three years in Le Touquet, he decided on Italy after all; not his home patch, but the more sophisticated north. Franco and Sara found a villa on a hill above Lake Como and the family moved there. Franco, always a fan of the American way, entered Nicholas and Fabio as boarders at the TASIS American School in Lugano, just across the border and a year later, moved them to the American School in Milan, where they both thrived. With the boys in boarding school, Sara and Franco travelled extensively and Franco took advantage of his fame as a restaurateur to make new friends all over the world – in New York, on the US West Coast, in Paris, Geneva and many exotic places. On his travels, he collected new recipes and began to plan his first book.

Keen that the boys should both complete their education in the United States and still restless, Franco planned to move full time to America. He set up a company on the West Coast as a vehicle for any opportunities which might present themselves. He busied himself with visa applications, only to learn that the US authorities had declared a moratorium on all new applications from Italy.

So after three peripatetic years, Franco decided on another change. Sara and the boys would be based in London, while Franco, still following his accountant's advice, would remain outside the UK. His family would commute at weekends, holidays and festivals. He bought an apartment in La Napoule, in Provence near Nice and back in London, Sara and the boys lived in a Georgian house on a private road in a smart corner of Dulwich.

Most days, Franco sat on his terrace in La Napoule, working on a memoir which he had begun in the mid-sixties. In 1978, *The Recipes That Made a Million*, with cartoon illustrations by Enzo Apicella, appeared. Its publisher had fond memories of meals at La Trattoria Terrazza. However, little of Franco's original memoir accompanied his recipes from the restaurants. It was, in the end, impossible for his publishers to present the book as a celebration of Mario and Franco's achievements. Although Franco's first draft, started years before, contained many references to their early days together, in the end he insisted that his final text exclude any reference to his former partner.

Perhaps this was his revenge for the many times when the media had quoted his partner, ignoring him. When his son Fabio showed me a box full of his father's memorabilia, there were no photographs of Mario and Franco together. Franco had cut Mario's face out of every picture which featured them both.

Franco began a novel about life in the restaurant business, but his new career faltered. For many years he had been suffering from nagging gastric pains and, in 1980, he was rushed into hospital in Cannes with acute pancreatitis. It was expected that he would recover, and after three weeks in intensive care, he was transferred to the main Nice hospital for a series of operations. During the third and last, he died. He was still only fifty-three years old.

Their differences instantly forgotten, Mario rushed to Nice to comfort Sara, and his two godsons, Nicholas and Fabio. A week later Franco was buried at La Napoule, in Provence, or, as he'd always insisted on calling it, the former Italian province of La Provence.

At Franco's funeral, Enzo Apicella and Mario stood together. As Franco had once said, Mario and Franco couldn't have done it without Enzo and Enzo couldn't have done it without them. But even more certainly, neither Mario nor Enzo could have done it without Franco. Mario was without doubt the heart of La Terrazza and Enzo the Michelangelo who had painted its ceiling. But Franco, with his dedication to detail and perfection in the kitchen, in front of house, on the door, in the service – was the *soul* of the business and of the Trattoria Revolution.

*Sara Lagattolla's favourite portrait of her husband*

*Mario Cassandro and some of the surviving Pasta Pioneers, photographed at San Lorenzo, Beauchamp Place, April 2006. (Back row, left to right) Valerio Calzolari (of Scalini), Antonio Trapani (Montpeliano), Antonio Carluccio (Neal Street Restaurant), Mimmo Mattera (Mimmo d'Ischia), Dante Betti (Beccofino),*

*Mario Paggetti (Scalini), Mario Vollono (La Terrazza), Franco Buonaguidi (San Frediano), Peppino Taboro (Alvaro's, Mr Chow and La Finezza), Pasquale Lunghi (Trattoo and Meridiana). (Front row) Lorenzo and Mara Berni (San Lorenzo), Mario Cassandro, Alvaro Maccioni (La Famiglia), Enzo Apicella (Meridiana). Photo: Terry O'Neill.*

## POST SCRIPT: 1980–2009

### Continuation of the old

Franco Lagattolla's early death did not signal the demise of Mario and Franco's business empire, but it did coincide with the end of its role as a fashionable innovator. Under its new owners, the company expanded during the late seventies with the addition of City Tiberio in Lime Street, the Villa Augusta in Queen Victoria Street, and Claudius in Sloane Avenue. But Spillers was taken over by the Dalgety Group in 1979, and eventually it sold all of the restaurants to Kennedy Brookes – part of the giant Forte conglomerate.

Although, at the time of La Terrazza's twenty-first birthday in 1981, Egon Ronay was still recommending all the original Mario and Franco establishments, a few years later they had been dropped from most guides. The nadir came when Kennedy Brookes announced, in 1991, that it would relaunch some of their twenty-one Mario and Franco restaurants as pasta and pizza outlets. The company's marketing head optimistically averred that its "new" concept would "go into the more cheerful, lower price, faster service market." The first to be rebranded with the "new" name of "Mario & Franco Pasta/Pizza" would be Don Luigi. It was to be followed by La Terrazza in Soho.

But Mario and Franco's family tree had continued to spread its branches, especially where talented restaurateurs were personally in charge of their own businesses. Several stalwarts, who had trained under the eagle eye of Franco Lagattolla, continued to maintain his standards through to the 1990s – some of them continue today.

Dante Betti's Beccofino in Draycott Avenue became the haunt of the motor racing fraternity; Mimmo d'Ischia was a home-from-home for the showbusiness residents of Belgravia; other pioneers, such as San Lorenzo, San Frediano and Pontevecchio, continued to serve variations of the original Terrazza menus.

"All the other restaurateurs look up to me," Mimmo Mattera told me in his Belgravia trattoria in 2006. He had been notorious for his huge medallion on a gold chain, exposing his hairy chest, shirt open to the waist. Today, in his late sixties, he is an establishment figure in a suit, still a well-built, good-looking man with a big smile – a large personality with a great deal of stamina. Night after night, his restaurant provided the setting for his performance and after forty years, Mimmo was appointed Cavaliere del Lavoro della Repubblica Italiana for his services to Italian gastronomy. He still remembers all his customers' names, especially those from his early days. When my brother and I went to Mimmo's in 1996 (we hadn't eaten there since the early seventies), he appeared at once to greet us smilingly, "Ecco... Mr Sutherland... and Mr Sutherland... *Buongiorno, benvenuto*, long time, *come sta?*" This, you cannot program software to do.

But, where once had been the elegant simplicity of a classic Enzo Apicella trattoria design, every single cranny of the restaurant's walls was covered with photographs of Mimmo, either with small children (whom one must assume are his own babies and then their babies), or with every conceivable showbiz or sporting personality – Julie Andrews is godmother to his son – to the very bottom of the N-list. Recently, I've learnt that he has agreed to sell the business and retire.

Another of the post-Mario and Franco generation of pasta pioneers is Antonio Trapani (easily recognised by his red braces), who has been the stalwart owner of Montpeliano in Montpelier Street for the past thirty-five years. Inspired by Mario and Franco's achievements in the late sixties, Antonio set out to emulate them. Although he was never employed by Mario and Franco, he has spent most of his life under their influence. He was a waiter with Mara and Lorenzo Berni at San Lorenzo for three years, saving as many tips as possible, until, in 1973, he moved to Mr Chow's Montpelier Grill. During the 1974 recession, in partnership with Claudio Pulze and Luigi Regganzani, he bought Montpelier, reopening it in April 1975 with an Italianised name. Eventually he bought out his partners and Montpeliano, now three times its original size, still attracts the Knightsbridge crowd as they tumble excitedly from Bonham's Auctioneers next door, to celebrate popping granny's jewellery. In 1984 he also opened Toto's in Lennox Gardens Mews off Walton Street, and this, too, has a loyal following, especially for Sunday lunch, though devotees of the original casual trattoria style might be confused by its formal, black-suited waiters.

In the Fulham Road, Franco Buonaguidi and Mino Parlanti, freed from the responsibilities of the Aretusa after its sale in 1972, bought the building next door to San Frediano and this popular trat grew from 40 seats to more than 80. Eventually, their empire was to become nearly as large and influential – in terms of introducing new customers to Italian food – as Mario and Franco's. Crucially, though, it remained in private hands. It spread across West London – Santa Croce on Cheyne Walk, San Quintino in Radnor Walk off the King's Road, San Frediano Ovest in Olympia, San Ruffillo in Harriet Street, even the San Domenico Hotel in Surrey. But they, too, overextended themselves and wishing for a quieter life, reduced the business to the original San Frediano, before selling that in the mid-1980s. (While Mino and Sergio both retired to Montecatini Terme, Franco Buonaguidi continued with his career, opening Vin Santo, another Tuscan trattoria, in Hollywood Road.)

Gino Santin, originally from Venice, worked as a Terrazza waiter, studying methods and menus, before starting Gino's in Ealing in 1971. Thirteen years later he opened Santini, a glossy upmarket restaurant in Ebury Street, catering for the most part to corporate clients and later he launched the equally successful L'Incontro (now Mauro for Santini) in Pimlico Road.

Alvaro Maccioni, after selling his business to the Golden Egg chain, soon found that he was not happy as a corporate Pizza e Pasta man. He withdrew from Golden Egg. In 1973 he went back to live near Florence, only to find, like so many returning restaurateurs, that he was regarded as a foreigner – an *Inglese*. He returned to London and set about creating a new Alvaro empire, opening first I Paparazzi in Soho and then, in 1975, La Famiglia in Langton Street, Chelsea, and La Nassa on the King's Road a few years later. (His first manager at La Nassa, Roberto Colussi, now runs Ziani's in Radnor Walk, while Franco Epifano and Juan Correia, two of his waiters at La Famiglia, have their own place, Numero Uno, in Northcote Road, in Clapham.)

Sandro Tobi and Mario Paggetti's empire encompassed Sale e Pepe, Sambuca and Signor Sassi. Like Mario and Franco, Paggetti and Tobi enjoyed a successful partnership based on the difference in their characters. "Sandro had all the business grounding and handled all the deals," his widow Wendy Tobi recalls, "while Mario, always very charming and efficient, managed front of house." Later, their ambitions differing, they separated. But because each partner had his own favourite among their restaurants, the split was as amicable as these things can be. While Tobi retained Sale e Pepe and Sambuca, Paggetti continued with Signor Sassi and brought in another former Terrazza alumnus, Valerio Calzolari, as his partner and opened Scalini in Walton Street. When Sandro bought Mario Cassandro's Mario Restaurant, its name was changed to Sandrini and it remained a success until Wendy sold it following Sandro's death in 2000.

In 1990, San Lorenzo expanded into the next door building, and remains choc-a-bloc full, in spite of some indifferent reviews. Usually negative notices were written by journalists who felt slighted that Mara or Lorenzo had ignored them. (It must be hard to maintain an exact level of friendliness and greeting to every customer after four decades.)

They have never taken credit cards, and this is not because of the commission charges. "The man from Diners Club came around at the beginning, to arrange for us to take their card," Mara says. "But he took one look at the restaurant and said, 'I'm sorry, you're too small.'" Since then, Mara, defiant, has always stuck to her principles.

> They have all been in here to try and persuade us to take credit cards, but we did fine without them and I don't see why we should allow them to treat us like that. Everybody starts out small.

**Taruschio's Tree of Plenty**

If walls could speak, those of the Walnut Tree Inn at Llandewi Skirrid near Abergavenny could tell the story of the Italian invasion of British food culture better than I can. The Walnut Tree is the legendary pub-restaurant which has enjoyed consistent popularity from its inception in a village in South Wales in 1963, to the retirement of the owners in 2001. "There is only one Italian chef in Britain," reported Christopher Driver in *The British at Table*, "whose style is as various, imaginative and self-critical as the cooking described in Elizabeth David's *Italian Food*."

Of all the accolades they've won during their forty years reign, the one Franco and Ann Taruschio mention most often and most proudly is that Elizabeth David once said that theirs was her favourite restaurant in the whole of Britain. By the time they retired, they had won many awards, and been featured in the *Good Food Guide* every year since their first appearance in 1965.

When Franco and Ann first took over the Walnut Tree pub, they really did have to assure habitués that spaghetti didn't grow on trees. Deep in the Welsh countryside where, as Ann understates, Elizabeth David's *Italian Food* had made little impact, they had to educate their customers about what they were eating. To begin with, locals thought the food that Franco cooked was, to say the least, extremely odd; they would mutter into their pints whenever they smelt garlic. When, as they grew bolder, Franco and Ann first offered dishes such as lasagne and cannelloni, only a few customers, who had visited Italy and had tasted them before, were prepared to eat them; the dishes had to be described in great detail before any local person would try them.

At first, their menu was half Italian and half French, but influenced by Taruschio's heritage (he had grown up in Le Marche), the Italian flavour grew. One brave customer, during the Walnut Tree's early years, ordered minestrone, followed by lasagne, followed by cannelloni; he believed Italians only ate pasta. The same man became a regular and having continued to eat there, tasted all Franco Taruschio's range of Italian-influenced dishes and saw the menu evolve from basic pasta, through regional Italian dishes, into an eclectic mix of what must now be described as Italian-influenced British food. He is probably the archetypical participant of the entire 1960s–1990s metamorphosis of British cooking.

Diners-out in South Wales learnt how to recognise good food as they tasted it; and they were prepared to queue for it, then pay for it. On the evening of the day the Taruschios retired, Ann and Franco escorted the new Walnut Tree owners to the front door as evening opening grew near. Their successors were astonished to see a queue which already stretched out from the front door across to the far side of the car park.

The Taruschios then explained that, having spent all day on the *mise en place*, they'd go on to handle the first sitting at seven, the second at eight-thirty and a third after ten o'clock.

"How *can* you cope with that?" was the not unexpected response.

**Time for Something New**

Standards were seldom so high in myriad copies of the Mario and Franco formula. Sloppy cooking and unhelpful service had become common – even in La Terrazza itself. My wife Felicity was lunching there in 1982 when she found a used toothpick in her spinach. It was clear that she was about to eat someone else's recycled leftovers. When she called the waiter to question him, he glared at her and walked away. Arrogance, complacency and disdain had crept into the revolution, and it was clear to me that the opportunities for enterprising young Italians to follow Mario and Franco and begin yet another pink-tableclothed, tile-floored trat anywhere in Britain, proffering *Petto di Pollo Sorpresa*, then succeeding without really trying, had well and truly ended. Something new had to come along.

That something new, as it turned out, was a broadening of the style of Italian restaurants, as well as the arrival of new available ingredients, both of which led to wider choice, therefore much stronger competition in terms of quality and value. Today, food from almost every region of Italy at every level of sophistication is available in Britain. As the Thatcher years brought increasing prosperity and made the discovery of Italian cooking more and more affordable for more and more Britons, Italy was increasingly becoming the focus of restaurant and food development in the UK.

In the space of a few years, Italianate influences transformed Italian food in Britain all over again and greatly increased its spread from the trattoria environment to homes and high streets all over the country.

Several, not immediately perceptible, influences were at the forefront of the changes. Antonio Carluccio's flight back to quality at the Neal Street restaurant, plus his popular television shows; Alastair Little's creation of "Modern British"; the River Café's Tuscan "home cooking"; the gradual divergence of British Italian restaurants into new and traditional, especially the lighter "modern" cooking of Gennaro Contaldo at Passione, Nino Sassu at Assaggi, and the "Chef," Giorgio Locatelli.

**The New Wave: Carluccio's Britalian Crab Parcels**

The first noticeable new development happened in 1981 when Antonio Carluccio took over as manager at the Neal Street Restaurant in Covent Garden. His changes in its menu and style advanced the growing authenticity of Italian food in Britain.

It wasn't Carluccio's ambition to be a chef. He began his career in the wine trade, first based in Germany. He didn't arrive in London until 1975. "I came to England for private reasons," he told me, "but the reason was too late. She had married someone else." Instead, he met and married Priscilla Conran and through her brother, Terence, he became a restaurateur.

After six years selling wine to trattorie – like Alvaro's La Famiglia, Meridiana, Pontevecchio and San Frediano – he felt confident enough to cook publicly in the 1981 *Sunday Times* amateur cookery competition. His success (he came second) prompted Terence Conran to ask his sister if she thought her husband might be competent to run a restaurant.

Although Antonio, as a wine salesman, knew the downside of a restaurateur's life, Conran persuaded him to have a go. He insisted, though, that he'd be useless at admin or finance. He made it clear that he would concentrate on style, menu and on being the front man.

The Neal Street restaurant is often regarded as the first of a new wave. When Conran launched it in 1971, it featured a modern un-trattoria design – white brick walls and tiled floors, yes; but nothing rustic. There were David Hockney pictures, mirrors and Bauhaus cane chairs. Egon Ronay called it an "elegantly simple modern restaurant" and, no doubt because of the Conran influence, it helped to create a style which has since become "Classic Modern British." (Loyd Grossman described Neal Street as "the precursor of the hip eclectic restaurant now so beloved by young British chefs." It was, he said, "very beautiful, if ever so slightly bloodless.")

The publicity which surrounded the 1981 *Sunday Times* Cookery Competition led to an offer for a series of television cookery programmes. He took immediately to the medium, and, within a few years, our friendly lunchtime restaurant host appeared every week on our screens at home. A plethora of cookery books ensued, followed by the chain of café-delicatessens which spread Antonio Carluccio's name across the country.

Carluccio agrees that Mario and Franco were the first Italians in Britain who enabled his countrymen to be proud of their country's cuisine. But he

*Maestros and old friends together at La Famiglia, April 2006. When Antonio Carluccio first arrived in the UK, he worked in the wine trade, and Alvaro and many of the other trattorie were his customers.* *Photo: Edward Lloyd*

feels that many Italian restaurateurs of their generation "got away with murder." Britons had little idea of how Italian food should really taste. Trattoria owners should, he believes, have made much more effort to present authentic dishes.

"When I arrived here, the love affair with Italian food was still in embryo. It was still trattorie and a very few restaurants," he says. "Italian food here was very much 'Britalian' food."

"Britalian," a phrase Carluccio probably invented, is one of his favourite subjects. Although he uses it in a slightly derogatory way, it could also be taken to mean an essential distillation of all that is excellent about the Italian attitude to food – of which Antonio is a prime representative. He fits my theory that if you put an Italian cook down on a desert island, he will immediately seek out the best ingredients and create delicious dishes with them; if you did the same thing to a classically trained French chef, he would probably wait until he'd found the correct ingredients to produce a correct recipe. Meanwhile, you'd starve.

Franco Lagattolla's *pollo sorpresa* is, for Carluccio, a prime example of an Italian chef producing food for the British in Britain – in Italy, it wouldn't have needed to be invented. But, in spite of his insisting on maintaining the purity of Italian cuisine, especially when it comes to non-Italians cooking it, Carluccio has actually been one of Britalian's great innovators. In his first book, *An Introduction to Italian Cooking* (1985) he gave the recipe for one of Neal Street Restaurant's favourite dishes, Crab Parcels, a ravioli he had invented using fresh crab from Cornwall. When we met at the Fulham Road Carluccio's, I encountered some other Britalian adaptations. The menu offers scrambled eggs with grilled pancetta on toasted ciabatta, or even better, there's a Great British Fry-up – except at Carluccio's it's known as *Colazione Magnifica* – eggs, grilled pancetta, sautéed mushrooms, tomato and toasted ciabatta. With a cappuccino and a fruit juice, it'll cost you just £7.95.

"You try to get the best egg with lovely yolks, the freshest mushrooms and herbs and then the pancetta must be nice and the bread has to be fresh ciabatta, lightly toasted," Antonio said. "The combination is very natural. But the Italians would never have a fry-up. So it's really Britalian."

The great comic Tommy Cooper once observed that most people in China didn't know they were eating Chinese food. For them, of course, it is just food. And now that's true here. We're eating ciabatta and pancetta and pasta and pizza and for us, too, it's just food.

**Saltimbocca of Monkfish; Alastair with a "t"**

When Alastair Little opened his eponymous restaurant in Frith Street, Soho, in 1985, his style of cooking placed him at the forefront of a new wave of Italian-influenced British chefs. Maybe, though, it was me who was responsible for the birth of Modern British Cooking. In *Soho Cooking*, part cookbook and part autobiography, Alastair Little tells how he got started:

> **In 1975, my cooking career was launched at the Old Compton Wine Bar. The chef left and I volunteered to have a go. The very next day, I was cooking eighty lunches armed with a copy of Elizabeth David's *French Provincial Cooking* and a self-confidence that can only be viewed as foolhardy.**

Alasdair (with a "d") was the chef who left. After six years in partnership with my brother Robin, and after opening three restaurants together, the recession had bitten, I had had just about enough of working from 8.30 a.m. to 2.00 a.m., so decided to go back to the public relations agency business, and Alastair (with a "t") took my place.

Within a few years Alastair became, as it was said on the BBC, the "Godfather of Modern British Cooking." The *Good Food Guide* for 1990 awarded four or more marks to fourteen restaurants in London, but only one of them offered Italian or Italian-influenced cooking. This was my successor's own business, Alastair Little in Frith Street.

"For many, this is the best most pleasant eating house in London," wrote Tom Jaine, editor of the 1990 *Guide*. Alastair's food was

> high on flavour, high on thought and inspiration, witty and wide ranging. Were a real enthusiast with a sense of the multivalence of various cooking traditions to devote a long weekend to the elaboration of a good meal, the food as you find it at Little's would be the result.

Two English chefs, Alastair Little and Marco Pierre White, epitomised the renaissance of British cooking in the 1980s. Marco Pierre's influences were all French, but, once he got going, Alastair's were Italian.

Having started with Elizabeth David in one hand and a wooden spoon in the other, Little's attention was first drawn to the possibilities of Italian peasant cooking by Marcella Hazan's celebrated *Classic Italian Cookbook*, and, as he continued his love affair with the colour and simplicity of Italian food, it was while he was chef at 192 Kensington Park Road that his distinctive, Italian-influenced style began to emerge.

> I started to sneak some Italian main courses on at 192. Simple things, like a big

chunk of roast veal or simple calves' liver dishes which I'd always enjoyed from La Terrazza days. The old *Fegato alla Veneziana* with onions at Bertorelli's was disgusting, but then when we went to Mario and Franco's, they served it with butter and sage, it was soft and tender, just wonderful.

His spell at 192 boosted his career because it gave him time to adapt his cooking and experiment further with his menu; also, many of 192's customers worked in the media, he got to know them and made friends with them, and many of them would help create the extraordinary media hubbub which greeted his eventual opening in Frith Street.

"I wanted to do a restaurant I would like to eat at myself," he said,

so I wanted it to be essentially informal but proper. I wanted to do it the way the Italians do it, to have proper cutlery, proper glasses. The one thing I always liked about Italian food was the way the Italians laid their tables. They made a fuss about it and they did it nicely. It was just right.

If you went into La Terrazza the spotlight was perfectly focused on the rose on the table, but if you went to an English copy, it was way off, pointing at the wall or at

*Alastair Little at his Tavola deli, 2007. "For the first time since I started as a waiter," he says, "I now have an ordinary social life."*

your ear. The Italians just did everything so nicely, so the food could be fairly average, but it all seemed right.

Reviews were instantly ecstatic. "Alastair gets more publicity than Princess Diana," was his fellow restaurateur Simon Slater's comment. Television and radio appearances followed massive exposure in print and all this naturally attracted general attention to his new style of simple, Italian-influenced cooking, which gradually became known as "Modern British."

*Saltimbocca* is usually a veal escalope wrapped in a slice of Parma ham, then sautéed. But in Alastair's adaptation of this classic Italian dish, he used monkfish instead of veal and this became one of his signature dishes. Another of the modern British menu trends which he is credited with starting – or at least adapting – is, as he puts it, "heaping things on toasted bread." He prepared simple Italian antipasti – ciabatta dressed up in a delicious way – as starters. These were enthusiastically embraced by the Soho dining public. In 1990, he charged £9 for borlotti beans and rocket on toasted bruschetta (bread grilled with oil) and *Gremolada* – grated lemon peel, garlic and parsley – a dish redolent of summer lunches outside the kitchen door; this would have been far too unimpressive in a restaurant a few years earlier.

"Food fashions come and go," he says, "and I was a food fashion at the time." But the time was right. Very soon his methods spread across the street, across the city and then across the entire country – "It was rocket with everything. Oil with everything. Everything sun-dried."

Influenced by Alastair, young chef acolytes transformed not only restaurants, but also many pubs, which having been sold off by the chains, metamorphosed into highly popular gastropubs, where the cuisine was often based on Little's original approach to simple Italian food.

**Ruth and Rose Cook the Pasta their Way**

In 1987, Ruth Rogers' husband Richard, the architect of the Pompidou Centre, the Stock Exchange, and numerous other iconic buildings, needed new offices for his practice. The building that they found, on the Thames Hammersmith frontage, already had planning permission for a restaurant. The site was a long way from decent lunchtime venues, so the husband and wife decided to create a canteen for his staff. That canteen has become one of the most celebrated Italian restaurants in

England – although debate continuous as to whether it is, sincerely, Italian.

When The River Café first opened, neither Ruth nor her partner Rose Gray had gained much experience in canteens, let alone the restaurant business. Ruth had entertained at home a great deal, and, she says, had a wonderful cook for a mother-in-law, but other than that, had only her experience of Tuscan cooking, gained from staying in their own and friends' houses there. Rose was trained as a home economist, but her only restaurant experience to date had been six months in the kitchens of a New York night club and a six-week stint at 192 Kensington Park Road.

When Ruth Rogers approached Gray in 1986 to discuss a possible canteen partnership, they found that they shared many of the same culinary views. Together, they adapted recipes and methods which they'd individually discovered in Tuscany, and as soon as they opened to the general public, the restaurant's menu and tastes were reflected in the food columns of magazines and weekend newspapers.

Due to its modern premises, natural and relaxed environment and short, simple menu, people at first compared the River Café's style with that of Alastair Little. Its early menus included *Ribollita Estiva* – a summer soup of chard, canelli beans, celery, carrots, tomatoes and oregano – char-grilled squid with red chilli and rocket, spaghettini with crab and main courses:- char-grilled sea bass, butterflied and marinated lamb with basil, aubergine funghetto and rocket, a bollito misto (mixed boiled meats) and pan-roasted grouse cooked with prosciutto, thyme and dolcetto jam – all of which wouldn't have been out of place on Alastair's menu.

As their success grew, the ingredients they used, mostly simple items to be found easily in Italy, became those that every British cookery enthusiast and restaurant-goer of the 1990s looked out for. Everyone wanted lentils, cavolo nero, mustard greens, rocket, pancetta, broccoli sprouts, buffalo mozzarella and every sort of bean.

The food historian, Gillian Riley, points out in the *Oxford Companion to Italian Food* that "Northern Italian food" is a concept unknown in Italy, and when I asked Antonio Carluccio if, in his view, The River Café's was authentic Italian, he harrumphed, "No, it's not,"

> It's very, very good food, but not Italian food, never was. The Italian food that she serves is her and Ruth Rogers' interpretation of Italian food. The Italian Academy of Food have been there and they say, "No way is it Italian food."

This doesn't bother me, and nor does it bother most other people. Restaurants don't have to be certified *Denominazione di Origine Controllata*. But what probably does annoy professional restaurateurs – and several other professional Italians – about The River Café is that Rogers and Gray have made simple quality seem so easy. Many of its critics repeat that in Italy there is no such thing as Italian food, only Italian regional food; so it is probably true that only a restaurant outside the country can take an objective view and present cuisine selected from across all twenty regions. Certainly, some of what one eats at The River Café is not often seen on the menus of Italian restaurants, as Ruth and Rose's food started out as home cooking, using recipes and methods they had learned locally, from their friends in their Tuscan farmhouses and from Richard Rogers' mother. As Alastair Little says, they gave us "an English person's view of Tuscany." When, in 1993, they first published their cookbooks, Rogers and Gray were, in effect, completing the circle; they brought recipes from domestic kitchens, evolved them into restaurant dishes, then took them back to their origins for the home cook.

Rose and Ruth both had a fairly blinkered view of the heritage of Italian food in Britain in the years before The River Café. Rose told me that she visited Italy several times as a student, then, on her return, had discovered that the food she had eaten at simple restaurants couldn't be found in England. Having been lucky enough to have tasted Italian food on its home territory, Rose never saw the point of any of the London trattorie of the sixties and seventies and still denies that there was any authentic Italian food to be found in London before The River Café opened.

La Terrazza, she remembers, wasn't quite like the restaurants she had visited in Italy. It was "relaxed and not stuffy," Rose continued,

> I saw that it was different and unusual. But I never thought the food was that great. Mario and Franco had a more sophisticated view than most restaurants in Italy in that period. Most of the restaurants in Italy were very local and simple, whereas Mario and Franco had a stylish interior.

When she and Ruth started, they had agreed that the kind of food they wanted to cook was the kind you find in Italian homes,

> and in those kinds of very traditional Italian restaurant that don't exist here in England. We wanted to make bread soups, very simple food, we didn't want to make the slightly poncy Italian food which started with Mario and Franco.

Hang on, I thought. I tasted that Tuscan bread soup first at San

Frediano in 1967. Was Mario and Franco's *Pasta e Fagioli* slightly *poncy*? Was San Lorenzo's Pigeon Casserole a meal for *wimps*?

How do Ruth and Rose respond to critics who say their food isn't the real Italian thing? "I very rarely hear that it's not Italian food," Ruth says briskly. "When Italian people come here they say how Italian it is. The River Café has been called 'The best region of Italy.'"

Rose, however, does have an explanation for Carluccio's view.

> Because we're not Italian, we take our recipes from every region. Most Italians only know the recipes of their own region, so if you talk to an Italian about The River Café, they don't get it, because they might come from the Veneto and we've got Tuscan or Apulian or Piedmonte dishes.

This is certainly true. I have heard reports from trattoria owners in Puglia and Tuscany of two visiting ladies, lunching with large notebooks. By the descriptions, they have to be Ruth and Rose.

Perhaps the above may explain why Ruth and Rose have found it difficult to employ Italians in their kitchen. They did, once, hire an Italian chef, but it didn't work out. "Lorenzo came from Liguria," Rose explained,

*Ruth Rogers and Rose Gray at The River Café.*
*Their one Italian chef just didn't work out, but they have created a new and widely extended family of non-Italian Italian chefs.*

"and he always wanted to make the pasta, but he would only make it the way his mother had taught him. We found it very difficult to get him to make it the way we wanted."

**Divergence – Traditional Trattoria and Modern Italian**

By the end of the 1980s, Italian restaurants in England had finally settled into the same sort of pattern that had always existed in Italy – elegant and expensive upmarket restaurants at the highest level of food and service, in cities (and particularly scenic villages), mid-market, medium-priced trattorie across the country and many café-restaurant and pizza chains which offer a quick, inexpensive and satisfying meal that most could afford. Italian food had arrived in the British mainstream, available at all price levels to all British customers.

In the upmarket restaurants, Italian food presented itself in two distinctive varieties, not based on the individual Italian regions. There were those which stuck to the formula established by Mario and Franco, and there were the "new Italian."

"Life was so much easier when we started," says Franco Buonaguidi, a partner in the original San Frediano. For him, the change in Italian restaurants and Italian food in the UK since he, Mino and Sergio had first opened forty years before is nothing less than another Italian revolution.

"I don't know if I would dare to open a restaurant today," he admits.

> The cooking is so different. Italian restaurants don't offer heavy food any more. It's more refined, more elegant. In the sixties, people were starting to discover Italian food for the first time and eating their first spaghetti and lasagne and veal, but the competition is so much harder today.
>
> There is a much broader choice and now that there are so many places, you've got to be good but also different to stand out from the rest. We three opened many restaurants together and we were successful. Mario and Franco opened many restaurants together and were successful. Most of the new Italian restaurants which opened in those days did well, there were very few which failed completely.

As the influence of Neal Street, The River Café and their imitators brought a new, lighter Italian cuisine, there were still excellent trattorie and restaurants with the same sort of menu as Mario and Franco and the San Frediano group had initiated. This led to a sub-division in restaurant guides and thus, too, in their customers' attitudes. Guides began to separate Italian restaurants into two categories – the traditional trattorie and the more modern establishments in which chefs had introduced more sophisticated presentation and lighter dishes. The Mario and Franco-style places continued to be run by hosts (people who would recognise their customers and know them by name) while the "modern" were more likely to be owned by chefs and non-restaurateur partners. In 2002 the *Zagat London* restaurant guide listed eighty-six of what they called "contemporary" Italian and fifty-seven "traditional," and a year later there were ninety contemporary and only forty-seven of the traditional. The 2009 *Harden's Guide* reviews no fewer than two hundred Italian restaurants in London – not including the chains.

**You don't have to be Italian**

Young restaurant-goers of the 21st century have already enjoyed many more years' experience of eating out than their parents' and grandparents' generation had. When La Terrazza, the San Frediano and San Lorenzo first opened, they were just as new, relevant and popular for their then middle-aged customers who had lived through the Second World War and rationing, as they were for my generation born after the war. Mario and Franco's British customers, whatever their ages, had rarely been to restaurants before.

It was not only the Italians who took advantage of the UK's growing love affair with Italian food. Social change, for the better, in Italy pretty well ended the influx of young Italians; now they arrive for six months or so as members of a fellow EU country; they come to learn English so as to serve tourists back home. The standard of living in Italy today is far higher than it was during the sixties and seventies and many of the Italian restaurants in the UK are staffed by Spaniards and Poles.

By 1990, it was possible to open an Italian restaurant in London without having any Italian staff; even the restaurateur didn't have to be Italian. At Orso in Covent Garden, a great eighties favourite which has lasted well, the menu was written in Italian and seemed at first glance to be entirely authentic (if a little inclined towards New York style). But on my several visits no Italians were visible among the staff.

Today, immigrant restaurateurs are longer limited to offering their own national cuisine. Many Spaniards, arriving in London and finding that Italian was the favourite restaurant cuisine, and that trattorie were Britons' favourite restaurants, opened their own Italian restaurants, giving them

Italian names, Italian menus and Apicella-style designs, but the staff spoke Spanish. The best-known example of this was the celebrated Leonardo Restaurant at World's End on the King's Road. Throughout the seventies, eighties and nineties it was popular with an increasingly middle-aged, Chelsea crowd; it was always packed for late lunches as well as from seven to past midnight. Every one knew that Paco and Pepe were Spanish, that it was a pretend Italian restaurant and that the food, although good, was not really authentic. But no one called their bluff, or seemed to mind. It was particularly popular with stars of the rock and acting worlds, though somehow not the hyped-up glamorous showbiz types; its customers may have been wild once, but now they were family-oriented people enjoying a quiet life. We would see Eric Clapton, with his agent, or Mark Knopfler having lunch with his children. When Paco and Pepe sold Leonardo, and it became a real Italian place, Frantoio, some of the Spanish staff stayed on, but it was a while before the food returned to the previous standards of Span-Italian.

In its own small way Leonardo's created a legend. If you had survived the sixties (perhaps been away and come back), on the next tables you'd see other contemporaries who had done the same, still eating Italian trattoria food as though Mario and Franco had never left. It was a great relief to see them.

**Gennaro, Jamie and the River Café Dynasty**

If, back in the 1990s you'd walked into the Neal Street Restaurant and salivated over heaps of different kinds of mushrooms – porcini, chanterelles, horn of plenty and many others – in the reception area, the wild ones had often been picked by Gennaro Contaldo, who shared Antonio Carluccio's passion for fungi. Gennaro worked with Antonio at Neal Street for more than a decade. Today he is well known for his *Passione* – the name of both his restaurant and his book – as well as for his role as the man who taught Jamie Oliver about Italian food. He is an important branch of the Spaghetti Tree, because his cooking remains grounded in the food of his native town, Minori, near Amalfi, where both Mario Cassandro's and Franco Lagattolla's mothers came from; his Italian influence is apparent in all Jamie Oliver's work.

Having arrived in 1971, Gennaro missed the beginning of the British trattoria boom, but over the following years he worked in the kitchens of Prego in Soho and at the Meridiana on the Fulham Road – coincidentally under former Terrazza and Tiberio chef Angelo Cavaliere. He started at Neal Street in 1988 and it was there that he first worked with the young Jamie Oliver. In addition to his role as mushroom selector and sous-chef, Gennaro toured around Italy with Antonio on his many television programmes, acting as his researcher, assistant and chief buyer, which was a foretaste of what Gennaro would later do for Jamie Oliver. The tours were an eye-opener on the regional differences.

"I had never tasted Bolognese or Milanese or Sardinian food when I first came to England," says Gennaro. "At home, we ate only the dishes of our region. Working with Antonio gave me a new opportunity to travel all over Italy, to gain more experience of the other regions, which added a great deal to my basic knowledge."

Gennaro believes that the Neal Street was a huge influence on the general correction and improvement in Italian food in London during the 1990s. "Before Neal Street," he says, "there were mostly trattorie. Not many real restaurants. There, Antonio Carluccio raised the standard of everything. It was about freshness, the best ingredients. Everything coming from Italy. Antonio was bringing traditions back to the table."

In Gennaro's first book, *Passione*, there is a recipe which epitomises the change of style of Italian food which Antonio and Gennaro introduced

*Gennaro Contaldo, interviewed in the cafe next door to Jamie Oliver's Fifteen trattoria in London.*

to England. His tagliatelle with preserved tuna, rocket and lemon juice contains on the one hand, simple and natural ingredients, assembled and heated through, rather than laboriously prepared, then cooked. On the other hand, it provides a sophisticated and unusual combination of flavours. When my wife and I tried it at home, it was so quick and simple to prepare, so fresh, natural and uncomplicated, that, like some of Alastair Little's dishes, it could never have appeared on an Italian restaurant menu twenty years ago. It was hard to believe that, even now, it had been developed as a professional restaurant recipe.

As it turned out, it wasn't.

"That was an original dish from my village," Gennaro explains. "It was very much a poor man's dish. We used to preserve our own tuna and wild rocket grows on the side of the hill."

While Alastair Little spawned a new generation of chefs who copied his Italian-influenced cooking in several "Modern British" gastropubs, The River Café's influence spread not only through Rogers and Grey's television programmes and books, but also through the many young chefs who worked in the open kitchen there and absorbed their principles of uncomplicated Italian "home" cooking.

Jamie Oliver, having left Neal Street, was discovered in the kitchens of The River Café when Rogers and Grey were filming their first TV series. Their other alumni include Hugh Fearnley-Whittingstall, who says his career as a food writer was kick-started by being fired by Rose; Sam and Samantha Clark who met there and then took themselves off to open their own successful Spanish-Moorish Moro in Exmouth Market; Lynette Barron, now at the Tangerine Dream in Chelsea Physic Garden, and Allegra McEvedy, who, with Henry Dimbleby, now runs the blooming healthy-fast-food chain Leon and says she learnt more working at The River Café than anywhere in her apprenticeships. Two of Ruth and Rose's kitchen alumni have opened their own successful restaurants overseas, April Bloomfield in New York, where she received her first Michelin star at The Spotted Pig and Darren Simpson who opened La Sala in Sydney. In 2007, in a blow for the River Café founders but a clear demonstration of the power of their reputation, their senior chef, Theo Randall, was poached to become the named star of a restaurant at the Intercontinental Hotel.

Some of the River Café's alumni are regarded as more expertly Italian than the Italians themselves. In late 2008, Theo Randall signed a lucrative deal to "create" a series of pizza toppings for Pizza Express.

**The Cantona of the Cantina**

In 1986, another major influence on Italian food in the UK appeared. Its impact didn't manifest itself for some years to come, but it was then that Giorgio Locatelli arrived from Lombardy to start as a commis chef at the Savoy. Subsequently he built on his experience in classical French kitchens, to bring yet another version of Italian cooking to London. In so doing, he has won two successive Michelin stars.

Locatelli opened the Locanda Locatelli in 2003 to ecstatic reviews – A.A. Gill of the *Sunday Times* gave it his first five stars – and within a month the restaurant was booked up for six weeks in advance. Locanda Locatelli became "the best Italian restaurant in Britain."

Like many before him, Giorgio has worked his way up from the bottom of the ladder. In his case, though, he had to do it three times: first in Italy, then in London and, finally, in Paris. He comes from the village of Corgeno, on the shore of Lake Comabbio in Lombardy. His parents ran the hotel restaurant La Cinzianella there – where he first learnt the rudiments of cooking. Within days of his arrival in Britain, he discovered that his job at the Savoy wouldn't materialise as soon as he expected, so he found work at an "old-fashioned" trattoria in Surrey, where he was shocked to be told to make "Chicken Surprise." At the time, he thought to himself, "this is something I have never cooked in Italy."

It was, of course, Franco's famous parmesan-garlic-and-butter Italianisation of Chicken Kiev, which by now had become the favourite Italian dish of the British trattoria-going public. By the mid-eighties, most customers in Italian restaurants across the country were finding this item on their menus. No Trat worth its salt dared discard it. It had become a signature dish of the next revolution – generically labelled by the food critics of the day as "boil-in-the-bag menus."

In 2003, when the BBC conducted a survey of British households' favourite meals, they found that there were three Italian dishes in the top ten. Spaghetti Bolognese was our preferred evening meal, risotto came ninth and eighth was 'stuffed chicken breast' – Franco's 1960 recipe. La Terrazza's most popular dish had not only been copied in the myriad trattorie that followed Mario and Franco's success, but also food manufacturers, and then supermarkets too, had taken up the recipe and today thousands of their customers buy it to heat and serve at home.

Giorgio patiently continued making his Chicken Surprises in Surrey until the job at the Savoy eventually did materialise and there he started to work for its head chef, Anton Edelmann. When he had time off, he was greatly inspired by his discovery of Alastair Little and was astonished to find someone not born in Italy, able to cook in such an original yet authentic way, creating new dishes imbued with real Italian feeling.

He could see that the new cooking of chefs like Alastair, Ruth and Rose, and the Neal Street coterie was making its mark. But, on his salary, he couldn't often afford to visit the smart places. Moreover, after four years in London, Giorgio was clear that the most famous names in the gastronomic world remained French. So, in order to ensure that he missed nothing in his education, he decided to apply for a job in Paris. Having been a sous-chef in London, he might have expected to land a similar role in Paris. Not so.

It was start at the bottom again: as a commis at Joel Robuchon's Laurent. Other young staff members in Robuchon's celebrated, modern restaurant were appalled when they found that they had to share their ranges and prep areas with the lowest of the low – an Italian (a wop, they called him), who, even worse, had been learning to cook in England, the one place where, everybody knew, no decent food was to be found. Eventually, though, Robuchon asked Locatelli to make him some pasta and, gradually, Italian dishes such as risotto and polenta were added to Laurent's menu, often used as garnishes for exotic seafood creations.

Locatelli began to see how he might be able to combine his native Italian knowledge with what he had learnt in Paris. He moved on to the Tour d'Argent, but, as he says, other than cooking 140 ducks a day for their celebrated speciality Caneton Tour d'Argent and once again, being hated as an Italian by French staff, he learnt little.

Somewhat depressed, Giorgio returned to Italy in 1992 to chill out and rethink his direction. The break could not have come at a better time. Having worked in classic French kitchens for two years, producing complicated dishes with many layers of texture and flavour, it was a huge contrast for him to go back home and enjoy more simple, natural food. Within a few months, he says, he underwent an epiphany. At home and during a month of travel round the Mediterranean contemplating his future, he rediscovered the pure pleasure of simple uncomplicated food.

Eventually, the phone rang in his home in Corgeno, and Giorgio learnt that he was invited by Mauro Sanna to return to London as chef of a new restaurant, Olivo in Eccleston Street, which opened in 1991. This was Giorgio's first chance to start to develop his own style. When Fay Maschler wrote a highly complimentary piece about Olivo in her *Evening Standard* column, it became popular. For those accustomed to trattoria food, it was a new experience. Instead of the traditional Apicella tiles, pink tablecloths and white arches, there were plain wooden floors, no tablecloths and blue-painted walls. It was there that Giorgio's celebrated style emerged. There were several unusual pasta dishes, seafood, grilled vegetables and many simple, innovative char-grilled main courses.

At this stage Giorgio got to know Claudio Pulze (the entrepreneur whom we met back at Montpeliano in 1974), who, with the chef Marco Pierre White, Viscount Linley and the actor Michael Caine, had opened The Canteen, in Chelsea Harbour. White and Pulze ate regularly at Olivo and eventually Claudio suggested to Giorgio that they should open a restaurant together. This happened at an opportune moment, as Locatelli had begun to disagree with his Olivo partners. Claudio Pulze's A to Z Restaurants partnership with Gordon Ramsay at Aubergine was the first in a succession of restaurants which made Pulze's name well known in the business; when Locatelli and Pulze finally opened Zafferano in Lowndes Street, with Gordon Ramsay as their third partner, it took only two months to become a hit, both with the Belgravia crowd and food critics. (While working there, Giorgio married Plaxy, the daughter of one of Mario and Franco's former regulars, the writer Clive Exton. She fondly remembers being taken to La Terrazza for Sunday lunch and watching their special children's film shows.)

"If tables are hard to come by," pronounced the *Good Food Guide* in 2001, it was because Zafferano was indeed "a special place." Giorgio led the way in introducing un-anglicised Italian cooking and his simple treatment of seasonal ingredients, such as a salad of early peas and broad beans with pecorino cheese and simple trenette al pesto, through to a stunning langoustine risotto, impressed many.

Giorgio's partnership with Pulze lasted seven years, before he started his own new restaurant, Locanda Locatelli, off Portman Square, and it was there that I went to see him with some sixties menus from La Terrazza, Alvaro's and San Frediano. I wanted to compare his menus with those earlier ones. Although Locatelli does slightly resemble his friend, Marco Pierre White – tall, dark and with a mass of long curly hair falling in all directions, Giorgio is more the philosopher-chef – a Cantona of the Cantina – than the tyrant of the kitchen. His staff are famously well looked after, mainly working a straight shift instead of the back-breaking, desperately tiring split shift. Like Rogers and Gray of The River Café, he has a reputation for getting what he wants done without the tirades of a White or a Gordon Ramsay.

As we talked, it soon became clear that for someone of Giorgio's experience, to study the menus that we ate from in the sixties and seventies is a form of anthropology; it's like discovering a human footprint, which describes the time and social circumstances that they represent. Looking at these old menus, as we sat in his tiny chef's office at the back of his kitchen, he could tell instantly where a chef came from and what produce was then available.

"You can see that they prepared certain ingredients in a certain way," Giorgio said,

> they were dictated to by the abundance of this or the scarcity of that. In those days the chefs and owners were still fighting for their Italian identity, to get away from French food. Now, we can put almost any dish on our menu and it will be accepted by some customers. But twenty, thirty years ago, if you opened an Italian restaurant, it took balls to put on certain dishes people had never tried. It was a great gamble to say, "Let's try quails and polenta."

With better quality produce, he continued, the food could be more authentic;

> In my early days here, there were cargo flights coming into England from Italy maybe once a week, but now it's every two hours. The whole market is more and more sophisticated and also micro-organised. Several producers and growers in Italy have started to bring their produce directly here to the UK. They sell it to us and then to someone else, then others follow and then they come over here every couple of weeks and eventually some food item which was hard to find is suddenly very easy and convenient.

I asked Giorgio how many of the dishes that the old Terrazza menu offered are still on menus today and how the then available ingredients would have changed. He looked up, then said, "I have someone who can tell you. Someone who was there." He opened the office door, stuck his head out and asked a commis to go and fetch Osvaldo.

I had heard of Osvaldo but had never met him. My friend Valerio Calzolari, formerly a headwaiter at the Trat and manager at Mr Chow, now the prosperous co-owner of Scalini, had lent me a photograph from the late sixties; he was one of a group of striped-jerseyed waiters photographed together with La Terrazza head chef, Osvaldo Antoniazzi.

Here, now, in the kitchens of the most prominent, modern Italian restaurant in London, was that same chef who linked directly back to La Terrazza. At last I would hear – from as it were the horse's mouth – how much Italian food has changed between the Trattoria Revolution and Modern Italian cuisine.

Still wearing his whites and blue striped apron from the lunch service, Osvaldo came into Giorgio's little office and sat down beside me. From his 1959 arrival in London from Bardi near Parma, Osvaldo's career is, he explained, virtually a history of the London restaurant scene. He started in the days when hosts, not chefs, were the well-known restaurant personalities and he was head chef in six different establishments, though never a celebrity. He created and re-created dishes from his own region and most of the other Italian regions. He has cooked city Italian food, trattoria Italian, peasant Italian, bourgeois Italian, northern and southern Italian and – whatever we decide what that is – Modern Italian. Whatever is required, he can provide it and provide it to a consistently high standard.

Mario and Franco hired Osvaldo in 1969 (a year after they went public) as head chef who would run the newly enlarged and upgraded kitchens at La Terrazza. He was a great success, producing more than 500 covers a day at what was one of London's busiest and most fashionable restaurants, but his name remained unknown to the customers. He helped to expand the menu to much more than La Terrazza's traditional Neapolitan dishes, was asked to help rebuild the team at Tiberio and, later, to relaunch Terrazza-Est when management changes occurred. In 1974, he opened his own place, which became very popular with the locals in Winchmore Hill – especially after local people began to travel to Italy for holidays.

"They'd come back and say, 'Chef, can you make this for us?'" he told me. "And I'd say, 'Yes, of course I can.'"

After eleven years on his own, Osvaldo sold up and became head chef at Luigi's in Tavistock Street, in Covent Garden, where he stayed for eighteen years. When he finally retired, he stayed home for two months, dry-curing his own bresaola in the cellar under his Enfield house. But this wasn't enough for him. He was bored.

One day, the phone rang and, as it transpired, Giorgio Locatelli, the most innovative and fashionable Italian chef, wanted the benefit of his experience. Would he come and work part-time at Locanda Locatelli? So at the age of 68, Osvaldo started work for the first time in a Michelin-starred Italian restaurant.

Giorgio greatly respects Osvaldo's knowledge and experience.

Having Osvaldo here makes a huge difference to us. He's brought us his thirty years' knowledge of buying meat and of the best way to cut and use that piece of meat. If we're thinking about putting on a new dish, we talk to Osvaldo. He knows what our London customers will go for and with his advice, when a new dish goes on the menu, we know that it will sell. When you're doing a menu of forty-eight items with only eighty covers, you need to be sure that every dish is pulling its weight.

"Has the old Mario and Franco style of cooking gone away?" I asked.

"Just look at places like Scalini and La Famiglia," Giorgio answered. "They are very much in the Mario and Franco style. They're always full and most of the British public's understanding of Italian food is based on what they do. I couldn't go back to the time of Mario and Franco and understand what they did. That's why I have Osvaldo here. He's the link."

Osvaldo is clear about the difference between his views and Giorgio's.

Giorgio has kept something of the old Italiana, yes. But he does everything in his own way. It's definitely far away from what we used to do in the past. He wants always to purify the Italian cuisine and take it away from French food. There's nothing that resembles French food on the menu at Locatelli.

"Mario and Franco were Neapolitan," Giorgio said. "Alvaro is from Tuscany, I'm from Lombardy. Osvaldo from Parma. We've all taken dishes of our own regions and produced them here in versions that we knew the British would like."

"Is there really such a thing as Modern Italian?" I asked.

"The River Café's not modern Italian. It's really traditional old Italian, more traditional than anywhere," he continued. "It's traditional Italian food, meat with little things that come with it, or pasta. It's a very straightforward way to eat."

Locatelli, clearly, doesn't see Carluccio's "Britalian" concept as derogatory.

Yes, there is such a thing. There were dishes invented here like *pollo sorpresa*. But that was to get away from the French Chicken Kiev. There's nothing wrong with that. All Italian food is based on a natural selection of what's available. A restaurateur's value is in how many people come through his door and whether they come back again. He either gets it right or not. Mario and Franco had more people waiting outside than they had inside. They got it right all the time.

*Above: Chef Osvaldo Antoniazzi at La Terrazza, 1969, with (second left) head waiter, Valerio Calzolari, now a partner at Scalini, and three waiters of the era. Photo: courtesy of Osvaldo Antoniazzi*

*Decades later, he was still at the top of the tree, working with Giorgio Locatelli at Locanda Locatelli (below). "The old style has never gone away," they said.*

**Digestivo**

Today there are plenty of people around who remember Mario and Franco. But few of them remember the dreary experience of eating out in the 1950s. Half a century after the opening of La Terrazza, London's restaurants offer a quality and variety of cooking which would be unrecognisable to a Rip Van Winkle who'd fallen asleep in April, 1959.

It remains a matter of debate as to which innovation has most contributed to the way we live, cook and eat today. Was it the emergence of imaginative, creative English chefs and restaurateurs? The pervasive influence of television and travel? The rise of brasseries, the changes in licensing laws, or the spread of chain restaurants that offered quality, economy and style?

To me, the part played by Mario and Franco and their Trattoria Revolution seems to over-ride them all. "At the outset of a thrilling decade," says the historian and former *Good Food Guide* editor Tom Jaine,

> Mario and Franco offered a potent recipe for living, one that encompassed visual style, welcome informality and new, delicious things to eat and drink. On the one hand, they waved goodbye to red plush and carpets and on the other, their food was lighter, simpler, more directly flavoursome than had been available within living memory.

Mario and Franco's effect was immediate, electric and had long-term consequences. The new generation of English chefs who came onto the restaurant scene in the 1970s and 1980s absorbed their influence and, without allegiance to any one national culinary culture, freely adapted all their learning into what became Modern British.

"The centre of gravity of restaurant cooking shifted eastwards and southwards," Jaine adds. "It shifted away from our obeisance to all things French and towards an exploration and celebration of the Mediterranean."

The Italian influence has changed not only the food that we eat, but also our ideas about the values of simple cooking, quality ingredients and freshness. What's more, in addition to bringing us their food, Mario, Franco and their Spaghetti Tree taught us how to enjoy eating, and the role a good meal has in celebrating life, love and friendship.

Today, as British families tuck in to their rolled stuffed chicken breast at home and in Italian restaurants across the country and, as Giorgio Locatelli cooks in his Locanda with Mario and Franco's former head chef at his side, the legacy of their Trattoria Revolution lives on.

## EPILOGUE

The King's Road, Chelsea, is different now. The Pheasantry, where nine-year-old Alicia Markova was discovered in the 1920s by Diaghilev, is a branch of Pizza Express. The Six Bells, to which Spike Hughes and his Decca-Dents would stampede after another 1930s recording session at the Chenil Galleries studios, has become Henry J. Bean's Bar and Grill. The Great Gear Trading Company, among whose fifty stalls you could find, in 1970, everything from an Afghan coat or a pair of hand-tailored leather trousers to a haircut or a full size water bed, is now a branch of Marks & Spencer.

All the other sixties lodestars – such as Bazaar, Just Looking, Hung On You, or Granny Takes a Trip – have gone the way of all fashion. Only the Picasso Café, dating back to the 1950s, and the Green & Stone art materials shop, have not yet been turned into the mobile phone showrooms or chain-store branches which make the fabled road almost as bland as any provincial High Street. As the chains have taken over the top end of the King's Road, individual shops are to be found further west and now most of the remaining cafés, boutiques, restaurants, chemists, galleries and bookshops are squeezed into the small area between Flood Street and Finborough Road.

Today, if you walk down from Sloane Square, past Sloane Avenue, there is no trace of the original Alvaro's restaurant, or of Mario & Franco's Don Luigi. Lower, the site of the Aretusa has changed hands so many times now that it seems more a site to buy and develop for profit than one which might ever become, or have been, a restaurant club. As I walk on past the Chelsea Potter, the Antique Market and Oakley Street, continue down past Paulton's Square, Old Church Street and through the chicane towards the World's End, there is precious little left of the atmosphere of excitement which in the sixties and seventies permeated the air of the most famous street in the world.

Having strolled beyond the reverse clock in the window of number 430 (where Malcolm McLaren and Vivien Westwood opened SEX and punk rock was born in 1972), you could glance into that café on the corner of Limerston Street, in case you recognise a recovering celebrity enjoying an orange juice after his or her weekly session at AA. Maybe you might peer through the steamy windows of the Mona Lisa to check if Clapton or possibly Mark Knopfler is enjoying a late breakfast. But there's absolutely no chance of booking a haircut at the long-vanished Todd's, where the air hung so heavy with incense and a Stone or a Beatle waited in the next chair.

In order to find a genuine, thriving reminder of the days when the King's Road was the centre of the universe, you must stroll a little further, until, just past the World's End pub, you turn right into a small semi-residential area. Langton Street is almost a village; it has a supermarket, a couple of galleries, a print shop and a newsagent corner store. But in a pair of terraced houses a few yards down, you'll find one of the most celebrated, long-established Italian restaurants in London, with a history which echoes back to the days of 1966.

If you'd happened to pass by La Famiglia, on the evening of 30 April 2006, you would have been witness to the restaurant equivalent of the Beatles' return to the Cavern Club.

The tables were backed against the walls, the room was full of flowers, the Tuscan wine was chilled and the beaming staff were in fresh crisp whites. In a new suit and red tie, beaming his trademark welcoming smile, Alvaro – one of those, like Elvis and Cher whose one name is instantly recognisable to fans – was celebrating the 40th anniversary of the opening of Alvaro's. He has continued night after night, to feed the "beautiful people" who made sixties London swing. Among the three hundred guests present were three generations of his clients, some who have been his constant regulars since 1966, when Italian restaurants were leading Britain out of food austerity and Alvaro's (its telephone number ex-directory), was the most influential, most fashionable restaurant, on the most fashionable street, when Swinging London was the centre of the world.

Alvaro had invited all of his regulars, or as many of us whose addresses he could find, and of course we'd all come to share his anniversary, the moment when the King's Road reached its pinnacle of fame. The actors Albert Finney, Terence Stamp and Rodney Bewes, the photographers Terry O'Neill and Bryan Wharton, the writers Len Deighton, Herbert Kretzmer and Peter Evans, the wrestler Mick MacManus, the trichology magnate Philip Kingsley, the former Harpers & Queen editor Willie Landels, the tailor Doug Hayward, the model agent Laraine Ashton, the broadcaster Ned Sherrin, the pirate radio pioneer Ronan O'Rahilly, the furniture design guru Zeev Aram, the model Paulene Stone, the restaurateurs Shura Shiwarg and Peter Boizot – Alvaro's long-term customers, arriving to share memories with old friends, dining again at Alvaro's, as though it was an April evening in 1966.

Alvaro was the celebrated host, but his guest of honour was the man who had given him his start in the business. At the height of the evening's party, Mario Cassandro arrived together with Enzo Apicella. With their deaf aids turned full up, the octogenarians circled the rooms, greeting and embracing their former colleagues, and laughing with fellow guests, who had been their friends for forty-five years.

As we left and I turned to catch a last glimpse of the mêlée of faces behind me, I could swear that – just for a moment – I saw another familiar figure. There, near the kitchen door, he stood with his hands behind his back, his glasses poised on the bridge of his nose, his eyebrows raised. He was gazing round the room and, as always, missing nothing.

## APPENDIX I: WHERE ARE THEY NOW?

Updated for Second Edition

A new generation of children of some of the protagonists in this story – Walter's son, **Riccardo Mariti**, at Riccardo's in the Fulham Road, Alvaro's daughter, **Marietta Maccioni**, at La Famiglia and **Laura Santin** at Santini – are all assisting in or running their parents' restaurants. As for the others:

**Osvaldo Antoniazzi**, head chef at La Terrazza in the early seventies, is still at work in 2009 – five days a week – in the Michelin-starred Locanda Locatelli. He has promised his wife he will retire one day soon.

**Enzo Apicella** continued his multi-tasking career on all fronts; cartoons, restaurant designs and his own businesses. He has designed more than 200 restaurants. In 2006, Enzo married for the first time, at the age of eighty-two.

**Fabio Benet** left Alvaro to be the manager of Barbarella near Stamford Bridge, where he remained for many years. He died in Italy in the late eighties.

**Dante Betti** left the Factotum Club in 1975 to open Salotto in Hollywood Road with Franco Palmieri, a former manager at the Meridiana. In 1982 he opened Beccofino, which he sold in 2006, then retired.

**Peter Boizot** opened the 50th branch of his Pizza Express chain in Manchester in the 1980s and sold his shares in 1993. He went on to own other businesses, including restaurants, hotels – and Peterborough United Football Club, as well as starting the Soho Jazz Festival.

**Luigi Bolognese** worked at the Ad Lib club with Dante Betti and later became a manager of the Meridiana. After opening Beccofino with Dante, he decided after two years to go his own way and, with John French, took over the Villa Estense in King's Road, which became J Arthur, a restaurant club.

**Franco Buonaguidi** and Mino Parlanti finally sold San Frediano in the mid-1980s. Mino retired to Montecatini Terme in 1986, and Franco Buonaguidi continued for a few years with another Tuscan trattoria, Vin Santo, on Hollywood Road. He now lives in retirement by the river Thames near Hampton Court.

**Valerio Calzolari** runs and part-owns Scalini, in Walton Street. It is always full and said to be one of the most profitable Italian restaurants in London.

**Antonio Carluccio** has now severed ties with his Café-Deli chain. In 1998 he was made Commendatore del Lavoro della Repubblica Italiana for his services to Italian gastronomy and, in January 2007, was awarded an honorary OBE.

**Mario Cassandro** died in 2011.

**Pino Cecere** ran the Leeds Terrazza for 15 years, and then opened Brio, a chain of four value restaurants in Leeds and Harrogate. He retired in 2008 and divides his time between Yorkshire and Puglia.

"**Michael Chow** the man and MR CHOW the dining experience are both international icons of today's cultural landscape," it says on his website. He is apparently "a living legend" – designer, art collector, film actor, as well as restaurateur. He lives in Los Angeles, and appears with his fourth wife and children in lifestyle advertisements.

**Giulio Cornoli** sold his branches of Verbanella in the 1990s, except that in Beauchamp Place, where he presided until he retired in 2007 after 46 years in the business.

**Carlo Corsini** was manager of the San Frediano, then opened Trattoria Conti in Leicester; later he managed the Falconiere in Old Brompton Road until he retired. He now lives in Normandy.
**Luis Duas-Leon**, "Spanish Luis", one of the only non-Italian room managers at the Trat, moved to Tramps discotheque in Jermyn Street, then continued as manager of David Niven Jr's Drones in Pont Street.
The **Lavarini** and **Fraquelli** families built up The Spaghetti House chain to more than 20 outlets until, in the 1990s, they separated into two distinct companies. Metropolitan Restaurants, under **Stefano Fraquelli** has Getti's, Zia Teresa and Galileo's Locanda. The **Lavarini**'s Spaghetti House group has nine restaurants across town.
**Franco Lagattolla** died in 1980. His elder son, Nicholas, is a vascular surgeon, while Fabio, the younger, has recently forsaken a career in technology and re-trained as a therapist.
**Pasquale Lunghi:** after Walter Mariti retired and transferred Ponte Nuovo to his son Riccardo, Pasquale worked for a while at Taberna Etrusca in the City. He retired in 2004.
**Alvaro Maccioni** rules on at the celebrated La Famiglia in Langton Street. Many of his staff have been with him since 1975. His daughter, Marietta, helps runs the business.
**Marcello:** nobody seems to know what has happened to Marcello, the waiter who forgot to put the plate down first.
**Antonio Marson** Trattoo manager for eight years, returned to Italy, eventually becoming managing director of the Hotel Splendido in Portofino. He now lives in retirement in a penthouse above the Grand Hotel in Alassio and, he says, he "owes everything to Mario Cassandro."
**Mimmo Mattera** sold Mimmo d'Ischia in Elizabeth Street in 2008 to the Santini group. He plans to retire and divide his time between London and his house in Italy.
**Giulio Nobilio** stayed on as manager of La Terrazza Manchester after the Mario and Franco group was sold to Spillers. He acquired the business in 1982, renaming it Giulio's Terrazza. He finally sold it in 2001 and is now a senior manager with the San Carlo group.
**Luigi Paglierani** and **Sergio Galassi**: on 10 May 1988, the bodies of Luigi and Patricia Paglierani and Silvana and Sergio Galassi were discovered at Luigi's farmhouse near Riccione on the Adriatic coast. All four had been bound hand and foot, then shot. The deaths were a mystery. Although the safe was open, nothing had been stolen from it. So what could be the criminals' motive? Could it be a revenge killing?
Could someone have had a grudge against Luigi? Could the Mafia have been involved? Why had Sergio and his wife stayed on at the coast, when it seemed they had planned to leave a day earlier? Could the robbery and wrecking of the house have been a theatrical effort designed to throw investigators off the scent? The police eventually agreed that the motive was unlikely to have been robbery. The method of the killings was also puzzling. Because the pistol was a typical Mafia weapon and all four victims had been expertly bound before their execution, it might have pointed to a Mafia killing. But the Rimini area has little history of Mafia activity and Mafia hit men would have been unlikely to kill the women. Italian investigators soon admitted they were baffled and contacted Scotland Yard for help. Although both civil and military police detectives worked on the case for many years, it has never been solved.

**Mario Paggetti** runs the highly successful Scalini on Walton Street with Valerio Calzolari. In 2007 his other restaurant, Signor Sassi, was sold to the regional San Carlo group.
**Walter Palermo,** one of the first chefs at La Terrazza, opened five restaurants in Soho and west London and still owns the Siciliano in Dean Street.
**Franco Serpussi** closed his Brompton Road trattoria Franco unexpectedly, overnight, and although he was thought to have spent time in Paris, he eventually reappeared as manager of a big hotel restaurant in Sardinia. He retired in the late 1990s.
**Robin Sutherland** followed his Mr Chow partnership with the Old Compton Wine Bar and Maunkberry's nightclub. He and I sold our two Small's restaurants in 1975. He moved to Texas where he opened Sutherlands in Dallas before relocating to San Francisco where he bought, and ran, the celebrated Bar with No Name in Sausalito. He died in London in 1998.
**Peppino Taboro**: following his provincial venture with Trattoria Conti in Leicester, Peppino returned to London to run Sambuca opposite Peter Jones. He managed La Finezza in Lower Sloane Street for fourteen years before retiring to France.
**Franco and Ann Taruschio** are nearly as busy in retirement as they were at the Walnut Tree. Both are directors of the Abergavenny Food Festival and Franco consults to many restaurant businesses. Upon their retirement in 2001, The Walnut Tree was acquired by Francesco Mattioli, who started his career at the Trattoo in 1979. Sadly, the restaurant failed and now has new owners, the local business man, William Griffiths, and the renowned chef, Shaun Hill.
**Sandro Tobi** died in 2000 in a tragic car accident near his house in Umbria. His widow, Wendy, continues running Sale e Pepe with Tony Coricelli as manager.
**Antonio Trapani** continues in his red braces at Montpeliano, which today encompasses three buildings. He also owns Toto's in Lennox Gardens Mews off Walton Street.
**Mario Vollono** stayed at La Terrazza for more than fifteen years and three changes of ownership in Romilly Street, until he finally left in 1979. He then ran Barbarella 2 in South Kensington, until 1995. He lives in retirement in north London and hangs out with his old Terrazza-Est colleague Luigi Destro.

## APPENDIX II: WHO SAT AT THE TRAT?

In 1966, after Mario and Franco hired Mario Vollono to take over from Alvaro Maccioni as the manager of La Trattoria Terrazza, Vollono started a book which contained details of its regular customers; against each name he noted details of their favourite tables and special requirements. This is his table list, as he wrote it.

**Table 1**: Vincent Price, Liza Minelli, Maurice Jarre, Margaret Gardner of Robert Cowan, C Andrea of BTA, Pamela Portman, Sidney Marks of Alfred Marks Bureau, Sir Norman Foster

**Table 3**: Conte Filo del Torre, Luigi Forni

**Table 5**: Norman Laden, Tony Rose

**Table 5bis:** Joyce Hopkirk (*Cosmopolitan*), Eve Pollard, Lesley Ebbetts (*Daily Mirror*).

**Table 6**: Francis Bacon, Jeremy Isaacs, Glenda Jackson, Judi Dench, Derek Eckart, Barry Humphries, Terry Nation, Ken Thorne

**Table 12**: Lady Carolyn Townshend, Michael Cudlipp, Julien Freud, Nigel Davenport, David Goldstone, Keith Waterhouse

**Table 14**: Egon Ronay, Edina Ronay and Dick Polack, William Davis, Margaret Allen, David Bernstein, Patrick Cahill, Bernard Levin, Bryan Forbes, Nanette Newman, Felicity Green, Warren Beatty, Michael Bentine

**Table 15**: Quentin Crewe, Jarvis Astaire, Vic Lewis, Sir Laurence Olivier, Telly Savalas, Sir Alec Guinness, Ronnie Corbett, Lord Montague of Beaulieu, Willie Landels, Angela Landels, Robert Carrier, Bobby Buchanan-Michaelson, André Previn, Wylton Dickson, David Lewin

**Table 18**: John Burrow, John Black, John Boulting, Roy Boulting, Hayley Mills, Tony Curtis, Theo Cowan, Charles Berman of United Artists, Michael Medwin, Spike Milligan, Bob Guccione, Al Mancini, Albert Finney, Tom Courtenay, Sir Richard Attenborough, Richard Gregson, Anouk Aimée, Jean Shrimpton, Kenneth Tynan, Elizabeth Harris, Rex Harrison, André Deutsch

**Table 19**: Franco Zeffirelli, Vanessa Redgrave, George Raft, Franco Nero, David Hemmings, Stanley Baker, Gayle Hunnicutt, Penelope Keith, Jerry Lewis, Anthony Barber, Terence Feely, George Lucas

**Table 20**: Laetitia and Ken Adam, Joan Collins, Ron Kass, Sophia Loren, Carlo Ponti, Peter Sellers, Britt Ekland, Mo Rothman, Frank Finlay, Thomas Clyde, Beryl Reid, Jack de Lane Lea, James Clavell, Richard Harris, Gene Gutowski

**Table 21**: Roman Polanski, Sharon Tate, Dennis Selinger, Steve Boys, Val Guest, Fred Zimmerman, Ben Fisz, Sam Spiegel, John Ireland, David Niven and David Niven Jr, Antony Quinn, Lady Antonia Fraser, Rupert Lycett Green, Richard Widmark, Simone Signoret, Anthony Mann, John Gilbert, Karl Malden, Elliott Kastner

**Table 22** Frank Sinatra, Jane Russell, Bob Hope, Danny Kaye, Albert Broccoli, Harry Saltzman, Sean Connery, Roger Moore, Luisa Moore, Lee Marvin, Otto Preminger, Laurence Harvey, Paulene Stone, Wolf Mankiewitz, Robert Wagner, Lionel Stander, John Schlesinger, Sammy Davis Jr, Peter Lawford, Lionel Blair, Jackie Collins, Oscar Lerman, Johnny Gold, Bill Hofner, Doug Hayward

**Table 23**: Pila Saville, M. Sloan, Micky Most, Donald Pleasence, Tobias Maxwell Shaw, Julian Holloway, Kenneth Cope

**Table 24**: Marcello Mastroianni, Anna-Maria Pierangeli (Pier Angeli), Maurice Binder, Ursula Andress, Jean-Paul Belmondo, Len Deighton, Jack Clayton, Patrick Lichfield,

HRH Princess Margaret, Lord Snowdon, Jocelyn Stevens, Martin Vickers, Lady Giovanna Stone, David Bailey, Catherine Deneuve, Marie Helvin, Dr Sacks, Joseph Janni, Stanley Flink of Print Brokers, David Frost, M. Erlight
**Table 24bis**: Dirk Bogarde, Alexander Walker, Adrienne Corri, Dame Diana Rigg, Archie Sterling, Brian Duffy, David Puttnam, Tony and Linda Richmond, Jenny Agutter, Peter Evans, Tanya Mallett, Terence Stamp, Lauren Bacall, Stanley Donner, Cyril Frankel, Sir Robin Day
**Table 25**: Dustin Hoffman, Omar Sharif, Caroline Pfeiffer, Leslie Caron, Sandy Lieberson, Leslie Pound, Raquel Welch, Alan Ladd Jr, Eduardo de Filippo, Michelangelo Antonioni, Monica Vitti
**Table 25bis**: Stanley Bilesky, Dudley Moore, Peter Cook, Kenneth Glancy, Jeremy Kemp, George Peppard, Ronnie Beck, Richard Johnson, Kim Novak, Pascal Petit
**Table 26**: Vincent Korda, Milko Rozsa, Erica Frei of Jaeger
**Table 27**: Susannah York, Andrew Lloyd Webber, J Adams-Peraticos, Terence Baker, Terry Donovan, Sir John Mills, Laurence Evans, Juliet Mills, George Walker, Michael Parkinson, Sir John Profumo, Valerie Hobson
**Table 28**: Sir John Gielgud, Pietro Annigoni, Evelyn de Rothschild, John Bates, John Siggins of Jean Varon, R. Schenk, Maina Gielgud
**Table 30**: R. Trevelyan of Hamish Hamilton, Jean Marsh, Michael Lindsay Hogg
**Table 31**: William and Fabio Samengo Turner, Trevor Chinn (Lex), Bing Crosby, Stanley Holloway, A. Jarratt, Eddie Kulukundis, Michael Winner, Robert Morley, Sheridan Morley, Alfie Garrett
**Table 32**: Charles Chaplin, Oonagh Chaplin, Geraldine Chaplin, Oliver Gregory, Christopher Lee, Dame Shirley Bassey, Sergio Novac, Ron Moody
**Table 33**: Richard Gillinson, Eric Swain
**Table 33bis**: Peter Dunbar, Denis Piper
**Table 34**: Alexandra Bastedo, Gina Warwick
**Table 34bis**: Jim Baker, Ridley Scott, Frank Cvitanovich, Molly Parkin, David Gillard, Alan Bates, Robin Sutherland, Adam Faith, Charles Llewellyn, Lulu, Alan McKeown, Roy Castle, Janet Street-Porter
**Table 35**: Tim Emmanuel, Oliver Reed, Spencer Jay, Steven Bond, J. Baldwin
**Table 36**: Chris Highams, the Dranes, the Landaus, the Roses, Virna Lisi, Bob Freeman
**Table 37**: Dennis Abey, Alan Parker, John Claridge, George Blaug, Clive Arrowsmith
**Table 38**: Suter Harris, Ronnie Kirkwood, George Dixon, George Baker, John Hogarth, Paul Hitchcock, Peter Beale, Julian Glover, Ingrid Pitt, John Swannell
**Table 39**: Pier Luigi, Michael Hunter
**Table 40**: Alan Bates of Bellair, John Stevenson
**Table 41**: Tony Bussman, Bob Mahoney, Cliff Richard, Jack Palance, Ron Kravitz, John Redway, Eric Morecambe, Ernie Wise
**Table 42**: Rock Hudson, Charlotte Rampling, Cilla Black, Jimmy Savile, Terry O'Neill, David Connolly, Simon Williams
(Other regular customers whose preferences were listed included John Huston, Darryl Zanuck, Robert Mitchum, Burt Lancaster, Joan Cohn, Marlon Brando, The Maharajah of Cooch Behar, Elizabeth Taylor, Richard Burton, Stanley Baker, Peter O'Toole, Dino de Laurentiis, Katherine Hepburn, Franco Nero, Franco Zeffirelli, Barbra Streisand and Elliot Gould.)

## APPENDIX III: AUTHOR'S FAVOURITES

Here is my personal list of a few Italian restaurants which represent Mario and Franco's legacy – good food, perhaps not always "modern Italian" but served in a warm and welcoming environment, without pretentiousness and with real people answering the telephone. I've not included the chains, but our local Carluccio's and Strada are both welcoming and good value.
Since I never eat puddings, I have no idea if what I eat is "average." So, where possible, I have taken the prices for each establishment as marked in *Harden's London Restaurants 2009*. These prices cover an "average" three-course meal for one, plus a half bottle of house wine, coffee, and include VAT and service.

**Assaggi** 39 Chepstow Place London W2 Tel: 020 7792 5501 Nino Sassu and Pietro Fraccari both worked at the Neal Street Restaurant. They opened Assaggi in 1996 and won a Michelin star in 2005. Nino's cooking is high on flavour and fresh produce. The food is simple, with superb ingredients in happy combinations; menus change daily. Must book well ahead. This is where we go for a special treat. About £60 a head.
**Bacco** 39 Kew Road, Richmond, Surrey TW9 2NQ Tel: 020 8332 0348 My wife and I have found this family-owned trattoria particularly welcoming, for dinner after the show at the nearby Richmond Theatre. The atmosphere is bustling without being too noisy and the service friendly and competent. About £35 per head.
**Como Lario** 22 Holbein Place London SW1W 8NL Tel: 020 7730 2954 Como Lario has been buzzing quietly along since 1969. I've attended several well-managed dinners for PR agency types in its private room. A new generation has taken over the management. £42 per head.
**Il Frantoio** 397 King's Road Chelsea London SW10 0LR Tel: 020 7352 4146 When new owners took over they at first changed only the name and the menu, making it more authentically Italian, but continued with the same team of mostly Spanish waiters. Later, improvements came, including better air-conditioning and new furniture and now, almost ten years later, it's thriving again. £42 per head.
**La Famiglia** 7 Langton Street London SW10 0JL Tel: 020 7351 0761 Alvaro Maccioni's long-lived Tuscan trattoria still provides interesting Tuscan specialities, especially pasta dishes. It continues to appeal to his ever-faithful sixties clientele and their children and grandchildren. The terrace at the back fills up quickly for weekend lunches or summer dinners. £47 per head.
**Locanda Locatelli** 8 Seymour Street London W1 Tel: 020 7935 9088 The best Italian restaurant in Britain, wonderful food, luxurious comfort, sensational wine list, but a computer answers the phone. £60 per head.
**Lucio** 257 Fulham Road London SW3 Tel: 0207 823 3007 Lucio Altana was headwaiter at San Lorenzo for ages. He finally plucked up the nerve, found backing and opened his own place in 2005. Although the rooms have a complicated layout, it is welcoming and its food is interesting; some of it unusual and very good value. £49 per head.
**Montpeliano** 13 Montpelier Street London SW7 1HQ Tel: 020 7589 0032 Antonio Trapani's restaurant with its sliding roof is a good place to eat on a sunny day at lunchtime, or on a warm evening. His staff are charming, and the food is consistent, although slightly clichéd. £62 per head.

**San Lorenzo** 22 Beauchamp Place London SW3 1NH Tel: 020 7584 1074 Although there's no direct link between San Lorenzo and Mario and Franco, San Lorenzo's head waiter, Giancarlo Saba, started his career at La Terrazza. (Don't go on Saturday for lunch.) £48 per head.

**Pellicano** 19/21 Elystan Street London SW3 3NT Tel: 020 7589 3718 Marcello Vargiu, the owner, worked at Santini in Ebury Street and then managed Gino Santin's L'Incontro in Pimlico Road. At Pellicano he offers excellent Sardinian-influenced food at reasonable prices, in a welcoming atmosphere. £44 per head.

**Riccardo's** 126 Fulham Road, London SW3 6HU Tel: 020 7370 6656 Riccardo Mariti took over the former Pontenuovo from his father after Walter, having sold his celebrated Pontevecchio, decided to retire. In the past ten years Mariti Junior has built up a reputation for good-value Tuscan food and an interesting menu. £42 per head.

**Sale e Pepe** 9/15 Pavilion Road London SW1X 0HD Tel: 020 7235 0098 The late Sandro Tobi's first trattoria, now owned by his widow, Wendy, and managed by Tony Coricelli. One of the best lunch spots in Knightsbridge. £46 per head.

**Scalini** 1/3 Walton Street London SW3 2JD Tel: 020 7225 2301 Both the owner Mario Paggetti (the ginger-haired one) and his partner Valerio Calzolari (with the handlebar moustache) worked at La Terrazza. They opened Scalini in 1985 and twenty-odd years later several of their dishes reflect the Mario and Franco heritage. £58 per head.

**Signor Sassi** 14 Knightsbridge Green London SW1 Tel: 020 7584 2277 This was a business lunch favourite when my office was next door. It was acquired in 2008 by Carlo di Stefano, who has kept on the manager, Donato Russo, and most of his crew. Noise levels are high, but the food is reliable. £50 per head.

**Vasco & Piero's Pavilion** 15 Poland Street London W1V 3DE Tel: 020 7437 8774 This is an excellent traditional family-owned trattoria with regional Italian cooking – in this case, Umbrian. £47 per head.

**BEYOND LONDON:**

**Brio Pizza** The Light, St Anne's Gardens, Leeds LS11 8EQ Tel: 0113 243 5533 Franco Pardini, former of La Terrazza Leeds, is a partner and executive chef at this trattoria-pizzeria. This Brio is one of a chain of four in Leeds and Harrogate. The atmosphere is bright and modern. The staff is well trained and the food is well prepared and good value. Snacks cost from about £6 per head, full meals cost about £25 a head.

**San Carlo** 40 King Street West, Manchester M3 2WY Tel: 0161 834 6226 A bright and buzzy modern trattoria with excellent seafood. Owner Carlo di Stefano says Mario and Franco are his heroes, and that many of the dishes in his restaurants are based on Franco's recipes. About £35 per head.

## ACKNOWLEDGEMENTS:

The author and publisher have made every effort to trace the holders of copyright material appearing in this book and apologise unreservedly if any have been overlooked.

It would have been impossible to write this book without the assistance of a large number of people. So many have offered their memories and help, that I am sure to have forgotten to mention some of them and I hope they will accept my apologies.

In a memoir such as this, even when supported by the recollections of so many participants in the story, there will undoubtedly be mistakes of fact, interpretation or omission. I'm grateful to those who have pointed out and corrected such errors and apologise for any which remain. Many interviewees recounted different versions of the same events and I apologise to them if the one I set out is not exactly the one they remember.

First, I owe enormous thanks to Willie Landels, not only for his prompting me to begin the project and for his support and encouragement throughout, but also for this book's elegant design. Willie and his wife, Josephine, spurred me to stop talking and start writing about Mario and Franco and the Italian invasion of Britain's food culture; they introduced me to many helpful contacts and friends.

My profound gratitude goes to Mario Cassandro, who gave so much time to remember the early days of La Terrazza, and to the late Franco Lagattolla's sons, Nicholas and Fabio, who shared their memories of their father and allowed me access to his papers and photographs. I also offer many thanks to both Enzo Apicella, who was most generous with his time and his extensive cuttings library, and Len Deighton, who not only agreed to contribute the foreword, but also recalled telling details of the earliest days of La Terrazza.

David Bailey, Brian Duffy and Bryan Wharton all permitted me to publish their photographs from the Trat Scene era. Alvaro Maccioni not only shared his memories but also helped me contact many of his customers and former colleagues and let the photographer, Edward Lloyd, take pictures on my behalf at his fortieth anniversary party. Adrian Bailey was generous with his time, produced many early photographs, and lent me his tape of an early interview with La Terrazza's partners.

I thank Egon Ronay, who most graciously permitted me to quote from several of his early *Guides* and his *The Unforgettable Dishes of my Life* and The Consumers Association/Which? Ltd, publishers of the *Good Food Guide*, for permission to quote from early editions of the *Guide*.

Holly Eley has been most helpful. Her work – and her knowledge of Italy – transformed my drafts into a finished product of a higher quality than I could otherwise have hoped for. Holly, thank you a thousand times.

I am very grateful to Yvonne McFarlane, who turned my original collection of interviews and anecdotes into a co-ordinated whole and guided me on many technical details; Anne Dewe, of Andrew Mann, took on a project from a completely unknown writer, and worked with great determination; I am very indebted to her for the encouragement and commitment she showed. I also thank Catherine Blyth, whose early analysis helped me to see the real story which underlies the events described.

Nancy Newhouse generously read drafts, providing valuable guidance. Terry O'Neill roused himself from his convalescence from a serious illness to take the picture of the surviving Pasta Pioneers at San Lorenzo. I am grateful to all those who attended, to

Terry for the memorable photograph and also to Mara and Lorenzo Berni for allowing us to hold the event at their restaurant.

I want especially to thank: Jo Sandilands for her inspirational advice and encouragement when the project seemed mired; Mary Killen Wood for help and advice from start to finish; Tom Jaine, who introduced me to several valuable contacts; my stepdaughter, Delilah Bosanquet, who proved to be an excellent researcher and co-ordinator; my energetic nephew, Tom Sutherland, of Tom's Records, Hay-on-Wye, who introduced me to several useful contacts; Wilf James, who diligently maintained the www.thespaghettitree.co.uk website; and Brian Porteous, who was a professional and imperturbable print production manager.

My thanks also go to the following: to Giorgio Locatelli, whose suggestion prompted Dan Saladino at BBC Radio 4's *Food Programme* to make the edition featuring *The Spaghetti Tree*, which in turn spurred several former Terrazza regulars to get in touch; to Stephen Wickham, secretary of the Capri Classic Car Owners' Club, who heard the *Food Programme*, made the link between the Ford Capri advertising of the sixties and the book, and contacted me with the splendid material from that advertising campaign; to Prudence Korda, an efficient photo researcher; to Franco Buonaguidi, who corrected my many spelling mistakes of Italian names and dishes: to everyone at MBE Earls Court.

I am also grateful to the other friends, trattoria customers and restaurant professionals, both working and retired, who gave interviews, help or support; these include, but are not limited to: Antonio Alfano of Ciborio, Sarah Anderson, Osvaldo Antoniazzi, Geoffrey Aquilina Ross, Laraine Ashton, Zeev Aram, Julian Bidwell, Dante Betti, Mara and Lorenzo Berni, Peter Boizot MBE, John Bowering, David Briggs, Piero Cassandro, Valerio Calzolari, Tommy Candler, *Comm.* Antonio Carluccio OBE, Pino Cecere, Nigel Chism, Pat Copeland, Chris and Francine Corbin, Giulio Cornoli, John Dickie, Susan Farmer, Jo Foley, Pietro Fraccari, Henrietta Green, Charlie Hicks, Jane Howard, Virginia Ironside, Jose Fonseca and Dick Kries, Angela Landels, Tim and Suzie Leon, Pasquale Lunghi, Marietta Maccioni, Fay Maschler, Nello Massa of Mondial Wines, Walter Mariti, Mimmo Mattera, Philip Muscutt, Giulio Nobilio, Mario Paggetti, Mino and Franca Parlanti, Franco Pardini, Tony Pirozzi, Eve Pollard, Mal Pullan, Rose Gray and Ruth Rogers, Helen Robinson, Laura Santin, Gay Search, Godfrey Smith, Paulene Stone, Rex Sweetman, Peppino Taboro, Franco and Ann Taruschio, Wendy Tobi, Carolyn Townshend, Antonio Trapani, Marcello Vargiu, Madeleine Waters, Lorna Wing, Giles Wood, Simon and Lucy (Fleming) Williams, and Colin and Lindy Woodhead. Thank you, also, everyone who lent photographs and gave permission for them to be used. I also thank several individuals whose valuable contributions remain anonymous.

Finally, I offer my widest and most devoted thanks to my wife, Felicity, who has borne these last three years of *trattoria* torment with the utmost enthusiasm, always ready with calming words, sensible advice and an excuse to stop work. As Rita Pavone sang it, *Come te non c'è nessuno.*

## BIBLIOGRAPHY


Bewes, Rodney *A Likely Story – The Autobiography of Rodney Bewes* Arrow, 2006

Blackburn, Susan (editor) *James Sherwood's Discriminating Guide* William Heinemann, 1975

Bon Viveur (Fanny and Johnnie Cradock) *Bon Viveur* Andrew Dakers, 1954

Bon Viveur (Fanny and Johnnie Cradock) *Bon Viveur's London and the British Isles* Andrew Dakers, 1955

Bradshaw, Jon (editor) *Bradshaw's Guide* Leslie Frewin, 1968

Carluccio, Antonio *An Invitation to Italian Cooking* Pavilion, 1986

Clarke, Nick *The Shadow of a Nation* Weidenfeld & Nicolson, 2003

Colpi, Dr Terri *Italians Forward: A Visual History of the Italian Community in Great Britain* Mainstream Publishing, Edinburgh 1991

Contaldo, Gennaro *Passione* Headline, 2005

Courtenay, Ashley *Let's Halt Awhile* (26th edition) André Deutsch, 1958

Crewe, Quentin *Well, I Forget the Rest* Hutchinson, 1991

David, Elizabeth *Italian Food* Macdonald, 1954

David, Elizabeth *Italian Food* (with new Introduction) Penguin, 1963

David, Elizabeth *Italian Food* (with new Introduction) Penguin, 1987

Deighton, Len *Len Deighton's London Dossier* Penguin, 1967

Dempster, Nigel *Nigel Dempster's Address Book* Weidenfeld & Nicolson, 1990

Douglas-Home, Sholto et al (editors) *Zagat London Restaurants* Zagat Survey (various editions)

Driver, Christopher *The British at Table* 1940–80 Chatto & Windus, 1983

Evans, Peter and Bailey, David *Goodbye Baby and Amen* Condé Nast, 1969

Farnes, Norma, *Spike – An Intimate Memoir* Fourth Estate, 2003

Forte, Charles *Forte* Sidgwick & Jackson, 1986

Fox, Kate *Watching the English* Hodder & Stoughton, 2004

Gallati, Mario *Mario of the Caprice* Hutchinson, 1960

Gray, Rose and Rogers, Ruth *The River Café Cook Book* Ebury Press, 1995

Grossman, Loyd *Harpers & Queen Guide to London's 100 Best Restaurants* Robert Houghton, 1987

Harden, Richard and Peter *Harden's London Restaurant Guide* Harden, various annual editions

Hazan, Marcella *The Classic Italian Cookbook* Macmillan, 1980

Holt, Christine and Hayes, James *Recipes for the Nation's Favourite Food* BBC Worldwide Publications, 2003

Hopkinson, Simon and Bareham, Lindsey *The Prawn Cocktail Years* Michael Joseph, 2006

Hough, Richard *Edwina, Countess Mountbatten of Burma* Weidenfeld & Nicolson, 1983

Houston Bowden, Gregory *British Gastronomy* Chatto & Windus, 1975

Hughes, Spike *Second Movement* Museum Press, 1951

Hughes, Spike and Charmian *Eating Italian* (and reprinted as *Eating in Italy*) Methuen, 1966

Jaine, Tom, Smith, Drew, Ainsworth, Jim (successive editors) *The Good Food Guide* Consumers' Association Editions, 1990–2006

Lagattolla, Franco *The Recipes That Made a Million* Orbis, 1978

Lawton, T.A. *Dining Round London* Noël Carrington, 1945
Leoni, Peppino *I Shall Die on the Carpet* Leslie Frewin, 1966
Levy, Shawn *Ready, Steady, Go!* Fourth Estate, 2003
Little, Alastair and Whittington, Richard *Keep it Simple* Conran Octopus, 1993
Little, Alastair and Whittington, Richard *Soho Cooking* Ebury Press, 1999
Locatelli, Giorgio *Made in Italy – Food and Stories* Fourth Estate, 2007
Postgate, Raymond and Ardagh, John (editors) *The Good Food Guide to London* Hodder, 1968
Postgate, Raymond (editor) *The Good Food Guide* Cassell, editions1951–61
Riley, Gillian *The Oxford Companion to Italian Food* Oxford, 2007
Roden, Claudia *The Food of Italy* Chatto & Windus, 1989
Ronay, Egon *Egon Ronay's Guides* Egon Ronay Organization Ltd, various editions, 1960s
Ronay, Egon *The Unforgettable Dishes of my Life* Egon Ronay Publications (Cookery) Ltd in association with Victor Gollancz (The Egon Ronay Cookery Series), 1989
Taruschio, Ann and Franco *Leaves from the Walnut Tree* Pavilion, 1993
Winder, Robert *Bloody Foreigners* Little, Brown, 2004

# INDEX

Note: References in italic are to illustrations. The names of La Terrazza regulars on pages 237–38, do not feature in the index unless they also appear separately in the text.